Reducing Risk

with

Software Process Improvement

Louis Poulin

Foreword by
Ron Radice

 Auerbach Publications
Taylor & Francis Group

Boca Raton London New York Singapore

Published in 2005 by
Auerbach Publications
Taylor & Francis Group
6000 Broken Sound Parkway NW, Suite 300
Boca Raton, FL 33487-2742

International Standard Book Number-10: 0-8493-3828-X (Hardcover)
International Standard Book Number-13: 978-0-8493-3828-1 (Hardcover)
Library of Congress Card Number 2004066281

Library of Congress Cataloging-in-Publication Data

Poulin, Louis A.
    Reducing risk with software process improvement / Louis A. Poulin.
        p. cm.
    Includes bibliographical references and index.
    ISBN 0-8493-3828-X
    1. Computer software--Development.   I. Title.

QA76.76.D47P683 2005
005.1--dc22

2004066281

Taylor & Francis Group
is the Academic Division of T&F Informa plc.

Visit the Taylor & Francis Web site at
http://www.taylorandfrancis.com

and the Auerbach Publications Web site at
http://www.auerbach-publications.com

Contents

v

List of Figures

List of Tables

Foreword

Risks are everywhere in life and most assuredly during the life of software projects. Risk is not always avoidable, but it is controllable. In his book *Reducing Risk with Software Process Improvement,* Louis A. Poulin addresses the dominant risk types still seen in too many software projects. He offers practical guidance on how these risks can be managed without waxing philosophical as some writers do when addressing the need for good software processes.

One can argue that taking a risk is part of doing business. Indeed risk taking is a business choice, one that cannot and should not be stopped. But there is a major difference with intentionally taking risks, assuming risks must always be taken, or not knowing when risks are being taken.

When a business must make a constrained choice, it may take a risk to try to achieve a desirable objective. I would add that when any risk is intentionally taken, the risk taker must be willing to live with any negative outcome if the risk should manifest as a problem. If the risk taker is not willing to live with the problem should it manifest, the risk should not be taken, it should be controlled. These types of risks I would categorize as chosen, understood, and appreciated when taken. The possibility of a downside is included in the taken risk. These risks are not avoided, but are managed to minimize the problem potential.

Not all risks should be taken. Too often a risk is taken not knowing that there is a simple, practical way to avoid the risk. The worst possible risks are those not understood, seen, or appreciated by the risk taker. These risks are not managed. The risk taker does not even know they are taking a risk. The downside is not anticipated as a possibility, and when it manifests, the risk taker says, "Well, that's the way it is." Well, it is not!

I was asked to be an expert witness in a software project suit. The situation was that Company A had contracted with Company B to deliver a software solution. However, the solution was late, overran budget, did not address all the contracted requirements Company A wanted, and was highly defective. I asked the lawyer what the defense of Company B, the contractor, was. He said they were pleading that this is the nature of software contracts; i.e., that they are late, overrun budget, misinterpret requirements, may not deliver them all, and are defective. "That's the way it is!"

I told the lawyer to defend by asking the judge if he would buy a car under these circumstances or would accept this as the state of automobile manufacturing. Clearly, he would not. But there was a time when automobiles produced by manufacturers did not work as well as the customers expected, as a result, there were many problems that were endured because there was no better solution without increasing the expense of the purchase to the customers. This had to change and did change as society became more dependent on the automobile and demanded better and safer products from the manufacturers.

Today in software, the state of poor and unacceptable quality is still too often a problem. We have improved. We have processes that when implemented lead to desirable solution delivery for both the customer and the provider. We know how to deliver good quality solutions, on time, on budget, and which address the expected customer requirements. But it is not always so. Why? Mostly because the software provider does not know or does not appreciate that it can be done and takes unnecessary risks. Software can be produced at lower cost, leading to a more competitive position for the provider, and to higher customer satisfaction which in turn leads to repeat business.

The problem is more pronounced when we understand that some software is life critical. When not life critical, it directly relates to the quality of life we all expect now that software is bundled in almost every hardware device we purchase. We as customers need and expect good, reliable software solutions.

Poulin briefly explains this industry problem and leaves the reader hoping there is a better way. There is.

While the book, "has been written to appeal to many categories of professionals," says Poulin, I believe it will be of most use to managers of software projects. A project team is needed to build and deliver the right solution, but the manager is needed to ensure the team builds the right solution. If the managers don't know how to build the right solution, believe it is possible, or understand why it is important, the team will be handicapped in doing its best.

It is sad to learn how wide poor practice remains in our industry. Poulin's analysis on poor or deficient practices is comprehensive for low maturity organizations.

Poulin lists the common poor practices as found for over 40 assessments of software projects. His data is consistent with what others have been finding for the last 40 years, which is why models like the Capability Maturity Model (CMM)* from the Software Engineering Institute were developed to help software organizations. These models are now widely used, thankfully. Unfortunately, not all organizations or managers use the models for whatever reason they find justifiable. If they have an aversion to models, then they should start with this book, which provides practical advice on critical practices.

It is a startling indictment of managers of software projects when Poulin notes that, "A deficient practice, in order to be listed, must have been observed:

Either in at least 50 percent of the assessed organizations,

Or on average, once per organization, by counting the number of times it was found to be the source of difficulties and dividing this result by the number of assessed organizations (a deficient practice may have been noticed more than once in a given organization, since the same practice may have been the source of several potential problems)."

Think about the criteria he uses to define deficient practices, one that I would say is liberal and forgiving to software organizations. No one would or should purchase a product that reflects mal-practice by those who build it. I am not in favor of lawsuits, but lawyers would have a field day with this data.

We as users of software may be part of the problem. We are too forgiving when we encounter defects. It is simple to reboot when a problem on a personal computer (PC) occurs. It is a nuisance or sometimes worse, but we reboot and press on. We all know when a new release of PC software hits the streets we will encounter defects. The suppliers even admit there are defects. Yet we users buy because we want the new function. We can't wait, and in turn we motivate poor practice by the suppliers. We need to become more demanding and with some suppliers this is an absolute must. The suppliers need to learn how to produce better software solutions, because it is possible. They can start by reading and using books like Poulin's.

As a consumer, I implore all software suppliers to put this book to good use. We might live with unavoidable PC reboots, but how would

---

* CMM and Capability Maturity Model are registered at the U.S. Patent and Trademark Office by Carnegie Mellon University.

you feel if the pilot on your next flight announced "Hold on, I need to reboot the flight system"?

Let me restate Poulin's set of practical practices. All of these are quite easy to put into use and are not difficult to understand:

- Understand the requirements before you invest too much in building the wrong solution.
- Plan the project at a level of detail that provides further insight into how to deliver the required solution.
- Measure and track the project at sufficient detail to ensure the project will be delivered as required.
- Ensure that all on the project understand the quality objectives and then assure that these are being met.
- Control project assets, especially changes that always happen during the project life cycle despite what some managers hope for.
- If you need to subcontract, manage the subcontractor to ensure you get what you want, when you want it, and how you want it.
- Provide appropriate process understanding, tools, and methods to the project team members so they can transform the requirements into the desired deliverable solution.
- Ensure that those who need to know are kept informed as the project evolves from start to finish.
- Admit that practitioners make defects and know that high percentages of defects can be removed before turning the work over to others on the team who are dependent on its quality level.
- Protect your customer and their interests at all times.
- Learn the value of defining processes critical to the project and keep these definitions as simple as possible, but define them so there is agreement.
- Prepare the project team members with training to enable their capabilities to deliver the best of possible solutions.
- Build a common cultural understanding of what the organization holds as values for delivering solutions to customers.
- Understand that risks will occur on projects, but risks can be evaluated and managed, so they do not become problems. Read Poulin's book to get a better understanding of what these practices require. These are not complex ideas to understand and they are not complex to implement. Poulin provides more detailed understanding of these in his book. If you cannot start with all the practices then at least start with some. My own personal favorites are:
- Reviews and Inspections, as these are the least costly to implement and have the greatest economic and customer satisfaction return.

- Training, as our industry is constantly changing, and even the best people on our projects must be enabled to demonstrate their capability to deliver; training enables these capabilities; training is a necessary precondition to best work.
- Building a Culture, as a team that understands its purpose and objectives will find a way to use the best practices in our industry.

I do not know anyone who comes to work to deliver poor products, to make defects, or to overrun costs on projects. People take pride in building something good, but sometimes the system gets in the way. The system can be changed but it often requires help to change. This book can help you change the system in your organization. I invite you to learn and understand how you can do better on your projects. I know you all can. I've seen it many times once the organization and managers decide that there is a better way. Poulin's book can enable you to do your best and find that better way.

Ron Radice
November 4, 2004
Andover, MA
www.stt.com

Introduction

This book describes observations made over a period of ten years in projects and organizations involved in the field of Information Technology (IT), focusing on the areas of software development and maintenance. It highlights the most frequently encountered problems because of poor processes, the term process being defined as the way material and human resources, methods, procedures, and tools are integrated in order to achieve a given objective. It also provides recommendations in the form of critical practices to implement to achieve successful delivery of software products and services.

These observations were compiled as part of an initiative started by GRafP Technologies in the 1990s to study risk in areas where there is a high level of human involvement. For example, train accidents mostly occur as a result of human inattention, not because mechanical parts fail. This is precisely what we, at GRafP Technologies, wanted to analyze and quantify, particularly the thousands of interactions that lead to deterioration of a situation, often to the point of generating a crisis.

Because our company has been involved in IT for many years, it is the field we selected to perform our investigation. We conducted comprehensive assessments and 40 of those constitute the source of information on which this book is based. Software development and maintenance offered us an endless source of material. For example, development environments riddled with defects, innumerable crashes (the dreaded message, "This program has performed an illegal operation and will be shut down. If the problem persists, contact the program vendor), incompatible versions, problems mysteriously appearing and disappearing, requirements that kept changing depending on the mood of the development team leader, release of improperly tested products to beat competitors, the shame felt by the development team when customers found the residual defects, suppliers unable to deliver on time, and the list goes on. In other words, institutionalized chaos: yet chaos that led to innovations rarely seen in any other industry.

Chapter 2 to Chapter 15 present the details associated with each area that was investigated along with the problems (or potential problems) the assessed organizations had to deal with. Whenever possible, I illustrated with anecdotes recorded during those assessments how the problems were related to deficient practices and what their impact was, or how mastering specific practices benefited the organization that implemented them.

Management topics tend to be the subject of the first few chapters. This was done on purpose, as customers tend to place a lot of value on solid management, and it will strike a chord with anyone who has had to deal with investors. Indeed, investors look on the management team of a new venture as the critical factor that will determine whether it is worthy of their investment. The technical nature of the venture is not that important to them; they often do not understand it anyway.

The chapters that come later do not necessarily imply that they are less important than earlier chapters; it is that certain software processes can only be implemented after others have been successfully deployed. Managing Requirements is one of the topics that should be given attention because uncontrolled changes in requirements have the potential of being the source of a lot of problems in an IT initiative. It is therefore addressed in Chapter 2. Peer reviews and inspections, which are described in Chapter 10, constitute a very important aspect of developing software-intensive systems, but they are liable to be the first item to be abandoned in an initiative when the pressure increases to deliver and time is running out. It is for that reason they are described in Chapter 10 instead of in an earlier chapter.

This book was written to appeal to many categories of professionals. Practitioners, for example, will probably be more interested in topics like Releasing Products, Deploying Services and Controlling Changes (Chapter 6), Developing Products (Chapter 8), and Reviewing and Inspecting (Chapter 10). Managers are more liable to focus on Planning (Chapter 3), Tracking Progress (Chapter 4), Coordinating (Chapter 9), and Managing IT Initiatives (Chapter 14). Customers and senior managers may focus on Assuring Quality (Chapter 5), Contracting Out (Chapter 7), Providing Services to Customers (Chapter 11), Focusing on Processes (Chapter 12), and Building a Culture (Chapter 15).

Readers who want an overview of the data on which this book was written should start with Chapter 16, where they will find a summary of the results obtained as part of the aforementioned assessments.

The method used to gather data and the principles on which it relies are presented in Chapter 17. Readers who are deductive by nature and who like to understand the principles on which an approach is based before getting into the more practical aspects of Software Engineering and Information Technology (SE&IT) will want to read Chapter 17 first, followed by Chapter 16, and then proceed to Chapter 2 through Chapter 15.

It is worth providing a brief explanation to help readers understand how the information was compiled. The assessments that were conducted focused on identifying deficiencies that contribute the most to problems experienced by organizations involved in developing software products and services. The following criteria were applied to extract the information presented:

- A deficient practice is listed only if it was missing or incompletely implemented, and its presence was needed to mitigate a potential problem (i.e., a risk).
- A deficient practice, in order to be listed, must have been observed:
  - Either in at least 50 percent of the assessed organizations.
  - Or on average, once per organization, by counting the number of times it was found to be the source of difficulties and dividing this result by the number of assessed organizations (a deficient practice may have been noticed more than once in a given organization, since the same practice may have been the source of several potential problems).

This book is intended as a reference for:

- Senior managers in organizations that have an Information Systems department (most of them do, although more are thinking about outsourcing it) to enlighten them on what they should pay attention to.
- For customers who want to know what they should be looking for when purchasing information technology-based products or outsourcing services.
- For investors who want to get a hint as to whether they should invest in IT companies, and what they should look at to make a decision.
- For practitioners who are looking forward to becoming managers.
- For project and application managers, who want to minimize the number of crises they will likely have to deal with. They should be encouraged to learn from their mistakes, but they should be commended for learning from the mistakes of others.

This is really what this book is all about.

Chapter 1

The Information Age

> If cars were produced the way most software is, daily break-
> downs would occur, consumers would have to go to the nearest
> garage to obtain replacement parts and proceed to fit them as
> best they can.

The information age is here to stay. Those who doubt it need only open
a newspaper or a magazine and check the number of times the terms
Internet, e-commerce, or multimedia are mentioned.

Computers were common household items in the early 1990s and
electronic mail (e-mail) was rarely used; 10 years later, e-mail had become
not only a part of doing business but also an important part of everyday
life. There is no question that this so-called information age has brought
with it a myriad of benefits. The World Wide Web, in particular, has put
at one's fingertips a volume of information that would only be available
in a large library, along with the power to search through that library
much faster than anyone could think possible less than two decades ago.
One can be justified in asking how people have succeeded to manage
their work, let alone their life, without it.

The innovating minds of a younger generation who, having been raised
with television, quickly associated with the potential software offers in
the information age. This led to new products and services that were
developed in a sometimes incredibly chaotic manner. The result has not
always been amusing. Personal computer (PC) users know this all too
well, when they install a new application or an upgrade and keep their
fingers crossed that their system will still work.

The information age has also brought its own share of problems: more information to sort through, and less time to plan and organize it. The information age has also an inherent propensity to foster individualism and to reduce physical interaction between individuals. One can easily communicate with people all over the world without knowing (and possibly without caring about) what's going on next door. As a result, the coordination and management skills essential to developing an information technology (IT) system whose scope requires a significant amount of teamwork have been sorely neglected.

The software component of the information technology has also shown to be particularly vulnerable to defects and the more serious cases have already been thoroughly documented. The amount of money that was invested in correcting the Y2K bug ($200 billion U.S. worldwide), whether the risk was real or not, is indeed an indication of the level of concern that existed in connection with software applications.

Yet, the forgiveness of customers in connection with software products and services never ceases to impress me. Rational people, extremely demanding in other areas, are willing to accept anything when it comes to software. People would unlikely show such tolerance to regular power failures or water shortages, whatever caused them. Likewise, who would put up with a car that constantly breaks down, does not start when needed, and stops at the most inopportune moment?

When Intel deployed a Pentium chip in 1994, slight inaccuracies in floating point calculations could result under certain conditions; people were quick to denounce it and demanded reimbursement. Intel finally had to replace the chip in all computers that had been shipped with the faulty chip at a cost of $475 million U.S. No incident caused by the faulty chip had ever been reported. A few years later, Microsoft released a faulty version of Outlook, its e-mail application, which included a security gap quickly exploited by the ILOVEYOU virus propagated in mail attachments. Users lost hundreds of millions of dollars as files and registries were damaged, and entire computer networks were disabled. Nevertheless, everyone seemed to have accepted that situation as a fait accompli, and those affected only acquired more software to get better protection against similar mishaps in the future.

Is this situation insurmountable or can something be done about it? In order to answer this question, we have to take a brief look at the history of software development.

The Old Software Ghosts That Haunt Us

In the early days of computers (1950s and early 1960s), the activity dealing with programming had more in common with optimization than with anything else. People developing programs had to have a detailed understanding of the machine with which they were working in order to fully exploit its features. Like today, these programs had to be stored in memory to be run. The difference was that in those days, computer memory was limited and expensive. Computer monthly leasing rates often reached tens of thousands of dollars and the use of computer time had to be minimized in order to make it available to as many users as possible. Therefore, the essence of programming was to come up with the most efficient programs in order to save on computer memory and on computer usage requirements. The trend to label programming as an art thus started in those days. Good programmers were those who had tricks up their sleeves and were able to take advantage of every feature of the machine they were working with. The use of systematic and disciplined approaches was considered as long as they satisfied these criteria.

This culture was passed from programmer to programmer through the late 1960s and the early 1970s, and computer science courses taught at the time simply helped establish it more solidly.

Between 1970 and 1985, two main classes of programmers evolved. One class was made up of programmers who developed software on mainframes and the other, of programmers who developed software on mid-size and small-size computers. Mainframe computer programmers, because of the sheer size of the applications they were working with, such as banking, insurance, defense, air traffic control, and meteorology, were more likely to follow a somewhat disciplined approach. Roles had been defined over the years to cope with the various responsibilities of working with equipment that called on different types of resources and skills. Mid- to small-size computer programmers assumed all these responsibilities individually and software development moved toward becoming a one-man show. As computers became more convivial and cheaper (the era of PDP and VAX computers), the concept of computer operator, which had been introduced to free computer programmers from the job of actually operating computers and their peripheral equipment, slowly eroded. Programmers became used to doing everything, from developing the flow charts, to writing the code on remote terminals, to testing and integrating applications, to loading disks and magnetic tapes, and to controlling the jobs that were being run.

The advent of the microprocessor in the 1970s and the microcomputer in the 1980s sealed the fate of mainframe software development. Computers became available at low prices, and the class of programmers developing software on small-size computers triumphed, bringing with them the culture they had developed over the years. As a result, the relatively well-defined processes that characterized mainframes were slowly forgotten, information technology proliferated, with undeniable benefits for society in general, but chaos crept in at each step of this transition and became institutionalized with the personal computer. We observed this state of affairs numerous times in the assessments we performed. A relatively mature process characterized centralized systems that often relied on mainframes whereas client-server and Web-based systems, which were largely made up of networked PCs, were generally characterized by a significantly less mature process, often bordering on being chaotic.

Paradoxically, even though the cost of computer memory decreased drastically, the need to design small and efficient programs remained. This was particularly true for one-chip microcomputers and microcontrollers (those found in all kinds of apparatus, from hard disk controllers, to telephones, to washing machines) in which the amount of on-chip memory, albeit very cheap, is also very limited. In addition, small programs executed faster and the response time was thus improved.

I was involved, in the 1980s, in large software development efforts. One of these undertakings called on more than 250 programmers working on a single project and a disciplined process had to be followed in order to keep the project under control. We had to hire junior programmers and we certainly experienced first hand the impact of the culture brought about by PCs. Several of these programmers left after a few months because they could not get used to the more rigid task allocation that such a large project required, not to mention the boring documentation that had to be developed before the interesting work (i.e. coding) could start. Having also worked on small projects in which programmers do everything, I must nonetheless admit that it has a very strong appeal. One feels in control, like driving a fast sports car, even though it often is a false perception, with the result that one ends up in the ditch in both cases.

Unfortunately, the truth of the matter is that large projects demand the involvement of a lot of people and require skills that programmers working alone or in small groups are unlikely to develop. OS/360 required 5,000 person-years to complete and it secured IBM's predominance on computers for years to come. However chaotic, it was nevertheless completed in three years, and at times, there were well over one thousand people concurrently working on the project spread out over different locations. Even if 100 very bright programmers had been mustered to carry out the work with a resulting threefold productivity gain, it would still have required over 16 years to complete (5,000 divided by 100 divided by 3). And this does not take into consideration the challenge of finding these 100 very bright programmers in the first place, let alone keeping them and training them to work together (one must assume that there would be a few prima donnas among them).

Regardless of which class programmers belonged to, software was destined to experience a troublesome growth from the beginning. Undeniably, software was seen as having a major advantage over hardware: it was easy to change. This, unfortunately, also became its major disadvantage. Indeed, since software was easy to change, disciplined methods to develop it only came very late. In hardware and particularly in the field of integrated circuit design, conversely, changes could be very costly and could result in long delays. One integrated circuit designer working at IBM told me that an undetected error in his design made him miss his allocated slot in the semiconductor wafer production facilities located in Singapore, and his project was delayed over six months because of it. It almost caused him to suffer a nervous breakdown and in any case, accelerated his hair loss.

This forced hardware designers to plan more carefully and to coordinate their activities with an emphasis on contingencies. Even though the term software engineering first appeared in the late sixties, software has yet to be structured into a full engineering discipline. The equipment needed to develop software is getting cheaper by the month and any individual with some talent and perseverance can have a go at it. There is no need to deal with organizational issues or to manage groups of people to come up with a good software product that can then be easily replicated at low cost. Indeed, talented individuals (artists in their domain of expertise) have written some of the best programs available today and there is a strong resistance in the field to adopt anything that could be perceived as an obstacle to individual creativity. The managerial skills required in established engineering disciplines are still largely improvised in software; this is often compounded by the fact that customers have themselves been led to believe that software is easy to develop (after all, kids do it!) and does not require intensive preparation and planning before code is written.

Developing software can very much be like writing a book; one individual can do it, but all successful authors agree that writing requires talent and a lot of discipline, much time spent researching the book topic, innumerable reviews, and perseverance. On the other hand, encyclopedias (which can be compared to developing large or complex software systems) are written by teams, and may require several years and involve a large number of people; each individual contributes his or her expertise, and this implies extensive management and coordination.

Two events occurred indicating that a lasting change may be on the way. First, the Y2K bug, and particularly the cost associated with resolving this issue, has made senior management much more aware of the challenges that software presents and forced them to look into what was going on in their IT groups. Then, the collapse of the so-called dot com has greatly contributed to making people aware that software engineering is a trade that requires skills, domain knowledge, expertise, know-how, a solid organization, and as a corollary, solid management. As a result, several organizations, other than those developing and selling software products and services, have started to ask themselves why they need an IT group at all. Their value comes from the assets they have accumulated, the products they sell, and the services they provide with respect to their business domain. These are essentially generated by their workforce, with its collective skills, its knowledge, its incentive to perform, and a clear understanding of what to do with the information it has. Their rationale is that establishing and maintaining knowledge capital, a concept first put forward by Paul A. Strassmann in the mid-1990s, in an area unrelated to their business domain and profit centers is simply not cost effective. On the other hand, organizations are seeking excellence in the organizations to which they are outsourcing or subcontracting their IT development and maintenance.

The introduction of the Capability Maturity Model (CMM) by the Software Engineering Institute (SEI), standards developed by the International Organization for Standardization, such as ISO 9001 (with the ISO 9000-3 guide for applying the standard to software), ISO 12207, and ISO 15504 have been key factors in catalyzing the move toward software process engineering, since it underscored the efforts required to produce high quality software. The military industrial complex had understood this a long time ago. It came up with military standard 2167 in 1968, laying the foundation for disciplined and controlled software development. However, the use of this standard has been limited to defense applications. It has rarely transpired to the non-defense industrial and commercial fields. In addition, even the Defense community was swept over by the PC revolution, and the 2167 military standard has all but been abandoned.

Many see a fundamental incompatibility between the CMM (replaced by the CMM Integration (CMMI)), and new development approaches, such as Agile methods. This is in fact a non-issue because both address different topics. Agile methods strictly focus on techniques pertaining to software development; the CMM (and the CMMI) strictly focus on managing software development.

The fact that the CMM and ISO standards have gained wide international acceptance, and that purchasers of goods and services are using them increasingly as a criteria to select suppliers, has heightened market awareness of the concepts put forward in software development models and standards. It will nevertheless take years before the cultural barriers that have been built over more than 40 years are overcome.

Chapter 2

Managing Requirements

> Whoever keeps changing direction, either on his own or on
> the advice of others, is likely never to reach his destination.

This chapter deals with the most common deficiencies related to controlling changes in information technology (IT) projects at the requirements
level. Depending on the scope of the IT project and the domain of
application pursued by an organization, requirements changes may come
from different sources.

For a custom-made system, an external customer typically issues the
requirements and the unavoidable subsequent requests for modifications.
In the case of a subcontractor, the prime contractor issues them. When
systems are developed for internal use, the customer is also internal and
an operational department may be in charge of specifying the system and
issuing requirements to the IT department.

For mass-market applications, the marketing department may assume
the task of identifying what users want through surveys and by keeping
a close tab on the competition. The result of these activities may take the
form of a list of desirable features, subsequently translated into a high-
level product description, which is then successively refined until it can
be used to drive product development.

In some other cases, the process is simplified to the extreme. The
original idea is the requirement and it is successively refined through trial
and error until those who initiated it and those who must implement it
share a similar vision of what the end-product will look like.

In any case, managing requirements acquires a particular significance
given that in the best of cases, 60 to 70 percent of the requirements are

known up front. Thirty to forty percent will be introduced along the way and these will be the cause of over 90 percent of the problems experienced in the project.

Ensure System Requirements Have Been Reviewed by Software Professionals before Forging Ahead

As software is becoming an integral part of information systems, the distinction between system engineering and software engineering is becoming fuzzier by the day. Requirements that need to be implemented in software constitute an increasing share of the requirements that systems must satisfy. This has usually been quite well understood by organizations involved in developing industrial systems, where system engineers/architects and software engineers/programmers often work hand in hand to define requirements or else, software engineers assume a system engineering responsibility. In manufacturing organizations characterized by a strong hardware culture and in organizations where SE&IT is focused on maintaining and operating Management Information Systems (MIS), this is not always the case. The software department in these organizations is often treated as a necessary evil.

Prestige and influence are usually at the root of this issue. In one of the organizations we assessed, there is a prevailing attitude that it is demeaning to ask the advice of software people, since these are perceived as individuals whose sole purpose in life is to do what they are told. The observed result is a series of unending changes for each developed application as there are always a few essential features that have not been taken into account in the requirements. Patches are applied over patches and, by and large, systems have grown to become unmaintainable. With time, the software group members have come to behave in accordance with what is expected of them: initiative is all but shifted, the work they have to perform needs to be specified to the nearest detail before they will start developing the application, and they have abdicated to third parties or to the users their responsibility of supporting the software after it has been delivered. In turn, this has contributed to reinforcing how the software group is perceived by the rest of the organization.

In another organization, those in charge of the system requirements are convinced that they know as much about software, if not more, as the staff from the software group. In many cases, this opinion has been reached after having hacked a few PC applications or browsed through the most recent computer magazines. In one instance, several million dollars worth of workstations bundled with applications were acquired without consulting the SE&IT department. It turned out that they were not fully compatible with the organization's corporate systems. The SE&IT department has so far refused to provide any significant level of technical support as they neither have enough resources familiar with the acquired systems nor do they have the time to invest in working out fundamental incompatibilities. As a result, these workstations have been grossly underused and they are inexorably becoming obsolete.

Establish and Enforce a Directive Stating What Must Be Done when Dealing with System Requirements

It should be common sense to think that if one wants a specific step to be performed, he or she will need to communicate it clearly to whoever has to perform it. Every parent knows that if a child is not told repeatedly to eat fruits and vegetables, and if this rule is not somehow enforced, the child will stuff himself with pop and candy.

It should be the same in IT projects. If it is management's wish that any requirements changes be reviewed and signed off, it should be easy to come across a directive to that effect in the organization. However, this is not what has been observed. In 23 of the 40 assessed organizations, changes to requirements were performed and authorized by word of mouth after a cursory review (sometimes in the form of a hallway discussion) had been conducted.

In one organization, changes to requirements need to be associated with a cost evaluation and the approval is linked to the expense authorization level of the signatory. The obvious evasion to this is to break down large changes into several smaller ones. But as the number of approved modifications is part of monthly progress reviews with senior management, a large number of modifications inevitably attracts attention and gives the impression of poor planning and poor design, neither of which directors, project managers, and practitioners want to be associated with. This organization has also developed a small binder (less than 200 pages) in which the entire process of carrying out an IT project is documented. It is therefore easy for a new recruit to skim through and get a good idea of the most important steps to follow (mandatory steps are in bold). The most important templates and forms are provided in appendices.

The largest impact by far that has been observed with the lack of policy regarding requirements is the loss of opportunity to create a shared vision in the project. Because it deals with requirements, which constitute the cornerstone of any development effort, this situation somewhat sets the tone for the remaining activities and their associated work products. Indeed, in all organizations where there were no clear and enforced directives on how to deal with requirements, the remaining phases were more likely to experience false starts and significant rework.

In one organization, the project manager all but relinquished his project responsibility prerogatives to the customer's representative. The latter happened to have a lot of experience with the application domain (air navigation simulation) and he was frequently on site evaluating the work and proposing changes to the project staff. The project manager, being involved in other projects that were more to his liking, tacitly agreed and relied on the customer's representative to keep him informed of what was going on as part of regular project reviews. The project manager and the customer's representative had worked together on and off for several years, so the direction the project took was not entirely surprising. Developers, who were constantly reminded that the organization's customers were paying their salary and had therefore to be treated accordingly, were only too happy to comply. However, an application that had been estimated at about $1 million ballooned to over $2.5 million, as change after change was incorporated into the project. Some of these changes had major impacts on what had already been done and called for extensive rework. Following a letter from the customer's contract administration department to the effect that the project was running late, an internal audit was carried out and the extent of the damage came to light. The customer's representative quickly adopted a hands-off approach and essentially claimed no responsibility, stating that in all his discussions with the project staff, whatever he said were only suggestions and had no contractual binding. The project was finally cancelled, and the contractor had to write off over $1 million, while the customer, who managed to recover its investment as part of an out-of-court settlement, did not get the system it needed and lost face in front of its own customers, to whom it had boasted of the system's capabilities. Not surprisingly, the customer's representative and the project manager, who took most of the blame, are no longer on speaking terms.

Train Those Who Have the Responsibility of Managing Requirements

Whereas technical courses abound in the SE&IT industry, training people in connection with the various management tasks that need to be performed in the course of a project is sorely lacking. For one thing, this type of training is rarely available from external sources and has to be developed in-house. External sources can nevertheless still be useful by providing training on requirements management concepts and tools to facilitate their application in real life scenarios.

Managing requirements is essentially learned on the job. This unfortunately often translates into dropping people who have that responsibility in the lions' pit without any form of preparedness other than a lot of goodwill to learn it.

Training on how to manage requirements deals mostly with issues like the negotiation and implementation of contractual changes, the coordination of requirements reviews, the application domain addressed by the project, and the process adopted to carry out the work. Understandably, personnel other than internal staff can hardly provide this kind of training.

The difficulty is that skills required to manage requirements are acquired by practice and unless mechanisms are in place to capture and to transfer them to others, whoever will assume this responsibility is bound to make the same mistakes over and over again. Those who have the knowledge do not necessarily possess the abilities (or the desire) to transfer it. This deficiency has been observed as a source of problems in over 33 percent of the assessed organizations.

Military organizations, among a few other select ones, have developed the infrastructure to do so through a combination of formal and on-the-job training. In one such organization, people who have acquired special skills are assigned to training positions for a limited time. In cases where they absolutely do not have the required aptitudes to assume this position, another individual who does accompanies them for some time in order to prepare and to deliver training material. The advantage of this approach is that the skilled individuals are still available to perform requirements management tasks while acting as advisers during training sessions.

One organization lost a significant share of the market in the telecommunications industry as a result of losing a good chunk of the most experienced members of its workforce, after a competitor had set up operations in the same area of town. Had it had the foresight to transfer some of the knowledge held by these members to others, the impact of this loss could have been greatly alleviated.

Document Project Requirements and Make Them Available to Project Team Members

It has been rather surprising to find, in the course of the assessments we conducted, that in nearly 33 percent of the organizations, the project team members' understanding of the project is largely based on hearsay. Meetings held for assessing requirements changes are then liable to turn into philosophical debates as people broaden the subject of discussions to camouflage their lack of a detailed understanding of what they have to discuss. After all, nobody likes to look stupid in such a meeting!

This situation is often the result of poor coordination in the organization and in the project. The requirements document may be in a filing cabinet somewhere or in an obscure folder on a server, but only a few people know about it, or else, they assume that somehow, this information has been spread around and everyone knows about it. At times, but this has been rather exceptional, information hiding was intentional and was the result of a few individuals who equated unshared knowledge with the power of controlling others. This situation is more likely to occur between a middle manager, who has built up a little fiefdom, and his or her subordinates, than between peers.

Nothing can replace a short session during which the requirements documentation structure is briefly explained to team members. In one of the organizations we assessed, this has been institutionalized. Someone has the responsibility of actually explaining up front the purpose and the architecture of the system to the entire project team and to whoever will be associated with the project in one form or another. This includes all technical staff, and at various levels of detail, quality assurance specialists, release and control personnel, technical writers, people in charge of administering contracts, and even clerical staff.

In one instance that illustrates the consequence of a deficiency in this area, a global positioning software subsystem was embedded in a navigation software configuration item; whereas the requirements were clearly stating that this subsystem was to be part of a different item. Even the customer did not detect the error as part of the project review meetings until a representative from the users indicated that given the operational context, the main use of global positioning data was for time tagging and not for navigation purposes. All the interfaces had to be redesigned, the documentation redone, and the data structure modified to consider this, and required an effort close to 1,000 person-hours. The decision to integrate global positioning data into the navigation configuration item had never been specifically taken; it just had been assumed that this was where it had to go as part of informal discussions in the course of regular technical meetings. Nobody had ever bothered to check what the requirements stated.

Take Basic Measurements of Requirements Management Activities and By-Products

Measurement is by far one of the most deficient practices in all of the organizations we have assessed. And yet, without measurements, decisions rely mostly on feelings and at best, on error-prone guesses often based on incomplete information.

The most common excuse heard in connection with measurements is that numbers don't tell everything. There is certainly some truth in that statement, but the reciprocal statement is that without numbers, anything can be said. The impact associated with the first statement, in our observation, is usually less detrimental than with the second.

As far as managing requirements is concerned, counting the number of change requests received and the number of changes implemented can be quite telling. If the effort invested in each of these changes, from analysis to verification of correct implementation, is also compiled, it can become a revelation. Unfortunately, IT organizations have a tendency of taking either too few measurements (if any!) or, of getting overboard and planning extensive metric programs that never get implemented.

In a particular assessment, a project manager explained to us how he had been converted to the value of measuring basic parameters. A lull had been experienced on his project and having all of a sudden a day to spare, he decided to plot the number of changes his staff had implemented as a function of time for the IT subsystem he was in charge of upgrading. This was a very crude chart, with the number of changes on the y-axis and the time on the x-axis. The slope he obtained indicated that at the rate changes were implemented, the subsystem would be at least 9 months behind schedule. All along, he had been utterly convinced that his project was in good shape and he had had no worries whatsoever. As a result, he called a meeting, first with his own staff, followed by one with his management and one with the customer to identify which changes were absolutely required and which could be postponed to another release. With the plan modified accordingly, he delivered his subsystem only two weeks late. The customer received a provisional release that did not include everything that had been requested, but at least it was functional. Furthermore, the discussions that took place to negotiate a workaround had allowed each party to establish a constructive relationship that handsomely paid off later on.

Yet this was not a project in which no management was performed. A project control department was in charge of collecting all progress data from all subsystems and generating earned-value reports. The problem was that detailed information was buried in the reported numbers and some of that information was also lost in the data collection process. This point does substantiate the aforementioned statement that numbers do not tell everything, but it also justifies the value of taking measurements.

Involve Quality Assurance Personnel when Managing Requirements

Practices related to quality assurance are also among the least implemented in IT projects. By and large, they are still widely perceived as providing little added value to a project. More on this in Chapter 5, which is dedicated to this key area.

As far as the application of quality assurance to managing requirements, 60 percent of the assessed organizations have been observed as exhibiting serious deficiencies in this regard.

The role of quality assurance personnel is often unclear, and project team members, including the project manager, usually consider that they are in the best position to fulfill quality assurance activities pertaining to managing requirements and for that matter, pertaining to the entire project. Theoretically speaking, this is a valid point. A system engineer or system architect is indeed well placed to verify the relevance of requirements changes and to conduct proper impact assessments before accepting these changes. However, this is not exactly what we are talking about here. Quality assurance in this area has more to do with the verification that the requirements management activities and by-products satisfy the standards, policies, and procedures applicable to the project, and if they don't, either they are relaxed or a conscious decision not to respect them is made, agreed upon by the interested parties and documented. If such standards, policies, and procedures do not exist, whether a system engineer or somebody else performs quality assurance activities may not make much of a difference; they would essentially be subjective. Quality assurance fulfills another role and it is related to placing a process under statistical control. This will be discussed in more detail in Chapter 5.

In addition, there is something to be said about the skills required to carry out a proper verification. It is difficult to have the same individual manage a project and perform the project activities at the same time (with the exception where the project is a one- or a two-person job). It is also difficult to have the same individual manage or perform project activities and at the same time certify that they have been done properly. Unless one deals with extremely self-critical and virtuous people, a doubt will always linger, at least from the customer's point of view, that corners have been cut, especially if the system does not meet all expectations. It is feasible to ask system engineers and system architects from other projects to carry out this verification, but it may not always be economically feasible to do so, not to mention that the continuity of the project tasks they are currently working on may suffer in the process. Furthermore, having personnel temporarily or permanently assigned to verify requirements management activities and by-products does not preclude the conduct of detailed reviews of proposed requirements changes. In fact, this is highly desirable, and will be discussed in Chapter 10.

The situation where the project manager essentially relinquished his project responsibility prerogatives to the customer's representative would likely have been avoided if quality assurance mechanisms had been in place. In all likelihood, the customer's representative would have been restrained after the first few changes had gone through these mechanisms.

A project manager in one of the organizations we assessed used quality assurance to his advantage in a good-cop, bad-cop scenario. Customers always want changes at the lowest possible cost; this is a well-known fact and quite frankly, it is also natural behavior. When the project manager met with his customer in the process of discussing changes, he played the good-cop role, assuring the customer that he really wanted to please him. It was the nasty quality assurance people, bean counters at heart, who objected to everything. He essentially used quality assurance as lawyers for his own protection, and notwithstanding all the jokes about lawyers, they come in handy in difficult times.

Conduct Reviews of Requirements Management Activities and By-Products

The assessments we performed showed that software professionals, by and large, are very well aware of the importance requirements have on the outcome of a project. This is not to say that no errors are made in this area, but rather when mishaps occur, it is more likely to be the result of unintentional oversights than willful mischief or sloppy work. The best approach to prevent such oversights from happening is to conduct reviews, and since requirements have a particularly high impact on the remainder of the project, management should be well aware of the activities carried out in connection with the way they are handled and of their by-products.

The importance of management reviews stems from the wide visibility managers have of the project and of the various issues that are at stake. Specialized software professionals are liable to make a decision regarding requirements, without having this knowledge, and this may result in undesirable consequences.

It happened to a senior software architect in a project we had assessed. With every good intention, this architect, during a meeting with customer representatives and in response to the latter's request, indicated that his subsystem could include a Microsoft Access front-end interface to an SQL server — whereas the contract specifically stated that this would be an option for which the feasibility would be studied and a decision made later. Ensuing meetings took place and finally, a decision was duly recorded in the minutes regarding this change. Everything was forgotten until the deliverables were submitted to the customer. Unfortunately, the interface was buggy and its functionality was not satisfactory to the users, which resulted in complaints from the customer. But to add insult to injury, the customer also criticized the fact that the submitted subsystem interface documents were not coherent with the other subsystems that had not contemplated an MS Access front-end. An agreement was finally reached with the customer, but it took several months of intermittent discussions, a detailed analysis of the discrepancies between the subsystems deliverables, and the intervention of senior people in the organization to negotiate a compromise.

Management reviews would more than likely have prevented this situation from degenerating into such a waste of time and effort. Granted, the architect had to shoulder some of the blame, but so did the customer representative who initiated the request in the first place. Both parties ultimately went through unnecessary bickering and for a while, their relationship was rather tense.

Chapter 3

Planning

Failure is the child of poor planning and bad advice.

Planning a project requires a significant amount of experience and knowledge. Unfortunately, whereas training on subjects such as Java, C++, Web servers, and so on, is readily available, managerial skills are learned on the job, commonly from past mistakes. More often than not, managers have only their own initiative to rely on regarding project planning techniques and issues to pay attention to.

Information technology (IT) also has this particularity that differentiates it from most other disciplines: there is very little historical data to rely on in order to prepare reasonable estimates of the work to perform. When a project is completed, the first reaction of the IT project staff is to put it behind them as fast as they can, jump into a new project, and make the same mistakes all over again. We have come across very few projects where time was taken to record lessons learned. In the few cases where the lessons learned were available, they were undoubtedly the most interesting project document to review, especially when they were substantiated with some figures.

Involve Software Professionals when the Project Is in Its Early Conceptual Stage

This is usually not a problem when the project is a pure IT project, for instance, the development of a software application. However, when there is material involved, such as mechanical equipment, or when software is embedded in a system, the IT component is often given lip service.

This has been found to be a particularly thorny issue in organizations that have a strong manufacturing culture. Government organizations and organizations that are focusing on management information systems are less affected by this condition.

It should be obvious, considering the importance IT has acquired over the last few years, that the involvement of software professionals needs to be secured early.

In a significant number of the organizations we have assessed, particularly in private industry, the culture that characterizes software professionals clashes violently with the rest of the organization's culture. Senior management are liable not to understand software and are unable to relate to the way software professionals conduct their daily activities. In one instance, a senior manager had all but given up and had come to have very little respect for anything that came close to IT. He had been burned so often by releases that did not meet deadlines, and new and unexpected problems the software staff came up with to explain delays that he refused to be part of meetings where IT would be on the table. He honestly felt that a bunch of self-interested individualists, who had no concept of what the word commitment meant, were holding him hostage.

Involving software professionals early in a project will increase the chances that problems will be identified early. It will also promote the team spirit on which successful deliveries critically depend. Software professionals should particularly participate in planning the overall project along with the other affected groups. This will greatly contribute to raising the awareness that abiding by promises made in the course of a project has a significant impact on its outcome. It is all right to make mistakes and to learn from them, but if the same mistake is made over and over again, there should also be consequences for the individual(s) involved.

Insist That a Plan Be Prepared and Specify What It Should Contain

Nobody in his right mind would venture into an unknown city without a plan or directions on how to reach his destination, and an idea of how much money he will need and how much time it will take.

Planning IT projects has always been difficult. For one thing, estimates are frequently based on guesses. When a new development is undertaken, there will necessarily be a lot of uncertainties. However, after IT applications have been developed over the course of several years in a specific business domain, there should be some trends that can be identified, even in the absence of hard figures.

The number of organizations where the preparation of plans was found to be an issue represents only 12.5 percent of all assessments. However, when the question of the plan content and relevance is addressed, this value jumps to 40 percent.

Having templates describing the format and content of a project plan can greatly facilitate its preparation. It is essentially the responsibility of management to define the content of what they want to see in a project plan. Once this has been achieved, the details can then be provided by whoever will assume the responsibility of preparing the templates. Initially, it is desirable to keep things simple and to develop templates for a specific project. Later on, as experience is gained in their use, they can be standardized and extended to the entire organization.

Typically, a project plan should at least contain the following elements:

- A summary description of what the project is all about (in order to be able to map it to the organization's objectives)
- A breakdown of the high-level deliverables
- The way the project will be organized, taking into account the structure of the organization in which it takes place
- A schedule
- A breakdown of the costs

Details that may be necessary for personnel who actually carry out the plan can be put in appendices.

We have had the argument thrown at us several times that if a project plan does not include selling features, the project's chances of going ahead will be reduced by as much. Our response has always been the same. Once a plan is prepared, it is because the project has already been approved, at least, in principle. Too often, personnel having the responsibility of preparing project plans want to hit two birds with one stone and address both issues in the same stride. As it is usually easier to focus on all the benefits that the project will have rather than on aspects dealing with its execution, the latter are cursorily described and the first step toward project failure has thus been taken.

Ensure the WBS Is Used Properly

The Work Breakdown Structure (WBS) is the result of breaking down a system into lower level components. One problem we have found over and over in our assessments is that the WBS is often misused.

A WBS is a representation of the products to be developed in a project. One common mistake is to include tasks in it. Elements that are not products should not be included in a WBS. Even though project management is a valid WBS element, its sub-elements refer to the products associated with project management, such as the project plan, cost-benefit analyses, and progress reports.

Tasks are defined, resources are assigned and schedules are prepared by mapping the WBS to the organizational chart. Figure 3-1 shows how a WBS should be used.

Mapping the WBS against the organizational chart results in work packages. These work packages are the element containing the tasks to perform and the schedule. For instance, a WBS element calling for the development of user documentation will result in a work package assigned to the group responsible for documentation. Essentially, they are prepared by each group of the organization identified as a participant in the project, based on the directives of the project manager, who then integrates them into the master plan, along with the master schedule. Cost accounts are then associated with work packages to support cost tracking.

Many organizations we have assessed mix tasks and deliverables, which makes developing meaningful plans much more complex because the plan must simultaneously deal with two sets of parameters (the deliverables and the tasks required to produce those deliverables).

Start by Estimating Size

The next planning hurdle consists of estimating the size, effort, and cost of the project.

The following is an excerpt of conversations I have had repeatedly with software managers:

"How do you measure the size of your applications?"
"We use developer-days."
"That's not size, that's effort."
"Well, this is what we use for size measurements."
"What would you say if I told you that the house you asked me to build for you will be 200 worker-days big?"
"That would not tell me anything about how large my house will be."
"That's precisely the point I am trying to make."

Size should be the first parameter being estimated. For a house, the number of bricks, the volume of wood used, and the number of square feet or square meters are useful size measurements, and when productivity ratios are also known, cost and effort required to build the house can then be estimated. In software, the debate has been raging for three

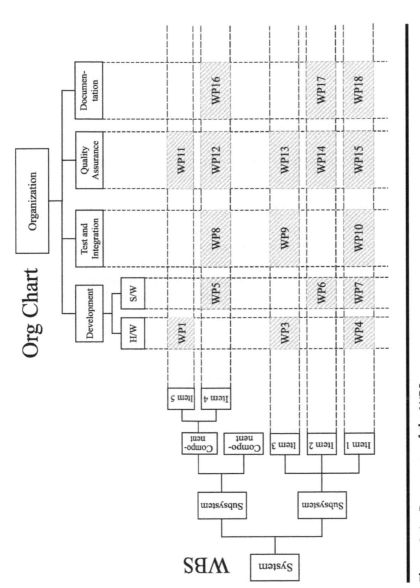

Figure 3-1   Proper use of the WBS

decades. Will it be source lines of code or function points or something else? As far as estimation is concerned, most organizations just guess. As far as size estimations are concerned, most don't do it. As it turns out, size is not explicitly stated, and effort is derived based on experience. The minus side is that experience disappears with those who have it and leave or switch jobs.

In all organizations we have assessed, we have seen only a few using function points seriously, which is unfortunate since they are relatively easy to apply and provide a good way to estimate all other characteristics once appropriate ratios have been established. By and large, managers and practitioners alike consider function points as an intellectual curiosity beyond the reach of anyone who has to deliver a real system. Few use source lines of code because many software professionals look at it as an approach easy enough to implement, but how one can actually make realistic estimates out of this is beyond their understanding. The kilobyte may be a very good measure to quantify size after a project has been completed, but to use it in order to estimate the size of a project is rather an abstract concept.

Those who actually have a methodical way of estimating simply break down the project in smaller and smaller components until, at the smallest level, the effort that will be required can be derived with some confidence. Given the rate associated with the category of personnel who will do the work, the cost can then be estimated. The only glitch with this approach is that these components from which other estimates are derived may not be independent variables. In other words, they are project-dependent and can't easily be used to estimate other projects.

Counting the number of components to develop constitutes one form of size estimation. If all components follow some organizational standard and if their nature and complexity are taken into account, this estimate can be used as an independent parameter to normalize all other mea-surements. These other measurements, such as work-days and $$, can then be expressed as work-days/component, $$/component, pages of documentation/component, and defects/component (and per type of com-ponents if they have been appropriately categorized). The source line of code constitutes the size estimate that has the finest level of granularity. Once normalized values have been obtained, they greatly facilitate esti-mation of other initiatives by providing ratios to be used together with size estimates to derive other estimates. They also make it possible to place the project under statistical process control, by measuring the limits within which these normalized values can vary, and detecting any non-random variations. The interested reader is referred to Annex A for a crash course in statistical process control.

At GRafP Technologies, we have wrestled with these issues like anyone else. Developers have a tendency to estimate effort and making them estimate size has been a constant battle. Function points were too abstract; source lines of code did not reflect new object-oriented methodologies and the use of code generators; pages of documentation were too subjective and too dependent on the author's style; classes were too broad to count; counting objects was inadequate because the number and complexity of methods had to be taken into account. At the beginning, we multiplied by two or three effort estimates developers were giving, depending on who was providing them. Indeed, they usually estimated the effort required to code and to perform some unit testing (the code will work the first time, right?). Integration, documentation, development of test cases, meetings, quality assurance, rework, reviews, and acceptance testing were all concepts that were forgotten when they generated their estimates. After deadlines were consistently missed, they were told to build some correction factors into their estimates to no avail. Finally, we settled on using a modified version of the COCOMO (COnstructive COst MOdel) approach. In COCOMO, one enters a size and gets effort and duration. The mathematical relationship is calibrated for a given environment using existing measurements if they are available, or as they become available after work has been completed.

We modified COCOMO's algorithms such that developers entered an effort and got size, expressed in thousands of statements (a statement could be the declaration of an object, the initialization of a property, an instruction in a method, a table declaration, etc.). The approach is represented in Figure 3-2. As we gained experience with the model, correction factors were refined to take parameters such as team experience and complexity of WBS elements into account. This approach made developers realize if their effort estimates made any sense, since it also broke down effort by phase or by iteration, and that there is more to software than coding.

Whichever approach is used regarding planning, it is worth keeping in mind that all project planning activities combined, whether they are performed by managers or practitioners, will represent 20 percent to 30 percent of the effort invested in a project.

Ensure That Auxiliary Resources Have Been Factored into the Plans

In battle, cold and hungry soldiers do not perform well. Likewise, in an IT project, software professionals who do not have access to the auxiliary

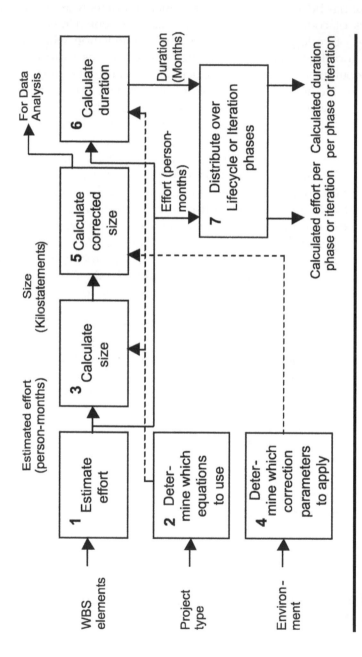

Figure 3-2   Size Estimation Approach

resources required to carry out the work will not be very efficient. Such resources may take the form of workstations, Internet access, graphics packages, simulators for testing, etc. They may also be more mundane, like having access to adequate storage space and secretarial services.

While preparing plans to acquire auxiliary resources, it is worth taking note that new methods and new tools will typically require four times the amount spent to acquire them in terms of training and support costs.

Identify, Evaluate, and Document Risks

If there is one sure thing in an IT project, it is that things will not go as planned and that there will be problems! The catch is that which problems will come up is unknown, as well as when or where they will come up. The more problems encountered, the greater the deviation from the plan. The greater the deviation from the plan, the higher the opportunity for more problems to develop. This is a vicious circle with increasing impact severity as time goes on, until either someone takes control and implements changes to prevent further deterioration of the situation, or the number of problems with which the project team has to deal exceeds its problem resolution capacity. If the latter case prevails, then the crisis has been reached.

In this context, it is not difficult to grasp the importance of keeping ahead of undesirable scenarios. In almost half of the assessed organizations, the lack of risk identification and evaluation was an issue that contributed to an average of 10 problems that subsequently developed in a project.

Note that what we are talking about here is not risk management. It is merely about identifying and evaluating undesirable outcomes in a project. It is essentially the instantiation of the French proverb: "Un homme averti en vaut deux"; or, "A forewarned man is worth twice as many."

Similar to the preparation of a project plan, the availability of guidelines for identifying and evaluating risks can make the exercise almost painless. In any case, the exercise is quite instructive and can even be fun. As part of our involvement in supporting IT projects and organizations after an assessment, we have implemented simple and successful approaches for identifying and evaluating risks.

For instance, in these organizations, at least three meetings are held during which the interested parties are gathered to discuss the highest risks each party envisions. Stakeholders who are at the same level of hierarchy attend individual meetings, which are moderated by an unbiased arbitrator. A defined process is established to prevent the meetings from deteriorating into recrimination sessions and to achieve consensus. At the end of the exercise, which can last from two to 5 days, depending on the scope of the project, the project sponsor is given the documented list of the most important situations to which he or she should give special attention, along with appropriate supporting information.

The exercise is typically repeated at least three times in the course of the project. Project personnel are usually eager to participate, since it gives them a forum to voice their concerns (they often have no other means of informing people who have the authority or the responsibility to address them). This also has the additional benefit of helping to establish a common vision of the project among participants.

Annex B contains a table that can be used to estimate risk exposure (i.e. the expected loss) as a function of the likelihood that a risk will occur, the vulnerability of an initiative to conditions that make it more or less likely the risk will deteriorate into the problem it suggests, and its impact should whatever protection is available fail to mitigate the risk or prevent its occurrence.

One problem we have found over and over as part of identifying risks is that by and large, people tend to identify problems; in other words, risks that have already materialized. This is different from identifying problems that are likely to develop (i.e. risks) based on problems that have been experienced in the past.

Ensure Management Reviews Commitments Made to Suppliers and Customers

Few organizations will give project staff a blank check to make commitments to suppliers or customers as part of the planning process. In most cases, it's not that project staff is not trusted. It has more to do with the fact that project staff may not have all the relevant information to make such commitments. Software practitioners would similarly raise an eyebrow if managers attempted to make detailed design decisions in a project.

The main deficiency observed in connection with this topic is that in more than half of the assessed organizations, ensuring that management reviewed commitments made to suppliers and customers (preferably before they have been communicated to them!) is essentially left to the good judgment of individuals. In these organizations, there is nothing indicating to the project staff the course of action before making promises.

The impact of this situation translated into undue cautiousness and hesitation on the part of those who were faced with the responsibility of participating in planning activities, or conversely, unrestrained recklessness.

In one case, a manager nearly brought his organization to the verge of financial collapse by submitting grandiose plans to customers which the organization had no means whatsoever of fulfilling. The result was that most customers cancelled the contracts on the grounds of non-delivery, and the revenues on which the organization was counting never materialized.

In most cases, a simple procedure attached to an e-mail will be sufficient to guarantee that management reviews project commitments, if quality assurance mechanisms are in place to ensure that it is followed.

Establish and Enforce a Directive Stating What Must Be Performed in the Course of Planning a Project

The most appropriate way for management of communicating to personnel what is expected of them is through policies and directives. This also goes for project planning. If people don't know what the minimal requirements are in connection with their work, they can hardly be blamed if they improvise activities associated with it.

The availability of policies helps project team members share the same basic notions on how project planning is to be performed. In order to be effective, they should be kept short and they should only state what is deemed essential regarding IT project planning. The details are typically described in procedures and interpretation memos that may be issued from time to time.

A full 55 percent of the assessed organizations do not have any policies associated with project planning. It has been our experience that personnel express a lot of doubt about the value of policies and the impact they have on a project. Yet, in the course of these assessments, the same people often stated that they did not know what the organization stood for and what was important to senior management. This is precisely the void that policies fill.

To use an analogy, policies are to an organization what a constitution is to a country.

Train Those Who Must Plan the Project

Planning a project is critical to its success. As mentioned earlier, up to 30 percent of the effort invested in a project is spent on planning, whether it is planning the overall project, planning design activities, planning tests, planning integration, or planning deployment. Yet, if one area lacks in skills and expertise, it is probably this one.

Managers to whom we talked repeatedly stated that as soon as they moved from technical positions to management positions, their training took a significant downturn.

Appropriate training in project planning does include formal classroom sessions covering planning tools and planning methods, such as the Earned Value approach. However, the bulk of training will most likely consist of on-the-job training, information seminars on interpreting procedures and guidelines that have been distributed in the organization, on writing memos, on the various administrative tasks, and the logistics associated with carrying out a project.

I personally had the chance of undergoing military training as part of the Canadian Armed Forces Officers Training Program. The part of the training that has been the most useful to me in my professional career are not related to the technical training I have received, which was thorough (and not always fun, especially the boot camp part!) but rather the organizational aspects of the job I had to do. A skill that has been easy to transfer to other facets of my professional life.

We have also found throughout the assessments that women seem to have a particular knack for planning. But then again, anyone who has to deal with a bunch of screaming kids, get them up and dressed in the morning, feed them, make sure they have done their homework, and have brushed their teeth before sending them to bed has got to develop some ability in this area.

Ensure That Individuals and Groups Are Informed of Project Commitments That Affect Them

Coordinating the various groups and individuals that have to work together on a project is probably one of the most challenging tasks a manager has to perform. At times, it can come close to herding cats, especially if the project has a large scope and is carried out in separate locations.

The issue of project personnel being unaware of events liable to affect them is far from uncommon. In some of the organizations we assessed, it came as a surprise to us (and also to the affected project team members, for that matter) that some individuals in two different groups were developing the same function of an IT application without knowing it, even though they met at regular intervals. In one instance, one group was actually working on implementing a function that had been removed from the plan two months earlier.

Keeping individuals in the dark, intentionally or not, will compound the coordination problems a project or an organization has to deal with, and it can lead to some cynicism. At one point in the course of an assessment, it came to our attention that several individuals had been aware for some time that acceptance testing of the application they were working on would probably fail, because a component delivered by a supplier was incompatible with some of the components developed in-house. When we asked them why they had not notified their supervisor, their answer was, "Nobody asked us. And anyway, in the ivory tower, they don't let us know what's happening, so why should we?"

Given the negative impact that such situations can generate, there is something to be said about managing by walking around.

Involve Quality Assurance Personnel during Project Planning

One proven approach to ensure that nothing falls through the cracks is to have quality assurance personnel play an active role during project planning. Having someone verify that planning activities and expected deliverables satisfy the applicable standards and internal procedures could have alleviated several of the deficiencies documented in this chapter. Yet 60 percent of the assessed organizations do not have any quality assurance performed during planning, the same ratio as for verifying requirements management activities and by-products addressed in Chapter 2.

In that sense, the role of a project manager is somewhat akin to the commanding officer of a ship. His or her job is to take the ship to her destination. On the other hand, the chances of succeeding will be that much higher if someone verifies that fuel and supplies will be readily available throughout the journey and at the stopovers.

Ensure That Management Reviews Project Planning Activities and By-Products

The proportion of organizations in which management do not pay much attention to project planning was relatively low at 18 percent. However, where this situation was observed (small organizations — those having fewer than 55 software professionals — have been found to be particularly vulnerable), this resulted in over 10 problems developing later on.

It is also significant to note that management reviews of planning activities and planning artifacts are performed in all organizations for which the likelihood of experiencing problems is less than 20 percent, i.e. one in 5 projects. The dramatic demise of one organization was partly due to a lack of such reviews.

Chapter 4

Tracking Progress

> Projects get in trouble one day at a time, and in the case of IT projects, the scarcity of visible and tangible end-products at each stage of the life cycle makes that a rule instead of an exception.

Tracking progress in an information technology (IT) project is essentially the continuation of planning after the work has started, based on collected or reported information. It should therefore not come as a surprise that the observations listed below are closely associated with those of the previous chapter.

Plans that do not change are, in all likelihood, plans that are not followed, unless they relate to trivial tasks that have been repeatedly performed in the recent past. This usually does not describe an IT project very well.

One common deficiency we observed as part of these assessments has to do with the preparation of detailed plans up front that then demand an unreasonable amount of effort to modify, as unexpected events occur. Either the plan is abandoned or only a token effort is invested to keep it up to date. The result is the same: improvisation slowly creeps in and eventually nobody really knows what is going on.

This is not to say that details are not important. However, details that are only guesses and wishes do not contribute much to the success of an IT initiative and can even reduce the chances of achieving it, since they are liable to mask important issues.

We have also found that the improper use of the Work Breakdown Structure (WBS) is frequently at the root of the problem. Often, plans contain both deliverables and activities, and a plan referencing design documents interleaved with design activities will be confusing. A plan should strictly be limited to identifying activities and resources to produce the deliverables identified in a WBS. Therefore, the design documents should be the title of work packages, and the activities should consist of the work required to produce these documents.

Ensure Management Reviews Changes to Commitments Made to Suppliers and Customers

Changes in commitments are as likely to happen as commitments, and because of their nature, they are liable to be given less attention. This is so because organizations believe that they still have the original commitments on which to rely. Original commitments are likely to be documented in a contractual agreement and are therefore considered as being the foundation from which work will be performed. Strictly speaking, this is entirely correct. On the other hand, changes made in connection with existing commitments and subsequently rescinded will bring bad blood in a project, which in turn will undermine the relationship between the parties for a long time to come.

As the old saying goes, whoever makes a promise may easily forget about it; the party to whom the promise was made will not. Establishing review and sign-off procedures will go a long way in preventing embarrassments and losses later on.

Ensure That Individuals and Groups Are Informed of Changes to Project Commitments That Affect Them

The assessments we have conducted over the years have allowed us to observe that between 30 and 40 percent of the problems that develop in an IT project are due to poor communication. The fact that people have a natural predisposition to take things for granted explains a significant number of situations we have been in a position to witness.

The organizations most affected by this condition are those having more than 100 software professionals involved in developing software products or services. In one such organization, this had degenerated into endless complaints on the part of the staff, who claimed that by the time the information they needed reached them, they often had to scrap part of their work, on the basis on false premises. For instance, a group that had to develop test scenarios and simulators for an online hotel reservation system found that the design group had made changes to the system architecture that made obsolete most of what had been developed. Senior management attempted to solve this issue by insisting that each project hold weekly review meetings and distribute minutes no later than three days after the meeting. However, this merely provided a means of voicing the frustration that had accumulated over the years, and the meetings were slowly abandoned, as first-line managers got tired of constantly being blamed for everything. An attempt was made to circulate all information relevant to projects among the staff. This was also abandoned as people complained that they had to go through piles of documents that represented little value to them, not to mention that the piles sometimes stayed on someone's desk for weeks before being passed around. The group manager finally decided to probe the project staff herself. She organized several sessions spread over a two-week period in which she listened to grievances and recorded the suggestions people offered. A consensus was reached to have each project maintain a bulletin board on the Intranet where all significant events would be journalized, along with the identification of a contact to get more information if necessary. After the system had been in use for about six months, weekly meetings were successfully reintroduced. The adopted solution had resulted in lowering the level of exasperation to the point where the staff was now ready to discuss in more detail items recorded on the bulletin board.

As will be seen in Chapter 5, Quality Assurance has a specific role in the establishment and maintenance of communication channels through which essential project information flows.

Ensure That Internal Project Reviews Are Held to Track Progress

Internal project reviews usually take place in 90 percent of organizations. Their usefulness, however, varies widely. In 60 percent of the organizations we assessed, we found that the project reviews are very informal and mainly held to discuss specific technical issues that come up from time to time. Progress assessment is qualitative, when it takes place at all. When progress is indeed assessed, the schedule is typically the only metric being looked at.

One organization claimed it always released its products on time and boasted of never having missed a deadline. After its IT projects were examined in more detail, it became clear that in order to meet its goals, the organization had to systematically trim the functionality of the released applications such that in the best of cases, only 50 to 75 percent of the initial functionality was provided. In addition, it was not uncommon for people to accumulate two to three months of overtime every year in order to achieve this result.

Software applications suffer from the inherent lack of physical by-products that are produced in the course of the development, particularly when a waterfall development life cycle is adopted, which is still by far the most prevalent. Progress can only be measured indirectly, unlike a physical structure (building a house for instance), where even non-experts can judge the advancement of the work with relative ease. Other life cycles have been devised to circumvent this limitation, mostly based on iterative and incremental techniques that focus on the old divide and conquer principle, in order to provide the equivalent of physical by-products earlier.

Managers of IT initiatives find it particularly challenging to assess progress objectively, unless they are extremely well versed in the technical aspect of the work. Not knowing where they stand, and often unable to get a better grip on the status of their project, they feel like they are caught between a rock and a hard place. On one side, senior management is applying pressure to have them deliver the product and on the other, practitioners are challenging them either to have the schedule relaxed or to provide additional resources. Conversely, technically oriented managers may be more at ease in judging progress, but have frequently been found to lack the project management and administrative skills that prevent them from anticipating impending crises.

One senior manager had devised a Machiavellian approach to handling this state of affairs. For essential projects, he had two teams perform the work, each one being unaware that the other was developing the same application. It was costly, but from the manager's viewpoint, at least he could have a better idea of how things were progressing, by comparing the two, while increasing his chances of getting something in the end. Depending on the progress achieved by each team, one would eventually see its project cancelled and team members would either be reassigned to other projects or simply let go. Not surprisingly, that senior manager was feared more than anyone by the project teams and this, in turn, had led to a rather unhealthy work environment. People chose to remain there, in spite of the treatment to which they were subjected, mainly because the work was interesting and they were given the opportunity to work with the latest technology, while acquiring valuable work experience on large projects.

Internal reviews have been found to be successful when the following conditions have been met:

- Meaningful and measurable parameters have been identified during planning
- External personnel are involved during the reviews to provide an objective assessment
- A strong culture for respecting commitments has been established

One small company (50 people altogether) that was part of our assessment sample initially relied on the third condition to assess progress and did its utmost to ensure that personnel felt free to provide status reports that reflected reality. Nevertheless, at times people bit off more than they could chew, and with the best of intentions, the impossibility of meeting the initially estimated schedule or cost became obvious. As new projects were undertaken, the first condition was combined with the third to prevent project team members from hanging themselves too often with the rope they had woven. The number of software components (tables, software modules, documents) that had to be produced in the course of past projects, along with their complexity, was used to establish scales on which personnel could rely to generate reasonable estimates. The number of components generated in the course of a project modulated by their complexity level was then compared to the original estimates to assess progress.

During these internal reviews, the quality of the components was also assessed based on the number and significance of the required modifications. Productivity was assessed by measuring the average number of components generated over a given period of time for various types of components (related to WBS elements). This data was compiled and managers subsequently used it to adjust complexity scales and define new categories when a lack of data correlation indicated that one type of component should be broken into two or more sub-categories.

The company also complemented this progress assessment approach with Earned Value management, with the help of internally developed Excel spreadsheets. This provided the quantitative feature of progress monitoring, and many developers had a rude awakening after being told of the variances that affected their tasks, while they thought all along that everything was fine. The company could have used commercial project management software to achieve the same results, but since their projects were relatively small (generally no larger than seven people), spreadsheets were sufficient, in addition to being easily integrated with their time reporting system, which also used spreadsheets.

Project team members also addressed technical issues during these meetings, and it quickly became evident that collecting data greatly helped establish up front the right focus for discussions. Managers used the collected data to assess the performance of project team members, to determine where they would be most effective and to identify coaching needs as appropriate.

The second condition, i.e., calling on personnel outside the project or the company during reviews, was used infrequently, and mostly when there were interfaces to other systems or when it relied on a particular expertise not readily available in the project. The company also used this condition as a last resort when a project appeared to be facing a crisis.

Track Risks

The identification, evaluation, and documentation of risks in IT projects are activities that are implemented in only half of the assessed organizations. Activities dealing with tracking these risks, closing those that are unlikely to occur, and identifying new ones as the situation evolves are performed in even fewer organizations.

The documents that were reviewed in the course of the assessments in which risks had initially been identified were rarely updated to reflect the actual project status. Initial risks were often still marked as current whereas the conditions leading to them had long passed. Likewise, there was little indication anywhere that problems that had been experienced had been anticipated.

In the organizations where risks are most likely to be taken seriously, tracking their evolution is performed periodically instead of being part of a continuous activity. Most people in the projects where tracking risks is performed in this manner recognize that it should be done continuously, but given the constraints under which they are operating, this is the best they can hope for.

Ideally, time should be allocated to discuss risks during internal project reviews, should it be only for the project staff to get an idea of what could go wrong and mentally prepare themselves for the possibility of undesirable events, let alone failure. On the other hand, risks should definitely be addressed during formal project reviews. Not surprisingly, tracking risks was less prone to subjectivity wherever progress was supported by hard figures. Numbers do indeed contribute to developing a clear mind. The table provided in Annex B can be used to that effect both to quantify exposure to risks during planning, and to track their evolution as conditions change.

We did observe that the reluctance of project team members regarding anything associated with risks is often the result of a "shoot the messenger" attitude adopted by senior management. Risks have the particularity that in organizations where a risk management culture has not yet been solidly established, senior management pays either too little or too much attention to them. In many instances, project personnel describe risks in a way as not to bring too much attention, since this is not necessarily a welcome event.

Indeed, once a project is under any form of scrutiny, one can always expect that something will be found that does not line up with the project team members' interest. Vague language is therefore largely preferred and risk statements often give the impression that they are well under control.

In one organization, an attempt was made to identify risks and to express them in terms of potential financial losses. It did not take long for senior management to react, and in this case, the attention paid to the risks expressed in this manner was way beyond what the project staff had anticipated. The project manager hurriedly chose to use a less conspicuous format and the Richter scale, created to measure the intensity of earthquakes, was deemed a much safer approach. A risk of one on the resulting scale was essentially negligible, whereas a risk characterized as a nine corresponded to a complete disaster, and any reference to a dollar figure was obliterated from all subsequent risk reports.

Organizational policies are particularly useful in preventing the occurrence of similar situations by clarifying up front what senior management wants and what the organization stands for.

Overall, these assessments showed that organizations identifying and tracking risks experience 40 to 60 percent fewer problems than those that don't. Very often, the mere fact of looking at what could go wrong will prevent a situation from deteriorating because those involved will have been aware of it and will have communicated it to others. On average, the absence of risk identification and tracking accounted for six major problems eventually developing in projects.

Institutionalize Formal Reviews

It is always a good practice to conduct reviews in a formal setting every once in a while, with senior managers present. Yet only 60 percent of organizations do so even though it has a high potential of preventing undesirable outcomes from developing in the course of a project. The formal setting conveys to project personnel the importance being given to the work that has been undertaken. These reviews do not have to be a call to all, but as many people as possible should be present so that everyone realizes their importance. At a minimum senior managers, the project manager, functional managers concerned with the project, and any other project stakeholder should attend. These reviews also offer an ideal forum for the customer representatives to voice their concerns.

These formal reviews should first be planned, for instance at the end of the specification phase, or if an incremental approach is used, at the end of each incremental release. The personnel we interviewed during those assessments indicated that at least one major problem was avoided by holding such reviews, for each of the six phases typically encountered in a project (requirements, design, code and unit test, integration, verification and validation, and deployment).

In one of the organizations we assessed, formal reviews are held at the end of each major phase of a project. There are typically two or three reviews per year for each project. The first review is held with personnel from the IT department to give everyone the opportunity to wash their dirty linen within the family. That review typically lasts one day. Then, shortly after, a second review is held with the customer representatives.

Most agree that these reviews have been very useful. Several sessions are conducted, depending on the aspect of the project to be covered, such that only those directly concerned with that aspect need to attend the corresponding session. Both practitioners and managers participate. Practitioners can see first hand the pressure to which a project manager can be subjected, and in some cases, it certainly helped them gain a better appreciation of the job, as senior managers or customers can sometimes ask tough questions. In addition, during the second review, they can hear the customer's feedback. For those who do not even know who the customer is, it can be a revelation. The reviews are usually not antagonistic. Senior managers or customers simply want to know what is going on, which is their prerogative.

Given that these reviews are not held every week, senior managers make it a principle to let everyone involved know that this is their chance to voice their concerns. The message is essentially, if you don't speak now, you will have no reason to complain later. In fact, it does foster a healthy and frank attitude, while reducing the chances that discontent and intrigue will creep in later. When reviews were first introduced, only the brave ones dared make a comment, but as personnel became used to the reviews, attendees made themselves heard. In addition, those who first brought up justified concerns saw the speed at which they were resolved when senior management got involved.

Eventually, this organization documented the approach to hold formal reviews, including presentation templates, guidelines, and checklists for their preparation. This greatly reduced the time people were putting in, while decreasing their blood pressure as they became acquainted with what was expected of them.

Take Measurements

If you don't take measurements, you probably don't know what is going on, at least not in clear terms, and it is likely that you are being optimistic. The biggest difficulty is to identify what should be measured. In fact, less than 40 percent of organizations collect meaningful measurements in the projects they have undertaken. In any initiative, cost and schedule are usually two essential measurements unless money is not an issue and time has no meaning, which is highly unlikely, especially if someone else is paying for the product being developed.

Other useful parameters as work is progressing are the number of defects that have been identified and need to be corrected, changes that have been made by the customer or that have been introduced by the team, and productivity.

Productivity is tricky to measure, especially if no size estimates have been made. However, if a WBS has been developed, then counting the number of components to develop is one way to get a rough idea of size. These components can be whatever has been identified in the WBS; they can be documents, tables, screens, functions, classes, implemented requirements, and so on. Anything that makes sense and appears suitable can be picked. Then, by counting the number of components that have been completed over a given period of time, and by averaging the counts over several periods, the productivity achieved in the project can be crudely estimated. Software spreadsheets can be used relatively quickly to derive ratios, such as the number of requirements implemented per month or the number of fixes made per week, and to display them in graphical formats for easier interpretation.

Productivity measurements can, on average, allow those involved in a project to implement corrective actions that will alleviate three major issues that would normally have a significant impact on the schedule. Taking measurements does necessitate discipline but the amount of time required to do so is not very large compared to the usefulness that can be gained from it.

In some of the organizations we worked with, management recognized that if left to themselves, people usually will not take measurements or will take them only for a while and will get bored. After all, how many of us are maintaining a family budget? When things are tough, we do, but as soon as the pressure eases off, we abandon it. Many of these organizations have therefore established a responsibility center for taking and analyzing measurements. The measurements are periodically fed back to the project manager who then takes whatever actions are necessary to bring the project back on target. Measurements may not be perfect and errors can creep in, but it is certainly better than relying on feelings and perceptions alone. In some other organizations, personnel assigned to quality assurance are assuming responsibility for this function, as will be seen in Chapter 5.

Keep in mind that in your next initiative, these measurements can come in handy when you are in the process of estimating it. In addition, defending one's estimates is much easier when one has access to historical data. Senior managers, usually being cost-conscious, tend to cut estimates. Defending your own with data from past projects could very well prevent such cuts, and save your neck should you have instead to give in and eventually miss your deadlines.

Establish Clear Roles and Responsibilities

The need to establish clear roles and responsibilities in a project should be understood. Surprisingly, we found that close to 40 percent of the organizations do not do it.

The idea is simple. First, make sure that everyone knows who has authority for what and who to contact in order to get action on specific issues. Second, establish the infrastructure that will enable everyone assigned to the project to communicate status and project information at the appropriate level of detail to personnel who can and do make use of it.

One would think that only small projects are liable to suffer from this ailment because of their higher likelihood to lack resources. That is not what we observed. It equally affects small projects and large ones. In a $100 million government project, the lack of clear roles and responsibilities was endemic. It started at the project director level and went all the way down to the executants. Everyone knew about it, yet no concrete actions were taken to correct the situation, as everyone waited to see who would take the lead. The director was close to taking his retirement and his replacement had not been identified. His main concern was to keep the boat afloat and to avoid making waves until he could get out of this mess. There was no project manager; someone had been assigned that role on a temporary basis, with little authority to do anything. Not surprisingly, the schedule was very unrealistic. The first major deliverables were supposed to be made in less than a year, and the staff knew that it was impossible given that work had not even started to produce them.

Establish Quality Assurance to Help Monitor Project Tracking and Supervision

Quality assurance is a topic most often left out of projects. A full 65 percent of organizations have not established quality assurance in their initiatives as far as tracking and monitoring is concerned. On average, one can expect that as a result, close to eight major problems will be experienced in the course of an IT initiative.

Project managers are often reluctant about being told that quality assurance personnel can be helpful in making sure that project activities are being tracked properly. They see that as their responsibility and a territory in which they should have absolute control. The truth is that project managers often do not have time to take care of the details in that area. They may very well instruct their team to track progress and to collect measurements, but that does not necessarily mean it will get done or it will get done consistently. Unless someone verifies that tracking progress and collecting measurements is being implemented across the board, chances are it is not what's on the minds of project team members.

Quality assurance can come to the rescue and be of great help to project managers. Project managers do mandate that certain activities be done and quality assurance personnel have the job, among other things, of verifying that these activities are being performed in accordance with project managers' wishes. I say among other things, because quality assurance also has the mandate to verify that project managers themselves perform activities that senior management has mandated. It may be the reason why project managers are not so keen to have quality assurance personnel too closely involved.

To use an analogy, politicians have the role of passing laws, to which they will themselves be subject, but without law enforcement agencies, those laws will be ineffective. This is one of the roles assumed by quality assurance. Unless one is dealing with an extremely virtuous group exhibiting unusual self-discipline, laws are bound to be broken, either on purpose or inadvertently.

State What Is Expected at the Organizational Level in Terms of Project Monitoring

This applies in particular to tracking progress in projects. If there are no written expectations in the organization that project managers can instantiate in their own projects, then they should take the initiative and explicitly state what their minimum expectations are to their project team members. After all, if the project fails, the project manager pays the price. For a project manager, claiming he could not get the best of each team member will not fly very high with senior management. Ultimately, it is the responsibility of the project manager to ensure that each team member gives the project his or her best shot. Yet, in over half of the organizations we assessed there were no such expectations, and by extension, there was none in the projects either.

For instance, a project manager should clearly state what is expected of the team leads responsible for specific deliverables in terms of progress reports. This statement should be kept at a relatively high level and not get into the details of how this is to be achieved. Essentially, it should fit on one sheet of paper and summarize the activities that must be performed and the information that must be submitted. If a specific approach needs to be followed, only a reference should be made to it. The implementation details should be left to the document in which the approach is described.

The idea of such a statement is that one knows what the minimum acceptable performance is; anything less than that will not be tolerated. The project manager can then leave to quality assurance personnel the job of verifying adherence to that statement and to the implementation approach, and to keep him or her informed of non-compliances.

We have observed that project team members generally welcome such direction when it is perceived as serving the team and not issued to satisfy the personal whims and ego of the individual in charge. People want to do a good job and any reasonable adult is aware that in a group setting, some basic rules must be set or the group will not function.

In one instance, the culture of the company was such that expectations for the team's performance had to be established by consensus. There were organizational policies in place but they left a lot of flexibility to project teams. The project manager had a kick-off meeting with his team where everyone had a chance to describe his or her vision of how the team should operate. No one came up with outrageous demands during this meeting, and overall, team members did not hesitate to willingly accept restrictions on what they could and could not do for what they felt would benefit the project.

In most organizations, this way of proceeding would be perceived as tantamount to the project manager relinquishing his responsibilities to the team and not doing his job, but in this particular organization, it was the vision the two founders had wished to instill in the minds of personnel.

Chapter 5

Assuring Quality

> Taking things for granted is an endless source of problems and
> the most heavily traveled road to failure.

Quality assurance, in my opinion, is the most misunderstood and poorly applied process in the software industry. It is perceived as an end of the road for whoever gets assigned that job. Yet, in reality, it is one of the most difficult and most important aspects leading to the establishment of a sound information technology (IT) infrastructure. After training (or lack thereof), it is the most significant cause of difficulties being experienced in the IT field. On average, 11 percent of the issues experienced in an IT initiative are the result of a lack of quality assurance. As a comparison, poor planning and poor progress tracking stand at 6.5 percent. Only lack of training is higher at 12.6 percent.

Quality assurance is most often perceived as a policing job. Few, if any, like quality assurance personnel to come peering into their activities and work products. It feels like getting a parking ticket or an invasion of privacy, and the usual response of the offender, like in the traffic violation analogy, is: why don't you do a useful job for a change?

This type of response is often the result of a misunderstanding of what quality assurance is all about. The only remedy is awareness. Quality assurance does contain a policing aspect, but its underlying objective is to ensure that the process is followed, that is, the way resources, methods, procedures, and tools are integrated in order to achieve the expected result. If the process does not work, then it should be changed and quality assurance personnel, having firsthand knowledge, can be very important contributors to changing the process. Until the process is changed, the role of quality assurance personnel is to ensure the current process is followed.

The main argument for making sure that the process is followed is that all measurements made with respect to the development or maintenance of a system are useless if they refer to a constantly changing process. The idea of implementing paradigms such as the Capability Maturity Model (CMM), the Capability Maturity Model Integration (CMMI), and six-sigma is to statistically control the process (see Annex A for an introduction to statistical process control). In order to derive useful statistics, the data on which those statistics are based must be reliable.

One cannot say that improvements have been made if no measurements are collected. Once a process is under statistical control, it can then be systematically improved and improvements can be quantified. But this can only be achieved after quality assurance has been implemented.

Establish a Quality Policy

This is essentially what ISO 9000 is all about and having a quality policy constitutes the basis for establishing the Quality System in an organization. The policy should clearly state senior management's expectations regarding quality assurance, such that it is clear in everyone's mind what is acceptable and what is not, and it must be enforced.

The challenge with quality assurance is that everyone wants it but nobody wants to pay for it. In fact, it turns out that quality assurance pays for itself and more. The catch is that in order to demonstrate this, measurements must be made, and measurements will not be reliable if there is no quality assurance. Out of the 40 organizations we assessed, 70 percent did not have a quality policy mandating which quality-related activities were to be carried out, and this resulted on average in 6.7 problems developing in the course of an IT initiative.

In many organizations, unfortunately, the quality policy is made of rubber. There is something written that presents grandiose and virtuous goals on quality, then there is the reality that sees senior management forgetting everything about these goals because they feel every situation brought to their attention warrants it. There is nothing wrong about bending the rules when the situation demands it; after all, it is the prerogative of senior management to do so. The problem is when there are several sets of rules, some being improvised on the spot, which then appear to be arbitrarily applied. When this occurs, it does not fall on blind eyes and deaf ears as far as personnel are concerned. Senior managers are then torpedoing their own quality assurance organization.

They might as well disband it because it is essentially wasted money. In fact, many would gladly do so were it not for customers who require that it be implemented. The quality assurance organization then becomes a facade for the eyes of the customer.

Quality assurance personnel should independently review adherence to the quality policy by everyone in the organization. Obviously, if a senior manager decides to derogate from the policy, this should ultimately be addressed by a senior quality assurance representative from the organization, not by someone who can easily be coerced into approving the decision without discussion. Such deviations should also be rare and result from exceptional situations. Most importantly, it should be documented and include the justification for derogating. The quality policy should be carefully reviewed before deploying it because everyone will have to live with it.

Assign the Responsibility of Assuring Quality

If the responsibility of assuring quality is not assigned, it will never get done. There are several ways of implementing quality assurance, which largely depend on organizational culture. The most common is the establishment of a separate group with a mandate from senior management. This group, in order to be effective, should have a direct relationship to senior management. The establishment of such groups is probably the main reason why quality assurance is perceived as assuming a policing function. They often have their own modus operandi and in the course of their activities, they are likely to have developed their own mini-culture of never entirely trusting the individuals they deal with.

In one of the organizations we assessed, experienced project managers assume the role of coordinators. There is no quality assurance department, the project coordinator position essentially includes it. This organization was part of a government department, and found this rather ingenuous way of implementing quality assurance in a way that was deemed acceptable to its employees. Being part of the government, where controls abound, senior management had envisioned that a traditional implementation would not work; personnel would rebel at yet another control or would lose motivation as a result of the perception that senior management did not trust them.

Personnel acting as project coordinators are not managing projects as such; however, they make sure that everything has been taken into account in the projects they coordinate. Because of their vast experience, they also help project managers and they sponsor new recruits to get them up to speed. Project coordinators meet on a monthly basis to recommend policies, standards, and procedures for the organization to implement, or changes to existing ones. They operate as a loose group in which ideas are exchanged on a regular basis, and because of their senior position in the organization, they have direct access to senior management. They ultimately attest that projects under their supervision are carried out in accordance with the rules in place in the organization.

Another implementation we have witnessed is through peer reviews. This is the approach the scientific community uses and in such an environment, it has been extremely successful. However, peer reviews do require an attitude of wanting to get at the truth, which is not widely found in private industry, driven by profit as it is, and in government organizations that are driven by politics. However, we have observed peer reviews, especially in small entrepreneurial companies in which there exists very strong leadership. In essence, the leader assumes the function of assuring quality and makes quality decisions based on the goals of excellence he or she wants the organization to achieve.

We have observed a form of quality assurance in one organization that we are at a loss to explain. In that organization, every individual does his or her utmost to implement quality in everything he or she does. Senior management fosters this attitude, but contrary to the preceding implementation, senior management has not assumed the responsibility of assuring quality; every individual in the organization has personally assumed the responsibility. The implementation appears to be the purest form of quality assurance there is, but we have so far been unable to describe it in sufficient detail to reproduce it somewhere else with any level of confidence that it would be successful. This form of quality assurance looks inherently unstable, yet extremely robust after it has achieved a steady state.

Train Personnel Assigned to Assuring Quality

Carrying out quality assurance is not an easy task. Unfortunately, as we have seen far too often in our assessments, personnel are assigned to perform quality assurance activities because they were not working on any particular project at the time, or they were perceived as not having any particular talent. Yet the skills required to perform quality assurance work are very real. A full 55 percent of the assessed organizations did not provide adequate training to their quality assurance personnel. As a result, 2.5 issues were experienced on average in projects undertaken by these organizations.

The analogy with the police always comes back. I remember a woman explaining to a neighbor that her young son really wanted to be a policeman. At that time, she was looking to send him to a highly rated private school. The neighbor's response was, "Isn't that a waste of money to send him to an expensive school if he wants to be a policeman?"

Personnel assigned to quality assurance must be able to communicate to senior managers, technical specialists, and customers. Their role, in addition to what was mentioned at the introduction of this chapter, is to ensure that essential information flows between senior management, customers, and project team members. To do this implies that they must be able to understand and talk intelligently about work statements, contract terms and conditions, management and technical processes, and management and technical topics pertaining to specific initiatives.

Training should not be limited to personnel assigned to quality assurance. Training should also include awareness sessions provided to personnel who will be interacting with quality assurance personnel to explain what quality assurance is and the value it adds to a project. I found that an overview of statistical process control is a big help, because most people understand the value of taking and analyzing measurements. Once people understand the final objective of quality assurance, it is much easier to accept it as part of their daily activities.

It is still very common in organizations to equate quality assurance with testing. One does not exclude the other, although quality assurance personnel can be assigned to test if they have the required skills, but quality assurance occurs throughout a project, from beginning to end, where testing happens at the end.

At Productora de Software S.A. (PSL), the organization referred to in Chapter 16, there is a core of individuals (3 percent to 4 percent of the staff) responsible full time for quality assurance. Added to that, 25 percent of the staff is trained in performing quality assurance activities, so when the full time quality assurance personnel are needed to verify technical design activities and work products, there are experienced designers trained in quality assurance who can add value to the verification available to assist them.

Prepare and Implement a Quality Assurance Plan

Once quality assurance responsibility has been assigned, personnel have been trained, and the organization is ready to start implementing it, the next step is to define what will be done.

Quality assurance focuses on verifying that the process is being adhered to in terms of development and maintenance activities, and that work products are compliant with that process and the standards it calls upon. For that to happen, a process first needs to be available, which also supposes that it is documented. That's a big assumption in organizations involved in software development and maintenance.

The process is often subordinated to the tools that are used in the organization. As for the way these tools are integrated with resources, methods, and procedures in order to achieve the expected result, otherwise known as the process, it is in people's heads. This is why process improvement often starts with personnel assigned to quality assurance. In order to do their job, they first need to capture on paper what the process is so they can subsequently verify that both development and maintenance activities, and the resulting work products, comply with it.

Ideally, a process should exist at the organizational level. That's usually a lot to ask, and establishing focus on individual projects should be the first step toward achieving this goal. As a result, it is likely that quality assurance plans will be different from project to project but one needs to start somewhere. Later on, as will be seen in Chapter 12, experiences accumulated over several projects or enhancements can be consolidated and slowly lead to a documented organizational process.

It is common that in order to implement quality assurance, personnel given that responsibility will need to document the process in individual IT initiatives before the plan can be prepared. Some compromise must be reached because documenting the process may take as much time as doing the project itself.

Based on our observations, the best way to go about this is to adopt an incremental approach. Quality assurance personnel, in collaboration with the project or the application manager, will document process components as they pertain to the software life cycle. They will start documenting the customer requirements analysis process, and then prepare the section of the quality assurance plan focusing on that aspect. While they verify that customer requirements analysis activities and resulting work products are compliant with this process, they will initiate documentation of the planning and tracking processes, followed by the software development (software requirements development, design, code, test, integration, and delivery) processes, including change management, and version control processes. At each step, as a process component has been documented, the quality assurance section will be prepared and implemented. Above and beyond the skills required by quality assurance personnel, it is necessary to add technical writing.

Once a project has been completed, there will be a documented skeleton process available if none existed. This process can then be refined in another project until the organization has a set of processes, one for each project at most. It makes sense to assume that the processes that have been written by the same individual will bear a lot of resemblance. If it is assumed that personnel assigned quality assurance responsibility talk to each other and act in a coordinated manner, then it is even possible to assume that an embryo of an organizational process will exist through cross-pollination.

This is the approach that was adopted by an organization that decided to implement quality assurance in the development of its applications. It worked relatively well, and even though people in the organization were very reluctant to accept quality assurance at first, a year later they were asking that a quality assurance representative be assigned to their project.

Quality assurance is one of the processes we examined as part of conducting our assessments. Typically, the technical staff chuckles when quality assurance is being investigated in an organization. They have no qualms about seeing quality assurance specialists being queried about their own activities. In fact, they are quite happy to see them grilled; in their minds, it is the rightful retribution for the pain they themselves have received from quality assurance audits and inspections. In the afore-mentioned organization, however, personnel were very protective of their quality assurance personnel and they came to their defense, trying to protect their representatives from undue questioning. This was unheard of, as the usual response is to let them have it.

One other aspect of quality assurance that needs to be clearly com-municated is that personnel assuming the responsibility cannot do every-thing. Frequently, engineering personnel expect quality assurance representatives will be able to define the entire management and devel-opment process, and not only verify that activities and work products are compliant with the process, but also review those work products and provide detailed technical comments: for instance, providing technical feedback on a detailed design document. This is an unrealistic expectation. In some cases, there may be instances where quality assurance specialists, because of their personal experience and background, will have the capability to meet that expectation, but this is exceptional. All that can be expected is that quality assurance personnel will verify that individuals with the right experience and knowledge will have reviewed that material.

Overall, the lack of quality assurance planning and implementation affected 43 percent of the assessed organizations and resulted in over nine problems that developed in each IT initiative later on.

Document Non-Compliant Items

"What is not written has never been said," according to the popular saying. This also applies to quality assurance.

As part of implementing the quality assurance plan, non-compliances will be detected, either in activities or in work products resulting from performing software development and maintenance activities. If non-compliances are not documented it is unlikely that they will ever be addressed. In fact, the task of documenting these non-compliances will be greatly facilitated if it is performed in accordance with a template, a procedure, or a checklist, so they are more understandable.

The data we collected proves this point. In one third of the organizations we assessed, non-compliant items were not documented and as a result, there were 12 outstanding issues on average in each of the IT initiatives we examined. When non-compliant items were documented, but still without respecting some standardized reporting approach, unresolved issues decreased to seven; in most cases, they were not resolved simply because they were not understood.

Non-compliances also provide a useful indication of the quality of the delivered products. By quality, I mean residual defects of course, but quality may also include time to market, if this is a parameter of importance for the organization (it usually is for commercial organizations). By having access to this information, cause and effect relationships can be established between non-compliances and overall quality, and appropriate corrective actions can then be implemented.

There are three ways to take care of non-compliances:

- Take whatever actions are necessary to make the product, the service or the activity compliant with the standard, the process or the requirement
- Modify the standard, the process or the requirement in such a way that will make the product, the service or the activity compliant
- Issue a directive to the effect that the product, the service or the activity will not comply to the standard, the process or the requirement

Each of these may call on senior management to make a decision, depending on the seriousness of the non-compliance.

We observed when problems are being experienced in IT initiatives, senior management understandably direct their subordinates to take corrective actions. Changes are introduced as fast as possible. Rarely are the collected data analyzed before implementing the changes, that is, if such data exist. Managers and practitioners just forge ahead to show senior management that they are giving heed to their directives. Changes made without taking and analyzing measurements usually modify the pattern of randomly distributed data. It may appear that an improvement has been achieved, but the fact is, nothing has, and the cycle repeats itself indefinitely.

Communicate Quality Assurance Activities and Results

Communication is the key to trust and cooperation. Quality assurance personnel who act like the KGB can hardly be surprised if they don't get any cooperation from project team members. They are despised, as they should be, and they do not add much value to an organization.

Senior management should insist that quality assurance representatives sit with personnel and resolve issues, if possible. The quality assurance plan should be a public document that everyone in the organization can look at. Having said that, it does not mean the quality assurance representatives should advertise ahead of time everything that will be looked at in an upcoming verification. But the dates, the topic, and the scope of a verification should not be kept a secret.

The findings resulting from the verification should also be communicated to project personnel, with the intent of resolving them if all parties agree, or to escalate to higher level management those for which an agreement cannot be reached. This requires yet another skill on the part of quality assurance specialists: diplomacy, or the art to do and say unpleasant things in a nice way.

Having this course of action documented really helps in conveying to all personnel the steps that must be taken in response to quality assurance findings. It does not replace awareness but it does help remove the contingency of viewing quality assurance personnel as informers. They are not; they prevent much nastier occurrences from happening, and they contribute to improving the capability of an organization with the information and data they collect.

One thing should be remembered at all times: what is not found in the process of assuring quality will be found by customers, and the price to pay will likely be much higher.

Have Quality Representatives Interface with Customers

Granted, quality assurance is not always a pleasant exercise to be subjected to. Yet, as a project or an application manager, having a quality assurance specialist sitting next to you when dealing with a customer, whether this customer is external or internal, can be a great help. It is like having a lawyer protecting your interests. However, as any lawyer will say, he or she must know the truth in order to be effective. One does not hide things from his or her lawyer; it is entirely counterproductive and it can eliminate all the benefits a lawyer can bring to a cause.

I have personally used, with great success, quality assurance personnel in this role when dealing with difficult customers, and as part of our assessments, we have observed others doing the same. In some instances, organizations have quality assurance representatives iron out the details of formal reviews with the customer's quality assurance representatives after management has got the ball rolling. This helps ensure that all aspects of a review will be covered and will be kept under control.

However, one question inevitably comes up, which is, what if the customer has not implemented a quality assurance function? This is not an infrequent situation, especially when customers are part of relatively small organizations. This also partly explains why over 55 percent of the organizations we assessed did not ensure that their quality assurance personnel interfaced with customers (half of them did not because they did not have a quality assurance function). In that case, our advice would be to have quality assurance representatives interface with whoever from the customer oversees the IT initiative. Again, as a reminder, this does not remove any accountability on the part of the project or the application manager; they still have ultimate responsibility for the success of the initiative. It simply implies that they have a resource to take care of the unavoidable details that must be taken care of in the course of their interactions with customers.

One argument often comes up during our assessments. If quality assurance personnel are responsible for ensuring that quality is embedded in the deliverables to the customer, yet they work for the organization that developed those deliverables, to whom do they actually report and which side do they take?

The answer is that they ensure that everything is done to guarantee that high-quality products and services are delivered to the customer, not because they take the side of the customer, but because it is more profitable for the organization. They report to the senior management of the organization that pays them, and senior management has the prerogative of issuing directives that quality assurance representatives may not like but with which they must comply. In that context, one can readily quote Lord Harold Caccia, "If you are to stand up for your Government you must be able to stand up to your Government."

Institute Senior Management Reviews of Quality Assurance Activities

Quality assurance must be very visible to be effective. Senior management should periodically review findings from quality assurance verifications. Only 45 percent of the organizations we assessed did so. Given that 75 percent of all organizations did have a quality assurance function in one form or another, we would have expected that the ratio would have been higher. For those that did not review quality assurance findings, it meant topics that needed attention fell through the cracks, and crises developed later on, as those topics invariably resurfaced.

Quality assurance findings reports tell a senior manager a lot about what is going on and how well things are going. The findings can be discussed during regular progress meetings, with the caveat that discussing them during meetings does not do away with the necessity of documenting them.

If most of the issues detected by quality assurance have been resolved at the project level, it tells senior management that people are working together to find solutions. For any remaining issues, senior managers are forewarned that they may have to get involved to make a decision.

In one organization, the quality assurance manager took it upon himself to send weekly quality assurance reports to senior management, who had never thought of the relevance of asking for such information. It turned out to be an eye-opener. Two, sometimes three pages of numbers and charts conveyed to them what they had always wanted. It took less than a month to have that practice implemented in the entire company. Eventually, everyone benefited: senior management, for being better prepared to make the right decisions at the right time; application and project managers, who saw their concerns and outstanding issues acted upon significantly faster; customers, who noticed improved response times from their IT supplier; and quality assurance personnel, who witnessed a marked improvement in their standing.

Chapter 6

Releasing Products, Deploying Services, and Controlling Changes

> Software applications to which corrections have been made possess an uncanny disposition to return to their original defective state in order to generate the maximum amount of inconvenience for the largest number of people.

Releasing products, deploying services, and controlling changes are basic activities in software engineering. We did not encounter any organization that did not do that. How well they did it is another story. Almost everyone in the field understands the implications of not doing it. In fact, any organization that develops products and services calling on Information Technology (IT) and does not control the versions of these products and services is unlikely to be in business very long.

This term, Release and Change Control, is also referred to as Configuration Management. People involved in real-time software development and embedded systems understand configuration management; however, the term is not commonly used in financial and information systems development. The term Migration is also used at times, though this refers to a specific aspect of releasing work products with the purpose of upgrading an existing system.

Whatever term is used, this chapter refers to the same activities:

- Collecting the latest components that have been developed, integrated and tested
- Releasing the resulting system to production
- Collecting bugs and identifying enhancements
- Making the changes necessary to fix those bugs, and to implement those enhancements in accordance with the priority they have been assigned
- Releasing new versions (or patches in the case where a bug or an enhancement needs to be implemented before the next planned release)

Out of the 40 organizations we assessed, only two did not have to assume responsibility for controlling changes and releasing work products, because they were outsourcing the development to a third party. They were essentially only taking care of managing the work.

Deficiencies in release and change control of software applications result, on average, in 1.25 issues in each release cycle. This may not appear to be very many, but one needs to keep in mind that corrective actions may be very expensive, especially when deficiencies have to be corrected after an application has been released to customers.

Establish a Repository for Baselines

A baseline is essentially a work product that has been reviewed, approved and for which future changes will be controlled. These baselines should be stored on a server or in a configuration management system where they will be safe. CVS, PCMS, Visual Source Safe, and ClearCase are examples of applications specifically built to control and store baselines.

This particular topic resulted in the highest number of issues in the development and maintenance of applications. Almost 24 percent of our sample either did not have a repository or it proved entirely inadequate in the sense that baselines were not controlled, which, for the affected organizations, resulted in an average of 10 problems later on.

One has to use judgment in establishing a repository. Because items that are stored in it will be placed under change control, and any modifications made to them will need to be reviewed, approved and duly recorded, it may slow down development drastically if it is implemented too early. This repository should contain at a minimum work products that will be delivered to the customer. However, in the course of developing products and services, intermediate work products sometimes need to be controlled as well, but without the rigor that formal change control requires. In those instances, we observed that it is common for organizations to implement additional levels of release and change control where it will be easier to implement changes. Some organizations reserve space on a server for intermediate work products or establish an intermediate repository that will feed the formal repository.

A small organization we assessed even did that by hand. Binders were kept in which documents deemed critical, including the code, were stored on CDs, and archived in binders. Such a system would not have worked in the development of a large system, but given the size of the application, it proved adequate.

Identify What Items Will Be Placed under Formal Change Control

At the onset of an IT initiative, identify up front what work products will be placed in the formal repository. If more than one level of release and change control is to be implemented, it may also be appropriate to identify what will be placed in each level.

It is common to place only code under formal change control. However, some other items may need to be considered as well. For instance, it may be desirable to place the initial requirements specification under formal change control after both the customer and the development team have reviewed and approved it. Likewise, tools that are used to develop and test that application may also be good candidates, especially if the application is expected to have a long, useful life. For instance, in the nuclear industry, we have observed customers requiring that changes be made to their system 8 to 10 years after it had been delivered. During that period, the original tools used to develop it may no longer be in existence or newer versions may not be compatible with the customer's version of the application. After establishing a repository for baselines, compatible software versions was the topic that resulted in the largest number of problems for organizations that did not give it enough attention, which represented a little over a quarter of the sample. Some customers don't take any chances. They require that the entire development environment be placed under change control and delivered to them.

Assign Release and Change Control to Someone

If nobody has the responsibility of releasing and controlling work products, it is unlikely to get done well, for the simple reason that it is not the most glamorous job. After all, setting up the repository, assigning read and write privileges, defining check-in and check-out procedures, and compiling bug reports and application statuses is not the most sought after task.

There is no need to have a full-time individual assigned to it unless we are talking about a large project. At a minimum, a project team member may take it on part-time. Some training is likely to be required; training on the tool used, for instance, as well as training on the approach to follow to release and implement changes. In large projects, making the development team members aware is also desirable to ensure that they know what to do regarding their own involvement in release and change control activities. In one case, awareness would have been very beneficial, since there existed some animosity between those assigned to maintain the formal repository and the development team members, who judged that their own release and change control procedures were more than adequate. Their feeling was that the group in charge of formal release and change control were bureaucrats whose sole contribution was to slow things down and make their life difficult.

One of the organizations we assessed found an innovative way of assigning volunteers to release and change control. Initially, it was the luck of the draw. Once the repository had been established, along with the process to maintain it, whoever added a component that made the system crash would inherit the job, until someone else did. That way of operating suited the culture of the organization, which developed graphics and animation systems. It would unlikely be acceptable for critical systems in which faults may be life threatening.

Have a Plan for Controlling Deliverables and Essential Work Products

All organizations that master release and change control have some plan of action. Sometimes, it consists of a few paragraphs in the project plan, while for large undertakings it could be a plan that stands on its own. This is essentially where release and change control, including problem reporting and request for changes, are described. It usually does not change much from project to project, other than annexes describing what is going to be placed in the repositories. Having it handy does convey the message that it is an important aspect of an IT initiative, while reminding development team members what their involvement is and what they are expected to do with respect to release and change control. For instance, in a particular project plan, templates for requesting changes and reporting anomalies were included in annexes, along with an explanation of what needed to be filled out, with examples and the links to accessing the form electronically. The plan itself was placed under formal change control, but everyone in the project could check it out.

This seems fairly simple and straightforward; yet one third of the organizations we assessed had no description of what release and change control activities consisted of or which had been carried out, which led to improvisation and problems later on because steps had been skipped or incorrectly performed.

Document Change Requests and Problem Reports

Surprisingly, almost 20 percent of the organizations we assessed did not appropriately document problem reports and change requests. In one case, it was not done at all. Changes and problems were discussed and whoever felt like taking them on did. It must also be said that this specific case applied to a small organization comprising about 15 software professionals. It managed to keep itself afloat, but there was a lot of wasted time and effort, and keeping track of what versions used by its few customers had been upgraded was quite a challenge.

It was inexcusable for an organization comprising about 700 people to operate this way. Indeed, it was unforgivable. The company experienced major problems and almost went bankrupt. Things must nevertheless be put in perspective. The risk of bankruptcy was not the result of a lack of problem reports and requests for changes; this was only a symptom of another much deeper malaise, that is, a lack of any systematic process to maintain, enhance, and develop IT-based systems.

Essentially, that organization relied solely on the memory of its staff and the notes people kept to remember what needed fixing and upgrading. This situation had not been planned that way; personnel of that company were as smart as people working in other organizations. The main problem was that the company grew extremely fast and had no time to organize properly. Any attempt to shore up the existing process always had to be postponed as new contracts came in. It became a relatively large company operating like a very small one, and every new employee who joined the organization quickly adopted that way of doing things and passed it on to others.

Interestingly enough, the common denominator of all organizations in which problem reports and change requests were not appropriately documented is that they all had problems. Their likelihood of experiencing difficulties exceeded 30 percent and reached peaks of 55 percent (as described in Chapter 16, the critical value has been empirically established at 40 percent).

All moderately mature organizations have established a problem reporting system and a disciplined process for handling changes, including review and approval of recorded anomalies and change proposals. Ultimately, both feed in the formal baselines repository.

Nowadays, there are free and easy-to-use problem reporting and tracking software applications available through the Internet, so organizations, even small ones, have no excuse for not having documented problem reports and enhancement requests. The most challenging task is to make sure team members in a project all do it more or less the same way. There is no secret to achieving this goal; documentation, periodic awareness, and independent verification.

Control Changes Affecting Baselines

Whatever is in the formal repository should be treated with the utmost care, because this is what ultimately goes to the customer. Residual defects that find their way out may entail very high correction costs. A power utility company we assessed had to correct defects several times over in each new release, because it kept building its applications with outdated components.

This is where changes may have the greatest impact. Without strict controls, baselines for which defects have been corrected manage to revert back to their defective state, because older versions are written over newer ones. It is imperative that the correctness and the integrity of baselines be maintained at all times, and regression tests should be performed to verify that changes made to updated components have not caused unintended effects on the baselines.

Accidents do happen, but there should be recovery procedures available, at least for critical code and data. In the middle of one of our assessments, a developer in the IT department of a government organization made an error in declaring a field of a table, which resulted in the deletion of all the data pertaining to that field. This was the consequence of improper regression testing and changes made under pressure. Transactions affecting that data had fortunately been recorded over the month and were still available. It was possible to rebuild the data, but it took several days on the part of many people. It so happened that the disk storage units were being repaired, so data was not backed up in real time.

One should never assume that code and data are safe. Complacency has indeed been the source of many costly errors. In the organizations we looked at, 15 percent of them had totally inadequate protection and recovery mechanisms of their baselines and were literally playing with fire day after day, while almost 40 percent implemented the use of these mechanisms by word of mouth only. Some of those organizations were relatively large and were providing services that, even if they were not life-critical, could have very serious impact on their customers.

Document What the Release and Change Control Repository Contains

Over 55 percent of our sample did not have any documentation on what the release and change control repository contained. The result was that personnel in those organizations did not know or only partially knew what functionality characterized baselines stored in the repository.

Not having that information just invites problems and reduces productivity. The best approach is to insist that developers write a small paragraph for each component they developed summarizing what its functionality and status are. The individual responsible for release and change control can then collate that information and make it visible to the development team. A word of caution here is to be brief and to the point. In one organization, a developer was particularly prolific and wrote page after page for each component he developed. Again, having templates and examples will go a long way in preventing either too little or too much documentation.

Conduct Baseline Audits

Because of its importance, the formal baselines repository should be periodically audited. These audits are normally conducted by whoever is responsible for release and change control, but quality assurance personnel can also perform them. However, it is more common for quality assurance personnel to limit themselves to verifying that someone has conducted such audits.

It is a common problem to build applications and realize later that some functionality is missing because not all components were collected to make the build, or some of these components are not the most recent. Two types of audits should be conducted to prevent that from occurring: functional audits and physical audits.

Functional audits focus on verifying that all the functionality of the application is accounted for. Physical audits focus on verifying that all actual components implementing that functionality are accounted for. Some of that verification can be partly automated. In some release and change control tools, the design components and the functionality they provide are specified early on along with all the actual components that will be coded, tested, and put under change control. The tool can then generate warnings if some of the components are missing or if additional components are put there by mistake. Of course, this assumes that the specification is kept up to date, as things are likely to change in the course of developing an IT system, and for that reason, even automation does not eliminate the need for audits.

This verification can also be done manually using traceability matrices (e.g., Excel spreadsheets) and checklists identifying all the components that will be developed and the functionality they provide. This appears to be rather burdensome, but like anything else, if a little is done every day, it is not so painful, especially for small projects. A disciplined team that has been told repeatedly to keep development folders up to date and to follow established documented guidelines will go a long way in facilitating such verification. However, when done at the end of a development, it can turn into monumental task prone to errors.

Half of the organizations we examined did not perform baseline audits. The consequence was more a question of inefficiency than anything else (on average, a lack of baseline audits resulted in two issues to resolve later on), since integration and acceptance testing usually identified residual anomalies. On the other hand, waiting until testing to detect the presence of defects is not always the most productive way of developing IT systems. There is ample evidence that methods maximizing the removal of defects before integration testing is initiated usually reduce overall development and maintenance costs.

Specify What Is Minimally Acceptable in Terms of Release and Change Control

These are essentially the policies and directives that we found were severely lacking in almost everything connected to the development and maintenance of software-intensive systems. Two thirds of the organizations we assessed did not have anything in this regard.

As was stated earlier in this chapter, most organizations that develop products or deploy services calling on Information Technology have implemented some form of release and change control; otherwise, they would not be in business very long. The lack of policies does not necessarily preclude the implementation of release and change control, but it leaves the door open to abuse or misuse. Policies and directives provide more mechanisms — and a low cost one at that — to prevent difficulties from developing in a project.

The establishment of policies specifically related to release and change control is sometimes not seen as a priority. It is more technical than planning or quality assurance, and since policies normally originate from senior management, the topic is not necessarily what is on their minds, unless disasters have been experienced in the past.

One thing must be taken into account in connection with policies. They usually come after a process has been defined. The reason is that making a policy for something that has not been defined is risky at best. Policies are at the base of any entity that regroups individuals who work toward a common objective. They should not change frequently because the introduction of a policy, if the staff takes it seriously, can be quite disruptive. If policies change constantly, then the staff will not take them seriously, and hence they will lose their value. Consequently, policies should be established after a process has been exercised for some time and has been found to be satisfactory.

Chapter 7

Contracting Out

> Blessed is he who does not know what he wants done, and does not ask someone else do to it for him.

Contracting out is something most organizations resort to, not only those involved in information technology (IT), simply because very few, if any, organizations have all the resources and the knowledge required to develop, enhance, maintain, deliver, and support their products and services. Even more so now, as a result of the new trend in outsourcing, which can be considered a form of contracting out. Where contracting or subcontracting usually implies a specific time limited task, outsourcing is more often associated with activities to be performed over a longer period. For instance, a company will contract out or subcontract the development of a system, then outsource the maintenance and operation of that system. Outsourcing is commonly referred to in connection with effectiveness and cost-saving measures, allowing an organization to focus on what it does best, where contracting out is more often referred to in connection with knowledge, expertise, and resources that must be acquired externally by the contracting organization.

For the remainder of this chapter, contracting out and subcontracting will be the terms primarily used, and the concepts to which they are associated will be deemed to apply to outsourcing as well.

Contracting out is not trivial and requires a set of skills that are not always available in organizations that decide to pursue that avenue. It requires strong negotiation skills to come up with beneficial conditions both for the contracting organization and for the supplier. A solid administration infrastructure is needed to put down in black and white what it is that will be contracted, terms and conditions of the subcontract, the acceptance criteria that will determine how the subcontracted item will be accepted, and finally, sound management to keep track of suppliers and to direct them properly. Those who are good at it benefit from a reliable supply chain that ensures their future growth.

Establish and Enforce a Directive Describing at a High Level the Steps to Take for Contracting Work Out

These steps are the rules of the land. No one is allowed to deviate from them unless he or she has the approval of the top individual in the contracting organization. These rules see that decisions are not made arbitrarily when work is contracted out, and that all aspects have been looked at, including requesting proposals, evaluating bids, and selecting the supplier representing the best value for the contracting organization. In a typical IT initiative, the lack of policy, misunderstanding the policy, or the lack of knowledge about the existence of a policy will be the root cause of two undesirable outcomes later on.

Keep in mind that the topics of all previous chapters, and some of the topics of the chapters that follow, will need to be applied before work is contracted out. If they are not, expect that problems will occur. In fact, from Figure 16-5 in Chapter 16, it can be seen that the likelihood of experiencing problems with respect to contracting out in organizations developing IT products and services is approximately the average likelihood of experiencing problems in Requirements Management, Project Planning, Project Tracking, Quality Assurance, and Release and Change Control.

Before a subcontract is let out, what exactly must be subcontracted must have been identified, along with the way subcontracted items will be integrated to the remainder of the system once they are delivered. Contracting out must follow a plan of action. The subcontract must be let out at the right time: not too late and not too early. For instance, if it is too early, everything may not be in place to verify that the delivered item is adequate. Subcontracted work must be monitored and controlled by the contracting organization, which must also verify that the contractor builds quality in the development of the products, and that the version and changes made to the subcontracted items are properly controlled.

The following question often arises in connection with contracting out: should the contracting organization impose its own process on the supplier?

Organizations that are good at contracting out, and have developed an internally shared vision on how to go about it, let suppliers apply their knowledge in accordance with their own process. After all, this is why suppliers were sought out in the first place. Requiring that suppliers follow a process with which they are not familiar is an added risk that should be avoided if possible. There may be situations where the contracting organization's customer will have specific requirements, for instance that documentation adhere to a given format. One of the organizations we assessed that had acquired a lot of experience in contracting out assumed the documentation formatting responsibility to make sure the customer would be satisfied. Another opted out of that responsibility, but worked closely with the supplier, which had been assigned the responsibility as part of the contractual agreement in which the close involvement of the contracting organization had been clearly stated up front. In addition, training for the supplier had been budgeted as part of the proposal the contracting organization had prepared for its own customer.

In any case, it is not a good idea for the contracting organization to abdicate its responsibilities and let the customer micro-manage suppliers. More often than not, this ends up in lawsuits from both sides and only lawyers make a profit.

Insist on Having the Supplier Submit a Plan

This should be done before work actually starts. For large subcontracts, this is usually not an issue, but for smaller ones, the urge to get the subcontracted item as fast a possible at the lowest possible cost often prevails over good judgment. We have done that ourselves and it has rarely resulted in a happy ending. Over the 40 assessments we performed, 27 had contracted work out and out of those, six had no plans from their suppliers.

The entire subcontract does not necessarily need to be planned in detail. If an incremental approach is being used, then it is quite acceptable to have the supplier submit a high-level plan, with details provided only for the first increment. What is important is that the plan be meaningful and clearly indicate that the supplier understands the work statement, and that the contracting organization is likely to receive what has been contracted out.

The typical approach to contracting out is for the contracting organization to issue a work statement in the form of a Request for Proposals to a set of pre-screened suppliers. Then, the potential bidders will repeat the work statement in their proposals, adding a few details to show that they do provide added value. I always found that this is not an approach conducive to getting a successful outcome. Some suppliers are very good at writing really nice proposals, with excellent vocabulary and nice pictures, but there is little under the surface.

Have the potential bidders prepare a plan as part of their proposal, but be realistic. Keep in mind that suppliers are as busy as you are, and they often lack resources to prepare detailed proposals. Suppliers estimate that they will win one out of 10 proposals, so the amount of work they are willing to put in preparing a proposal will be heavily influenced by a low hit ratio. But if they know what they're doing, they should already have plans at their disposal that can be tailored to the work statement.

Some organizations, instead of issuing Request for Proposals, especially when the work is relatively small, will visit potential bidders to scent them out, that is, to see for themselves what they are like. An experienced assessor will be able to say within a short period whether it is worth doing business with a given organization. The way people interact, the language they use, layout of their office space, and their process documentation can tell a lot about an organization. Asking the receptionist about the company is also a very good source of information. Insist on seeing as many people as possible during the visit. Speaking only to the public relations and marketing personnel will not tell you much. Those people are trained to present the most favorable side of the organization and to hide what should not be shown in public. Based on the assessors' inspections, which may last from half a day to a day, they will select a shortlist of potential bidders, and issue a request for proposal only to a few of them, and possibly to one only. When this is the case, then it is perfectly justifiable to request that a detailed plan be submitted. The bidder will be more inclined to do so, knowing that his chances of winning the contract are that much higher.

A business friend was interested in doing business with a potential supplier who offered to develop a marketing software application for his company. This individual was very tempted to negotiate an agreement with that supplier, whom he had visited once, but not being an expert, he had not been able to judge the soundness of going ahead, even though what he had seen had impressed him. Wishing to apply due diligence, he called me and I offered to perform a quick audit, if he paid my traveling and living expenses.

I called the supplier and explained to the president the last step my client wished to take before signing a contract, which was worth several hundred thousand dollars. I told him that I would visit him in a week's time and I listed the topics I would examine, namely the process his company was following to develop applications, and the people to whom I wanted to talk. Three days later, the supplier called my business friend, to say given his current workload, he could not afford to pursue my business friend's recent offer. Reading between the lines, my business friend rightly deduced that under the shining surface the supplier had shown, the sight was not so pretty and the contractor had decided that having it uncovered was not worth the contract he was after.

It turned out to be a good investment, since this friend was so impressed with the potential loss that in all likelihood I had prevented, he hired us to perform assessments of all suppliers with whom he was considering doing business.

Agree with the Supplier on How Progress Will Be Tracked and How Contractual Changes Will Be Made

The best way to avoid problems later is to have frank discussions with a supplier on how you intend to proceed.

First, baseline the plan the supplier has sent, after changes you deem relevant have been incorporated, and after you have approved it; and use it to track progress. If this is made clear to the supplier up front, he is more likely to ensure that the plan is realistic. In contracting organizations where plans were neither reviewed nor approved, 12 significant problems on average were experienced later on.

The plan should have been built based on the Work Breakdown Structure (WBS), and therefore, it should contain tasks, and these tasks should be traceable to the deliverables that are defined in the WBS. Organizations that are good at contracting out make sure that there are a lot of deliverables, even if they are small, to ensure that the supplier is never left unchecked for long periods of time. For that matter, a deliverable may be a progress report, and it is quite acceptable to have weekly reports. These reports should be read; if they never change, it may be because the supplier is experiencing no problems and everything is fine, and in that case, reports should indicate clear progress. Or, maybe progress reports don't change because nothing much is being done.

It is also a good idea to specify up front how changes will be made to the contract. A good contract is an insurance in case things turn ugly, and having a lawyer review it is desirable, keeping in mind that the clauses that are listed will probably never be exercised. One thing to remember is that there must be trust. A contract, however well written, will never replace trust. It can only reduce the losses you are liable to incur. In any case, if the contracting arrangement turns sour, you, as the contracting organization, will not have the product or the service that had been contracted out, and this will be a loss that will never be entirely compensated by legal action. A contract change procedure understood and shared by both the contracting organization and the supplier can go a long way to smooth out the ripples of contractual arrangements.

As part of our work in assessing the development of products and services relying on Information Technology, we have seen repeatedly organizations spending a significant amount of time preparing Requests for Proposals, evaluating bids, and issuing subcontracts. Then, after both parties have signed off, the engineering departments of both the contracting organization and the supplier forge ahead and do something only vaguely related to what has been specified in the contractual agreements. Usually, personnel from the contract department of the contracting organization has only a fuzzy idea of what is going on, and when they find out, that is if they do find out, then personnel from the legal department roll in and everyone blames everyone else.

On the other hand, we also observed contracting organizations and suppliers where everyone knew that the subcontract would not result in what was required, but no one could or would take the initiative to modify the contractual agreement. Obviously, negotiating effective contractual agreements requires a balance between strict adherence and allowance for making changes when they are required.

Hold Progress and Coordination Reviews with Suppliers

Holding frequent reviews is the best way to get what you want and to make sure that work is progressing to your satisfaction. This is as valid for work performed internally as it is for work that has been contracted out.

Unfortunately, both people from the contracting organization and the supplier are normally busy, and if they can avoid spending time in reviews, they will gladly use that time to do something else. In other words, if there is nothing forcing them to keep in touch, inertia will prevail, which is more than likely to result in disappointment later on. This is another reason why policies and processes are so important. They instill discipline, and quality assurance personnel from the contracting organization will be more than happy to ensure that these reviews are held, and held in accordance with what has been defined.

Incorporating in the contractual agreement the frequency of reviews and the participants in those reviews (by function if not by name, since they may change in the course of the subcontract), along with their expected outcome, is a practice that should always be implemented. This is something that differentiates organizations having a lot of experience in contracting out from those that do not. Contracting organizations are always in contact with their suppliers.

These reviews include management reviews, technical reviews, and interchanges between personnel from the contracting organization and personnel from the suppliers. The result of these reviews should be documented somewhere, either in a project notebook or electronically in the form of notes in a folder, in a database, or in an electronic agenda.

I purposely left the topic of formal reviews to the next section to stress the difference between informal reviews, which are discussed here, and formal reviews discussed below.

Conduct Periodic Formal Reviews with Suppliers

There is something behind the saying that familiarity breeds contempt. The formality associated with certain reviews can go a long way in putting things back in perspective and reminding suppliers of their role and responsibilities in the work that has been contracted out to them. The word "client" is too often forgotten, especially when those performing the work have expertise that their client lacks. However, the client has the money and without that money, there will be no work. Formal reviews contribute in subtly communicating that concept.

Formal reviews may be conducted once or twice a year, and at least once in a project, independent of its size. These reviews have the objective of letting suppliers present their progress to date and summarise the functionality of the product or service they are supplying, along with discussing any outstanding issues. Formal reviews are normally attended by senior management from both the contracting organization and the suppliers. Formal reviews will often provide the incentive to conduct the less formal reviews and interchanges discussed in the preceding section.

Formal reviews can also protect suppliers from customers who claim that since they are paying, they have all the rights. For example, it is fairly common in large projects to have formal requirements and critical design reviews. After action items have been addressed following these reviews, any requirement or design changes, depending on the type of review conducted, will entail additional costs.

There is no doubt that conducting formal reviews at selected milestones helps everyone gain better insight into how the work is going. In fact, we found that in those organizations that did not do so, an average of 20 problems developed later on.

It is also advisable to define the way these reviews will be held. This will benefit personnel from the contracting organization who will be in a better position to prepare a relevant list of items to review, and it will also benefit personnel from the supplier for preparing appropriate material, especially if they have never participated in such reviews.

Involve Quality Assurance Personnel and Personnel Responsible for Release and Change Control

If you want suppliers to deliver quality products and services, then have your quality assurance personnel check that the suppliers' own quality assurance personnel are fulfilling their role and responsibilities appropriately. There is no other way, as far as we have concluded from our assessments. Of course, this presumes that the contracting organization you represent has personnel assigned to quality assurance.

Like anything else, the best way to ensure that an activity is being performed in accordance with your wishes is through verification, and verification is a full time job, not something that one does in his or her spare time.

Only 40 percent of the organizations we assessed had implemented full or partial quality assurance for contracted work. Sixty percent did not have any. For those, this lack of quality assurance over suppliers resulted on average in 15 issues in the course of a project.

Likewise, personnel responsible for release and change control in the contracting organization should oversee corresponding activities performed by suppliers. This normally takes the form of functional and physical audits, which essentially means that verification is performed to the effect that everything is accounted for, physically and functionally, as far as components making up the product that has been contracted out are concerned. It will be the job of personnel assigned to quality assurance to check that this has been done.

We observed one extreme in connection with that topic. One organization having subcontracted the development of an application had stipulated that intermediate deliverables had to be provided by its supplier during the coding phase. Most of these deliverables had not been integrated and were not yet functional. Therefore, they could not be tested without having access to the development environment and its associated material and human resources. The only way to verify that something was being delivered was to perform physical and functional audits, which the contracting organization never bothered to perform. After problems arose with the supplier, someone proposed to examine what those deliverables actually consisted of. To do that, the contracting organization, not having the expertise to perform such audits on its own, acquired the services of a consulting firm. To the utmost concern of the contracting organization, most delivered components contained only headers and comments as to what these components were supposed to do. No code had yet been developed, even though progress reports indicated that coding was over 65 percent complete.

This finding unleashed a full audit by the contracting organization, which discovered that the supplier had experienced serious difficulties over the past year, from both a financial and organizational perspective, and was desperately trying to gain time in the hope that things would get better. Eventually, the supplier declared bankruptcy, and the whole application was written off.

As mentioned in Chapter 6, deficiencies in release and change control of applications developed internally result, on average, in 1.25 issues in each release cycle of a system, where deficiencies in release and change control of applications that have been contracted out result in three, that is, an increase of 140 percent.

Ensure That Acceptance Tests of Suppliers' Deliverables Are Performed, Complete, and Documented

Acceptance testing is sometimes neglected by contracting organizations. The deficiency that caught our attention during assessments was not that acceptance tests were not performed (7.5 percent did not do so, which resulted in 17 issues later on), it is rather that they were improvised. Acceptance testing was too often left to the discretion of whoever received the products or services that had been contracted out.

The biggest impediment was that no process was defined for performing such tests, with the results that they were often incomplete, and results were not properly documented. This was noted in almost 50 percent of the organizations that did contract out IT development and maintenance. Even though the lack of a defined way to perform acceptance tests was not as severe as not performing them at all, it nevertheless resulted in nine problems that had to be dealt with later on, which resulted in additional cost and wasted time.

In some of the organizations we assessed, it sometimes took several years before suppliers were notified that there were significant residual defects. Some of those defects had been discovered much earlier; they just did not get documented, and, as a result, they were never reported. In some cases, corrections were made as part of the warranty that had previously been negotiated, but in other cases, corrections fell under enhancements, which resulted in additional costs for the contracting organization. In other cases, suppliers had gone out of business, and the contracting organization had to pay a hefty price to get those defects corrected. In one case, the cost of corrective actions was so high that the contracting organization abandoned the product and initiated another project to replace it. As far as we know, the contracting organization has not learned anything from that lesson (or it has forgotten all about it), which leads us to presume that the whole cycle is going to be repeated again.

Train Those Responsible for the Selection and Management of Suppliers

Contracting out is a trade like any other, and personnel who must coordinate and perform this task need to be trained. Writing solid agreements, knowing which clauses are important, and negotiating with potential suppliers are all aspects that personnel involved in contracting out must know. Some of that training can be acquired from external sources, but overall, a large part of the training must come from within the organization. Indeed, no one outside of the contracting organization can teach personnel about its rules and regulations, and about the way of doing business in the organization. Seminars, short meetings, and peer reviews (to be discussed in Chapter 10) constitute very efficient mechanisms.

It is not uncommon to see untrained personnel assigned the job of negotiating with suppliers and writing contracts, especially in small organizations. In fact, in a full 30 percent of the organizations we assessed, personnel assuming that responsibility had received no training. Of course, good judgment is a big help, and some people do have natural abilities to deal with suppliers but most do not. In one of the projects that a small company had initiated, the project manager had been assigned that task and had received no specific training to that effect. He did as well as he could, and it was a good thing that his counterpart acting for the supplier did not know any better. Between their blunders and false starts, they both managed to pull through it because it was in their mutual interest to succeed, and neither organization had the resources to correct that situation, while both benefited from benevolent senior managers.

Some of the organizations we came across as part of our assessments could have taken either of the contracting organization's representative or the supplier's representative to the cleaners, without even trying or having malicious intent. In one particular instance, the supplier, which had personnel with a lot of contracting experience, took it upon itself to coach the personnel of the contracting organization on how to perform contracting-out activities, pointing out to the individual from the contracting organization the mistakes she was making or was likely to make if she forged ahead. This was rather unusual, and mainly resulted in the individual from the contracting organization having established a good relationship with her counterpart, while readily admitting that she knew little about contracting out, and indicating that she was more than willing to learn. In most cases, at least from what we have observed, the typical behavior is to pretend one knows it all and adopt an autocratic attitude that prevents any amount of goodwill on the part of the other party.

Chapter 8

Developing Products

> Developers have a gene that urges them to make major design
> changes as the delivery date approaches.

Having covered basic management themes associated with an information
technology (IT) initiative, and those deemed critical to its success, it is
now time to turn our attention to more technical topics. The development
of products, either to use internally in an organization, to sell, or to use
in the deployment of services, will be the focus of this chapter. After all,
even though management is critical to the success of an IT initiative,
without technical activities that result in tangible components, there will
be no product and there will be nothing to sell or to use.

This is what technically oriented people are interested in, to the point
where they often leave management aside and charge ahead with design-
ing and building a system based on their understanding of it. That is, not
necessarily based on what the customer wants. The fact is, and we have
observed it over and over again, while the customer is talking, or when
they read what the customer has written, they start thinking immediately
about what the solution should look like. This is closely related to the
valuable skills they have; they are very good at solving problems. It's their
job and it is what they are interested in.

That's why in any IT initiative, seasoned managers are necessary and
it is also the reason Chapter 2 through Chapter 7 essentially covered
management topics. "Striving to better, oft we mar what's well," said
Shakespeare. This is the motto of managers. It is also why in many such
initiatives, those same managers issue the notorious directive: freeze the
code; no more changes will be accepted from now on. This is because
they know that if they let engineers and programmers have their way,

the product will never get out. There are always features that the programmers have not had time to implement or that they thought, while they were building the product, would make it so much better. And they are perfectly willing to spend their own time and money to implement them. In fact, one should be wary of an engineer who says that the product is good enough; it is probably because he or she is no longer interested in it.

Having said that, I praise the perfectionism of engineers and programmers each time I must travel on a plane.

Define the Format That Work Products Must Follow

This should be one of the first tasks a manager should assume when an IT initiative is started, after the Work Breakdown Structure (WBS) has been prepared and the main deliverables are known. It does not have to be done at the onset of the initiative for all work products inclusively, but it should be carried out before activities dealing with a specific set of work products are well underway. If a similar initiative has been done before, whatever format was used may still be relevant and should be considered. After all, there is no need to reinvent the wheel each time a project is started. Maybe minor adjustments are all that will be needed.

By format, I also mean defining what each section of a document should contain. Because most of the work products generated in an IT initiative will consist of documents (architecture, diagrams, feasibility studies, operation manuals, code, test plans, test cases, etc.), reviewing them and finding mistakes will be greatly facilitated if documents of a given type are all written using a boilerplate.

In one organization where development went very smoothly, section managers sat down together and ironed out all the details of the formatting at least two months before activities related to a given development phase was planned to start (design, for instance). First, the table of contents was defined, and then under each item, the information it needed to contain was described. This was repeatedly refined and reviewed until everyone was willing to live with the result. Sometimes, when there was enough time and the complexity of the document warranted it, they also asked one or two senior developers to use it to prepare a sample of the corresponding work product. Adjustments were made as appropriate, and after department managers had reviewed and approved it, it was issued as the official template to be followed for the upcoming activity.

Over 40 percent of the organizations we assessed had not taken the time to develop such templates. Yet, all the developers we talked to stated that it would make their work much easier if they had them.

In some cases, the templates already exist. For example, DOD-Std-2167 contains Data Item Descriptions (DIDs) that consist of templates precisely for various deliverables associated with software development. Even though the standard itself is no longer officially mandated in software development, it can still be used as a guideline. However, keep in mind that heavy tailoring may be required because developing a system fully compliant with the 2167 military standard can be very expensive. Other templates have been developed and some are available free on the Internet.

It may be more relevant in an IT initiative to develop templates that are better suited to the way people work, and to the life cycle governing IT development or enhancement activities. Nevertheless, it never hurts to check what others have done before.

Ensure That Appropriate Methods and Tools Are Available

The availability of tools during development is usually not a major problem. There are some minimum required tools in terms of material resources; otherwise, the technical staff will not have the capability to do its job.

Managers, on the other hand, are always a little suspicious about acquiring tools because it is something that can easily be abused. I must admit that their doubtfulness has some justification; technologists have developed a reputation for being easily swayed by the advertising of tool manufacturers. In addition, as a new tool is acquired, it is not so much the cost of the tool that becomes an issue as the cost of making personnel proficient at using it, which can easily represent three to five times the acquisition cost. However, training is usually the last thing on the minds of developers; they want to play with it and learn by themselves all the features the manufacturer claims the tool has. During our assessments, we had the opportunity to observe on numerous occasions all kinds of software development packages on shelves, obviously unused and gathering dust. In some cases, at least developers were using them as bookends, so they were not entirely wasted.

One department manager we came across in a particular assessment had cooled down the taste of developers for new tools by insisting that whoever pushed for the acquisition of one would have to learn it, train all personnel in the team, and act as the resource person for at least six months. The number of requests went down drastically.

Methods are more problematic, because many organizations do not have any; they rely on the method that the tool suggests or promotes. The consequence of this is a proliferation of methods as new tools are acquired, to the point where sometimes development becomes a tower of Babel, with multiple platforms and technologies, each being supported by a multitude of tools and methods.

Yet, appropriate tools can be instrumental in making an IT initiative a success, in the sense that they can greatly improve productivity. Appropriate is the keyword because they must fit the work that has to be done; not too complicated if the project is relatively simple and not too primitive if the project is large and complex. In the 12 or so organizations where tools were deemed inappropriate, this resulted in over 10 obstacles on average to be surmounted in the course of developing their product.

Often, the most appropriate tools are the ones that the team knows best and is most familiar with. In some cases, the existing tool suite must be complemented by additional components, but if an entirely new tool suite must be acquired to complete a project, an organization would be well advised to assess if it is worth undertaking the work.

Conducting an inventory of what an organization has at its disposal and rating each tool in accordance with its frequency of use can be a very useful exercise and can help managers make better decisions regarding tool acquisition.

State What Is Expected in Terms of Adherence to Development Processes

The least that should be done is to insist that templates prepared for carrying out technical activities and developing work products be used, along with tools made available to the team. This is done in less than half the organizations that made up our sample, with the consequence that some developers, either by ignorance or through a misunderstanding about the necessity to use them, were going about it their own way. In almost all cases, the overall result was poor coordination, unnecessary rework, and more mistakes, which just increased the project cost and needlessly frustrated the team.

E-mails normally suffice to communicate to the technical staff what is expected, as quality assurance representatives can be counted on to make sure that adherence is respected.

Take the Time to Train Members of the Technical Staff on How to Perform Their Tasks

Inadequate training is by far the primary cause of troubles during development. On average, one can expect that in the development of an IT system, 14 issues will come up because of inadequate training. This was the case for over 40 percent of the organizations we assessed.

The most frequent complaint we heard about training is that it is not provided on time. It is either too early, so that when the time comes to apply what they have learned, personnel have forgotten a good part of it; or it is too late: They have already made all the mistakes the training taught them not to make.

Another aspect of training found to be sorely lacking is in the field of application for which a product is developed. Technical personnel feel that they rarely have a good understanding of the business domain in which their product will be used, and the solution they come up with does not match what the users have in mind. The managers we interviewed told us that users have always been more than willing to take the time to show development teams what they do, what their challenges are, and what could make their lives easier. They cannot always express their wishes in terms that developers can easily understand, and at times, the developers had first to be given an introduction to the terminology characterizing the users' business area. But goodwill was certainly there on the part of the users.

When training personnel, keep in mind that teaching them how to implement the process that has been defined for the initiative should also be taken into account. People can hardly be blamed for not adhering to something they know nothing about.

The tools that are used in development have also been a concern at times. In one initiative that presented particular challenges and where resources were in short supply, with the stress that this entailed, people who joined the project were given the tools documentation and told to read it. That was the extent of their training. Crises developed one after another. Project team members were asked to assume responsibility for deliverables about which they knew next to nothing. The team's capacity for solving the problems was less than the rate at which new problems were occurring, and people were constantly edgy, expecting the worst to happen each time an unexpected event occurred. One team member who had hoped to be transferred to that project because of the high visibility it had and the glory that seemed to surround it was much disillusioned after having obtained a transfer and was soon longing to return to his previous team, working with less advanced technology but with peace of mind, in a structured environment.

From our observations, coaching is probably the most efficient way of transferring knowledge. What makes it difficult is that an organization must have reached a certain level of maturity and stability before using it effectively. Effective coaching in an atmosphere similar to the situation described in the previous paragraph is wishful thinking.

Ensure That Comprehensive Software Requirements Have Been Developed before Moving On

Granted, they will never be perfect and they will change in the course of the project. This does not preclude the use of iterative and incremental life cycles, such as Extreme Programming or SCRUM. It simply means that before moving on with developing the entire system, an increment of that system, or an iteration of that increment, ensure that you know what you are doing. Without requirements specifications, you are blindly forging ahead and you will pay dearly for it. As unavoidable changes come up later, there will be no way of knowing what the impact is on the entire system (or on the increment or iteration), and the work will proceed on a trial and error basis.

Unfortunately, developing requirements specifications is difficult and requires skills that software professionals do not always have. One of them is the ability to write and express ideas clearly and logically. Software professionals, especially the younger ones, have other abilities of course, like being able to navigate the Internet, find the information they need, and implement a component that does exactly what they want it to do, but that component is standing all by itself and there is no easy way to relate it to the whole picture. Graphic methods have been developed over the years to help elicit requirements and document them in an unequivocal way, but the fact remains that clearly written text is still critical to communicate requirements so that all stakeholders have the same understanding of what the IT system will do.

In one large project, management had developed a requirements writing style guide calling on simple English, with a glossary of terms to use and even terms not to use. In addition, project team members who had unique writing abilities were singled out to take on that responsibility and to act as chief editors. One of those individuals had graduated in law and had a degree in computer science. His requirements specifications were simply superb, and one does not wonder that a large number of leadership positions end up being filled by lawyers. They can write and communicate their ideas like no one else!

Large and successful organizations usually have established a function (business or system analysts) solely dedicated to eliciting and developing software and system requirements from the set of customer's requirements. Smaller organizations have to make do with what they have. They can get some solace in the fact that they are not alone. For 10 percent of our sample, eliciting clear and logical requirements was a challenge and resulted in over 14 issues later on, most of them major. The only advice we have is to hire or temporarily acquire a resource with experience and natural abilities for that task, if none is available internally.

If what we observed can be of any help to personnel taking on IT initiatives, think about maintaining a traceability between customers' requirements and software requirements as this elicitation is being performed. It will greatly facilitate maintenance later on. In addition, if the first version of a project is being developed, make sure that the architecture for the whole system is being developed in parallel. We have observed where this was not done, and when upgrades were undertaken, possibly years later, there was no overall system architecture. Naturally, managers responsible for those upgrades had no desire to assume the cost of developing an architecture that would only benefit future upgrades and other managers, especially when senior management insisted on keeping costs down. As a result, it kept being postponed and the cost of rework it entailed amply covered the cost of having it done in the first place.

Develop Operational and User Documentation Early On

We noticed that in all mature organizations, this is taken on as the product is being developed. Having personnel develop documentation early compels them to have interaction with the development team, and because they must understand what the product will do in order to document its functionality, it raises questions and forces developers to explain the product's features. Inevitably, they will come across inconsistencies and convoluted solutions that should be simplified. A good technical writer with good common sense can do wonders in an IT project, especially if his or her vocabulary is sprinkled with the simple word Why. They should not be shy in using it either; better them than the customer. I feel it would be very good for engineers and programmers to be put on the hot seat every once in a while and be forced to answer questions from users and customers as to why their product is so complicated and difficult to operate.

In some cases, documentation is written by the developers and maybe edited by technical writers. It is certainly better than nothing, but the quality is rarely as high as when it is written by technical writers from the start.

In any case, having user documentation even in draft form is a very good tool to discuss functionality with users and customers. This is a document they typically understand and to which they can relate. Think of it as a cheap prototype that you need to make anyway, so why not take advantage of it.

Operational documentation may not be as critical as user documentation from that perspective, since technically oriented individuals will mostly use it, and they share common characteristics in the way they express themselves, not to mention that organizational boundaries have little meaning for them. Technology unites them, not organizations.

Plan Testing Activities and Test Thoroughly

Typically, a lot of time is allocated to testing in early phases of an IT initiative, and as the schedule slips, this is where the extra time will be borrowed, with the result that testing is usually cut short to get the product out. Most organizations perform adequate testing but for 10 to 20 percent of them, reducing the amount of testing to the bare minimum resulted in over 25 issues on average to be tackled later in each of their IT initiatives, which sometimes presented huge costs.

By testing we mean unit testing, which is typically performed by developers, but mostly integration and system testing. Integration testing focuses on verifying that all software components work together where system testing verifies that software components that have been integrated with other system components (e.g. peripherals, networks) function properly in their intended environment. System testing is sometimes combined with acceptance testing to demonstrate to the customer that all requirements are implemented.

Like documentation, testing should be planned early on. In fact, as soon as the requirements specification is stable enough, the planning of system testing should start, and as design activities start, the planning of integration testing should also begin. In initiatives under the responsibility of seasoned managers, test plans are developed in which test strategies are described, each test is mapped to one or more requirements, required tools and facilities are identified, and test scenarios are documented. As the product takes shape, test cases are developed and ultimately executed by individuals independent of those who developed the components making up the system.

Small organizations are more likely to be affected by deficient testing because of their chronic lack of resources. As a result, the developers end up performing all testing, and because they can't wear two hats at once, testing takes a back seat and is only performed at the end. In addition, because developers like to develop, planning also takes a back seat and ends up being improvised. In all cases where developers tested their own components, there was trouble. It's human nature, pure and simple. They are so sure that they have thought of everything that they do not actively look for flaws. Yet those flaws are there, just waiting for customers to find them.

This was apparent in a particular project that was started in a small enterprise employing around 15 people. The president of the company insisted on performing some verification of the product himself before it was shipped and without fail, within an hour of using it, he uncovered defects and omissions. He finally decided to pair up developers and made each accountable for the residual errors in the components that the other had developed. That did not entirely solve the problem but it certainly brought the point home that testing was to be taken seriously, especially after he told the staff that from now on, the number of residual errors was to be a factor in determining pay raises.

Collect and Analyze Defects

Organizations mature in developing their products because they gain knowledge of the defects they are making and they take appropriate action. This requires that those defects be documented. If not, they may not be corrected, depending on their visibility and criticality, but it is highly unlikely that they will ever be analyzed. They will happen again, somewhere else or later on, in other circumstances. This was effectively the case in one third of our sample.

One of the templates I referred to earlier in this chapter should specifically address defect collection and analysis. As an organization matures, further analysis will help find their root cause and systematically eliminate them. This does not happen by itself. The truth is that entropy will prevail and a group of individuals will take the easiest way out if given the opportunity. Quality is a cultural trait that needs to be nurtured and constantly reinforced, and measurements take a leading role in communicating its benefits. We have observed in the course of our assessments that where defects were collected, analyzed, and tracked, it was because senior management had strongly mandated that it be done.

We found that quality assurance representatives typically assume this task, simply because there is rarely anyone else who will volunteer. Managers are too busy coordinating the work, keeping the costs down, fighting fires, and making sure the product will get out soon enough after the delivery due date has passed. And developers have little interest in finding out.

Defect collection and analysis often starts after an organization has experienced major problems. The CEO of Productora de Software S.A. (PSL) admitted that his company had not always been mature. At one time, it lost $2 million U.S. because of the poor quality of its products. The company was quite small at the time and that brought it close to bankruptcy. This triggered a systematic approach to collecting and analyzing defects in every IT undertaking to keep them under control and to prevent them from reoccurring.

Measure, Measure, and Measure, But with Circumspection

Measurements were addressed in connection with Requirements Management and Tracking Progress, in Chapter 2 and Chapter 4, respectively. In the course of developing products, measurements should be taken to at least determine the quality and the functionality of deliverables. Typically, this will be expressed as the number of implemented functions and the number of residual defects identified through tests and peer reviews (see Chapter 10), possibly classified as a function of their severity, at specific milestones during a project.

Measurements are also particularly useful with respect to defects, the topic of the last section, because they can be used very effectively to communicate to the staff where improvements have been made and the improvements to be pursued (e.g. decreasing the number of residual defects per unit size).

More advanced ratios can be thought of, for instance, measurements related to components development compared to measurements related to work progress, into estimate productivity (e.g., number of units produced per day, cost per unit size). Another measurement of interest is the number of defects injected as a function of defects that are being corrected.

If similar outcomes can be expected when the same process is being applied to the development of different components, measurements can reliably be used to determine what improvements can be made. The process is then said to be under control.

It is not known before the fact if a process is under control or not. There is a widely held myth that measurements must follow a Gaussian (or normal) distribution before they can be used. This is entirely false. In fact, statistical techniques such as the one described in Annex A are used to determine if measurements are randomly distributed and to exclude those that are not in order to assess overall performance.

We witnessed two lines of thought regarding measurements. Some endorse the establishment of a stable process at the organizational level before attempting to use any statistical method. Others promote the use of simple statistical methods as soon as it is practical to do so, because taking measurements for the sole purpose of taking measurements is useless. Furthermore, it is not known if a process is under control or not until measurements have been taken. By applying simple statistical methods, it can be determined faster if the measurements are indeed useful.

In any case, what came out of our assessments is that it is not easy to know ahead of time what measurements will be useful. One can expect to proceed by trial and error before a standard set of measurements is defined in an IT initiative, not to mention that measurements may be collected haphazardly at the beginning and may lead to erroneous interpretation.

From what we observed, we advise organizations to promote the collection of a limited number of measurements early in their individual initiatives, particularly measurements that can easily be justified like size, cost, effort, number of defects, and number of changes, and to use simple statistical methods to assess their relevance.

One has to be careful because measurements can be fudged, especially when personnel feel that management uses them to assess their individual performance. I mentioned that quality is a cultural trait and measurements are part of that culture. In PSL, everyone collects measurements but no one is afraid of the use that will be made of them. This is not necessarily the case for organizations exhibiting a lower maturity level.

In one particular organization, senior management mandated that measurements be systematically collected. However, shortly thereafter, some of those measurements were used to determine which sections were the most productive. As soon as this became known, personnel started to play the game. For instance, they inflated the number of defects in order to come up with artificially high defects resolution rates. Others selected a small measurement unit to estimate size, because that way, they could show that a larger number of units were produced by unit time. It lasted about a year and the whole measurement scheme was abandoned. Worse, when someone else raised the subject of taking measurements a few years later, there was immediately strong resistance on the part of all who had experienced the earlier fiasco.

Involve Quality Assurance Personnel Throughout

Quality assurance involvement is paramount in making sure that development activities and resulting work products proceed in accordance with what has been defined earlier for the IT initiative. It is pretty well a sure thing, if quality assurance is not involved, all good intentions will go out the door and plans will become wish lists. For most of the 40 percent of the organizations we assessed, where a quality assurance function was nonexistent for all practical purposes, this is precisely what happened.

In some initiatives, quality assurance representatives also conduct testing, thereby the confusion that sometimes arises with quality control. However, as we have seen in Chapter 5, quality assurance stretches over the entire life cycle of a project, not just the end of it. As a result, it is well positioned to collect and analyze measurements, which is something developers are always reluctant to do and managers are too busy to take on. For instance, the situation described in the last section could have been avoided if quality assurance had assumed responsibility for measurements. Of course, this presumes that there was a quality assurance function, which wasn't the case in that specific organization. Because of their visibility, quality assurance representatives can also contribute to inform management of what works and what does not, in order to bring changes that ultimately benefit the initiative and the organization that sponsored it.

Unfortunately, the relationship between development team members and quality assurance is rarely one that fosters cooperation, unless the development team have been repeatedly made aware of its value, and quality assurance is staffed with competent and motivated individuals.

Periodically Review Development Activities and Results

This is specifically for anyone who has a management responsibility in an IT initiative. All organizations that do well in developing and maintaining products calling on Information Technology conduct regular reviews. The frequency varies, but we have not seen anything less that bi-weekly. Sometimes those reviews occurred every morning, for half an hour. Only 20 percent did not hold them on a regular basis, and in each case, it was either a source of problems down the road or a symptom of the problems currently being experienced.

These reviews also provide a nice opportunity to involve quality assurance, especially if senior management attends them. In fact, there should be an agenda item solely on quality assurance, should it be only to make it visible to all team members. Periodic reviews by management are essentially established as part of building up the process in an organization and I would go so far as to say part of the culture of an organization.

I remember our involvement in a specific organization specializing in project management where individuals, project managers for the most part, worked alone or in pairs managing initiatives involving the development of advanced electronic systems for internal customers, with the help of subcontractors. There rarely were group meetings, even though they had been quite frequent a few years earlier. As years went by, this essentially became the way of doing things in that organization. Several years later, a new senior manager came on board and his first move was to tell his staff that from now on, there would be a meeting every week.

There was one more meeting and the idea was quickly abandoned. He had been the target of so much cynicism and the lack of cooperation became so evident from everyone that he found it totally hopeless. He left the organization less than a year after he arrived.

It was actually pathetic to observe individuals talking about the good old times and the team spirit that prevailed then, yet, doing everything to undermine any attempt at reviving it. All this to say that if managers do not make a conscious effort to meet with their staff and find out what's going on, disinclination to action will pervade everything and everyone.

Chapter 9

Coordinating

> Inertia prevails in everything, and groups that need to coordinate their activities will tend to select osmosis as their preferred approach, unless they are forced to do otherwise.

Coordinating is what managers spend most of their time doing, and it is not easy. Some have natural abilities to do the job and some will never be able to. It is simply not in their nature. It takes a combination of organizational skills, dynamism, an interest in doing many different things at the same time, the ability to grasp the essence of a topic quickly, and foremost, the willingness to delegate.

An orchestra must have a conductor to perform well, and likewise, a team of individuals involved in maintaining or developing a software application must have someone to coordinate the activities of the team and its interaction with other groups. People who are great coordinators are rare; most of those assigned the task manage to do a decent job. Others, if they know themselves well enough and realize that they lack the required skills, may opt out of assuming that responsibility and focus on perfecting what they already do very well. On the other hand, some may decide to make the effort and learn the skills that will make them good at bringing together a group of individuals, each with his or her own abilities, in order to achieve a common goal.

It can be learned, but for some, it may turn out to be more difficult than for others, which does not mean they will not excel at it. In fact, in the course of our involvement with many organizations, sometimes returning after several years had elapsed, we have seen individuals come out of their shell and surprise everyone around them, even surpassing those who appeared to have everything going for them.

A woman in particular comes to mind. She was extremely shy. Yet, while remaining shy and constantly fighting her natural inclination to stay in the background, she became one of the best managers I have ever come across. Because she was shy, she never tried to grab all the attention; instead, she let others shine. Her superiors were no fools and saw that she did have the rare talent of leveraging the strengths and abilities of those who worked under her direction.

Document Stakeholders' Involvement and Their Commitments

One thing we observed during our assessments is that those who are good at coordinating leave little to chance. They choreograph everything. This is not evident during execution of the activities that have been so coordinated, but make no mistake about it; even though everything may seem improvised, they are following a precise plan of action. In fact, in some organizations, this is the gist of what the project manager does. The application manager takes care of managing technical activities. In that context, the project manager solely acts as the project coordinator.

For an information technology (IT) initiative involving several teams, possibly distributed over various locations, the key is communication and one of the key artifacts that should be prepared is a list of those involved, their coordinates, their roles and responsibilities, what they have committed to deliver, who will be tracking the status of commitments that were made, and to whom issues should be escalated. It is frequent to have the project manager or his or her delegate take care of preparing that document; in any case, the project manager will likely be the individual to whom issues are escalated.

Even for small IT initiatives, we had the opportunity to notice the usefulness of such a document. The most mature organizations we assessed prepared this coordination plan, as it is sometimes called, either before holding a kick-off meeting that brings together all the stakeholders or preferably after a draft had been developed.

Over 65 percent of the organizations we assessed had no document describing the roles and responsibilities of those who had a direct involvement in their IT initiatives, let alone stating what their commitments were. During the interviews we conducted, it was a recurring theme on the part of engineers and programmers who stated that they rarely knew who was responsible for what. In a particular assessment, even the project manager told us that the architect had for all intent taken over control of the project because he had managed to get the ear of the senior manager sponsoring the work. Even though a coordination plan may not have prevented such a takeover, at least it would have made it more difficult and it could have forced senior management to take visible action. This state of affairs had literally split the project into two groups: those supporting the project manager and those allied to the architect. That did not contribute to the team's efficiency.

Define How Issues Will Be Handled

An important aspect addressed in a coordination plan is a description of how issues affecting several stakeholders will be handled, particularly those that cannot be resolved at their level. In other words, issues that need to be escalated.

What quickly became obvious to us is that documenting and communicating to everyone in the project a way to describe a concern, to pass it on, and to get feedback on its status, can go a long way in reducing the number and frequency of crises resulting from unresolved problems that drag on forever (such deterioration of issues into crises was nevertheless the lot of 25 percent of the organizations we examined). This corresponds to implementing the handling of issues as part of a routine or an automated mechanism. This helps prevent the personalization of the hot buttons that are raised, and contributes to avoiding situations where blame is laid out at the feet of those who dared claim that things were not perfect.

Another approach we have seen is to let quality assurance representatives handle them. Because they are used to raising red flags and they normally get the attention of senior management, they are more likely to do it in a way that will take the pressure off those who can't find a solution on their own and may be reluctant to rattle the cage. In addition, as we have seen in Chapter 5, it is also the responsibility of quality assurance personnel to see to it that essential information flows between the stakeholders of an IT initiative.

In one organization, this was also complemented with monthly informal brainstorming sessions during which personnel could raise in confidence, issues and difficulties they were facing. Several sessions were held during which all participants were at the same level in order to guarantee the free flow of information. Quality assurance personnel, for whom those sessions provided a way of acquiring information to support their upcoming verification activities, facilitated them.

Ideally, escalating issues should take place in the open with everyone involved at all hierarchy levels. This we observed in one organization where the collection of measurements had been institutionalized for a few years. Because most activities and work products were quantitatively characterized, there was no need to hide anything, since issues came out through the numbers and graphs that were displayed throughout the company bulletin boards.

Ensure That the Tools Used by the Various Stakeholders Are Compatible

This is an issue in one IT initiative out of five. This definitely gets in the way of achieving efficient exchanges of work products and information, and throws a monkey wrench into the best coordination intentions.

Incompatibilities in electronic mail systems, different versions of software applications and incompatible network resources are usually the main culprits. The most common situation occurs when two or more departments, most likely located in separate buildings, find themselves working on the same initiative.

It can sometimes be trivial, like not having access to each other's telephone lists, or it can be more complex like being unable to access each other's documentation because of a lack of bridges between different networks, or working with different sets of templates, methods, and procedures.

In one particular instance, it became necessary to temporarily relocate the staff of one organization to the premises of the other. Murphy's Law came into play, and the organization that had to be relocated was the one that had the largest number of personnel to move.

Train Managers in Teamwork

This topic usually drew a chuckle out of engineers and programmers we interviewed in the assessments we conducted. Some managers possess natural skills that make them good team players, while others would benefit from training on subjects such as team building, team management, group dynamics, and on establishing, promoting, and facilitating teamwork. The training can take several forms, including seminars, tutoring, mentoring by a dynamic and experienced manager, and participation in the organization of social, cultural, and sporting events.

Close to 73 percent of the assessed organizations were found to exhibit deficiencies with managers who lack teamwork abilities, which resulted in 4.6 issues that affected the outcome of IT initiatives. This finding was initially taken with a grain of salt, because we thought there was an expression of some bias. However, when we explored the deficiencies associated with teamwork on the part of development team members of the same initiatives, that is, everyone in the team but managers, we came to almost the same result. Sixty-eight percent of organizations were experiencing difficulties in that regard, which resulted in 4.5 issues on average per initiative.

The most recurring complaints were individualism, poor people skills, dictatorial inclinations, and inability or unwillingness to cooperate. In some environments, it appeared that middle managers were building their little kingdoms and were adamant about preventing anybody else from meddling in their playground. In other instances, it was senior members of the technical staff using their knowledge and expertise to build up their influence. In mixed environments, it was indeed a fascinating psychological experiment to observe the team members' behavior, male and female, especially when they were in their twenties. The younger ones in particular were quite interesting to watch. Their comportment was rather obvious and their next move could be predicted with some accuracy, but as a whole, they were fresh and natural about it. The older ones could get nasty when they decided to play that game.

One organization, where senior management was at a loss on how to instill teamwork within its walls while putting a damper on the relationships that were developing between the male and female staff members, opted to sponsor sport activities. Soccer and softball teams were formed, games were set up between departments, and ultimately, between neighboring companies. Some players were excellent athletes, but overall, the quality of the games was horrible. Nevertheless, people from all teams were having a good time, and victors and losers enjoyed sharing a few drinks after each game. A special prize was given to the team that lost the most games. But more importantly, everyone participated, including those who had little talent in sports, and in our opinion, it greatly contributed to fostering cooperation between team members, and between managers and practitioners.

At Productora de Software S.A. (PSL), parties are periodically organized and impromptu gatherings arranged. The fact that a particularly good discotheque in town is located right next to the company also helped. The company sponsors most of these events to invite everyone to share some time together. It is part of the culture of that organization, a topic that will be covered in more detail in Chapter 15.

Ensure That Software Professionals Are Represented when Defining System Requirements with the Customer

Making sure that software professionals participate in the system requirements definitely helps in coordinating the activities of the IT development team with other groups. Where the involvement of IT professionals was an afterthought, we did notice that cooperation presented much more of a challenge. This particularly affected organizations that developed systems or deployed services in which Information Technology was but one of the called upon disciplines.

Problems related to requirements usually take their source at that level. Software professionals are not simpletons and they understand that poor requirements will inevitably lead to costly modifications later on. In other words, and this stems directly from our observations, the problem is not so much that insufficient attention is paid to requirements, it is that coordination among stakeholders is insufficient. This, in turn, leads to poor requirements because of misinterpretations and poor understanding of what the requirements are. This affected almost one third of the organizations we worked with and it resulted in the most serious ordeal as far as requirements were concerned: 14 outstanding issues on average in each initiative with peaks of 22. In fact, this ranks as one of the 12 most serious deficiencies we came across in all of our assessments. Organizations that did best are those where software application managers worked closely with system managers, equipment managers, and business managers when interacting with customers and users. In cases when software professionals were involved later with respect to requirements, that is if they were involved at all, changes were inexorably needed because the requirements sometimes made the implementation too complex.

In a particular government project, a new health service to the population was devised without involving IT professionals up front. Everything went fine until database administrators, after having analyzed the system in more detail, told one of the senior managers sponsoring this initiative that a subsystem that had been selected required that half of the existing data be converted. In addition, some of the data that was required to provide health services administrators with the information they needed had to be captured electronically. It was estimated that at the very least, this would add one year to the project. The project went forward anyway, but additional problems were encountered in the data conversion, which had been underestimated because users did not record data the same way. Ultimately, the entire project was cancelled. Some parts were salvaged to upgrade the existing system and extend its useful life.

Implement Regular Reviews with Representatives of the Various Groups Involved in the Initiative

This sounds easy. It isn't, as corroborated by over 45 percent of the initiatives characterized by a multi-disciplinary team. All those concerned need to be available at the same time. It also assumes that they will all be cooperative and that the final outcome has more importance than the specific needs of each group being represented; a very big and sometimes naïve assumption. Some may actually want to see the initiative fail because they will lose influence if it succeeds. For some, it will be the reverse; they want it to succeed because it will allow them to get rid of those who have been an obstacle to their plans of expanding their power reach. Some others could not care less; they have been parachuted in this and frankly, they have more important things to do.

In every assessment we think we have seen it all, until the next one comes along. Coordinating review meetings involving stakeholders from many disparate groups can be like herding cats, wildcats that is. When an initiative is well circumscribed, calls upon only one or two disciplines, and involves a few stakeholders that are all co-located, one manager can handle it, possibly supported by a review board that provides advice and support as needed. In cases where several representatives stand in for many disciplines, the organizations that do well usually bring in a team of managers who have worked closely together in the past in similar initiatives to coordinate the program. This team is in charge of calling the shots, including organizing reviews where they visibly support the team member acting as program manager, while actively listening to what each and every representative has to say.

In a case of the initiative described in the previous section, there were a large number of stakeholders each having his or her own agenda: health administrators, system managers, software managers, nurses, doctors, psychologists, and I forget a few. Trying to identify a common thread that would keep all of those individuals focused on the project goals was next to impossible. There were a few prima donnas among them as well, experts in their field, who were not going to stay quiet while amateurs imagined they could tell them how to do the work they had performed for umpteen years.

In another organization where a similar initiative had been undertaken, a single individual was placed in charge with a team of managers who were more acquaintances than close associates. The work spun out of control within a couple of months and it was clear that the manager was way out of his element and really wanted out. Senior management brought in a team of four seasoned and pragmatic managers who took over and in less than a month, the project was back on track. Weekly review meetings were held, and every discipline had to be represented; anyone who skipped more than two meetings in a row without sending a delegate was liable to be dropped and replaced. Stakeholders who had been labeled as uncooperative were listened to and their arguments were taken into account if they were reasonable; in other cases, they were simply discarded and replaced by others.

Identify and Manage Critical Dependencies between Stakeholders

In a project where there are several groups involved, critical dependencies are bound to happen. This does not happen only in large initiatives. We have seen small initiatives involving from 12 to 15 people in which stakeholders represented four to five different groups. Those actually present special challenges because of their small size, which means the same personnel are bound to both manage and carry out the work. As a result, coordination suffers. There is simply not enough time and resources to do that activity well.

Critical dependencies should be documented in the coordination plan described earlier in this chapter. The idea is to identify and to discuss critical items to be provided or critical activities to be completed, who will provide or complete them, when, and how acceptance will be assessed. This presented a challenge in half of the organizations we assessed. Most of the time, the problem was due to commitments made without an appreciation of what they implied. At times, we have seen promises made by individuals but deliberately wrapped in a lot of verbiage because they had no intention of keeping them.

In fact, when one deals with initiatives calling upon different nationalities, everyone must proceed with caution. In some cultures, people don't always mean exactly what they say. Sometimes, what sounds like a commitment is only a way of being polite and showing that one can be counted upon to cooperate, no more. Indeed, it is a personality trait found in every nationality, but which is modulated by the culture in which one grew up.

The problem is compounded if whoever makes such empty commitments is allowed to get away with it. I recall work we did in an organization where one individual kept proposing new activities as part of a project to develop a customer relationship management system for an external customer. During monthly review meetings, which by the way were much too infrequent, he kept proposing new activities and new deliverables. While keeping in perspective that our mandate was temporary in that organization, we tried to warn the project manager, who was relatively new on the job that he would do well to follow up because this sounded more like delay tactics. What also confused the issue is that the individual making those proposals seemed to be doing it partly because he was not in his element; in other words, that was not his usual behavior. Furthermore, he had a position in the company that called for some respect. In any case, over a period of five months, little progress was achieved in the area under his responsibility, while its scope increased every month, until he made his final proposal...a feasibility study!

Communicate Again and Again

Communication is without a doubt the most essential aspect of coordination. The lack of communication and the inability to communicate efficiently have been recurrent themes in over 60 percent of the organizations with which we have been involved.

The existence of quality assurance does alleviate part of the problem, since one of its roles is to ensure that essential information is passed on to the stakeholders of an IT initiative. However, quality assurance representatives are not cheerleaders. They do not motivate individuals nor do they see to it that everyone cooperates and is aware of who the other stakeholders are, what they are entitled to expect, and what is expected of them. That's the role of the manager assuming the overall responsibility of the initiative in which those stakeholders are involved.

Measurements can also be used effectively to communicate the status of outstanding inter-group issues and of those that have been resolved. Mature organizations do take advantage of the measurements they collect pertaining to coordination, since these can be quite useful in providing an indication of existing and upcoming difficulties. For instance, the amount of effort invested by one group to support another may very well provide hints that something that will not be to the taste of everyone is brewing in one or both groups.

Coordination meetings are necessary in any work involving several parties. Yet very few organizations actually know how much time is invested in those meetings and how efficient they are. In most of our interventions, when we started compiling time spent in meetings, people were always surprised at the numbers we showed them. While many managers were often reluctant to send personnel on training for half a day, they did not think twice about various groups of three, four, or five individuals spending their time (sometimes wasting it) in series of hour-long meetings in the course of a few days. Person-hours then add up quickly.

A manager told me that she could feel the pulse of her project by reviewing who was charging time to what. By setting up cost accounts appropriately, she was able to see if she needed to spend more time coordinating and communicating, and that often came just in time to avert a mess.

Manage Expectations from the Start

The best way to reduce the number of inter-group issues is to take whatever steps are appropriate to prevent them from occurring in the first place. Because multi-disciplinary teams provide an endless number of opportunities for events to deteriorate, setting the record straight right from the beginning will save you a lot of grief later on. State up front what is expected of all stakeholders in their relationship with each other.

Individuals generally want to work in an environment conducive to harmonious interactions with each other. However, it usually is desirable to remind them of the points to which they should pay attention when dealing with members from other groups. There should be rules to that effect that are documented, communicated, and enforced, with managers leading by example, and they should include the boundaries that should not be crossed under any circumstances.

We observed that in the few organizations (one out of four) where there were basic policies and directives governing interactions between people involved in multi-disciplinary teams, even though these policies were only common sense, coordination was much easier and the cooperation of people was assured from the beginning.

Chapter 10

Reviewing and Inspecting

> Constructive criticism is achieved by teaching individuals that truth and accuracy must be pursued relentlessly, albeit without ever compromising the respect of those for whom this criticism is intended.

This chapter deals with reviews and inspections, most specifically with reviews conducted by peers of the author of a work product. Inspections, peer reviews, walkthroughs, structured reviews; these are all terms that are used interchangeably in software engineering. Yet the activities that they entail are rarely carried out consistently in the course of developing a software application.

Peer reviews are the norm in the publishing industry. An associate editor of a popular newspaper told me that someone other than the author reviewed, at least once, the most benign articles — even those that have a life of a single edition. Articles and commentaries that were likely to be recurring were reviewed seven times. He was amazed when I told him that most organizations that develop and maintain software do not conduct peer reviews.

The editor-in-chief of a popular magazine told me that every article is thoroughly peer-reviewed at least three times (in addition to editorial and typographical reviews) before it is published. Even though budgets have shrunk over the years and the company, like most organizations, has restructured its operations (fewer people doing more work), peer reviews constitute one activity for which no compromises were made. Likewise,

The Economist, one of the most influential magazines in the western world, despite its relatively small distribution, has institutionalized peer reviews of every single item it publishes.

As discussed in Chapter 16, the highest contributor to failures in the information technology (IT) industry (52.7 percent) is the lack of peer reviews. The following observation may contribute to helping software organizations learn more about peer reviews and adopt them: successful software organizations will invest on average, 24 times more effort in implementing productive peer reviews than the average organization.

Why is it that peer reviews in the publishing industry and in the scientific community are widely accepted while they are the first items to be dropped from the priority list in the software industry? Given the strong analogy between publishing and software development, one would expect to see peer reviews performed in all software organizations, with no exceptions. From our observations, the most likely answer is that they are essentially a low-tech approach in a high-tech environment, in which the culture of defect-free products has yet to take root.

Mandate Reviews and Inspections

The best way to ensure that peer reviews are performed in an IT initiative is to mandate them. Unfortunately, two thirds of the organizations we assessed did not. Without a directive of some sort, you can be sure that every reason will be invoked in order not to do it. The most common is: if peer reviews are conducted, we will not meet the schedule. After all, there is always enough money to do things 10 times over but never enough to do them right the first time. Well, the schedule is usually not met anyway, and the first version of the product is riddled with bugs or the initial service suffers from a myriad of false starts.

In some organizations, every work product is subjected to a peer review. In others, a list of work products is prepared for which peer reviews are mandatory. In any case, the statement mandating that peer reviews be conducted is unequivocal; unless there is a documented derogation originating from senior management, the affected work product will not be released to production.

The biggest problem by far with issuing such a directive is if some practice has not first been established, it may simply result in peer reviews whose sole purpose is to rubber-stamp the product to review. Organizations that have not yet mastered a somewhat disciplined process are particularly vulnerable to this outcome. It means that before mandating peer reviews, some experience should be acquired in conducting them, even if only informally.

Peer reviews are indeed unlikely to be successfully implemented in an environment where crises happen. Peer reviews provide so many benefits that they should be introduced as early as is practically feasible. The stimulus for implementing peer reviews often comes from the benefits a manager has experienced as part of a previous job. We have come across senior managers discussing peer reviews with their peers from other organizations who convince them of their usefulness.

In an organization where we had tried to convince management to adopt peer reviews, we had to use a different strategy as a result of the resistance we encountered. We convinced senior management to conduct a comparative analysis. Two projects happened to be starting at approximately the same time. The manager of one agreed to introduce peer reviews in his project, where the other would run his project as he always had, that is, a lot of meetings interspersed with improvised reviews. In fact, the first manager did not have much to lose; if peer reviews were successful, he would be rewarded for having made the right decision; if not, he had the perfect scapegoat, namely us.

Both projects went ahead, in a rather competitive spirit. The manager of the project in which peer reviews were conducted did become slightly worried at one point as reviews took their toll; progress was slowed down and it looked like the second project would finish a solid month before his. Then, tests started and the first project quickly overran the second. Bugs detected in testing were relatively minor and were quickly corrected. The second project became literally bogged down by a module in which repeated changes had to be made, and with each change came a new series of bugs that called for more changes. Peer reviews were adopted across the organization shortly thereafter.

Train Peer Review Participants

This is particularly important in the case of peer reviews involving a relatively large number of participants (five or more), but from our data, it happens in only 20 percent of the organizations we worked with. In peer reviews, the author of the work product may feel intimidated at receiving comments from several reviewers. He or she may be inclined to agree to all comments or to take a defensive attitude that will not bode well for the future. In one case, an author and a reviewer were on the verge of settling their differences in the parking lot and would have if another participant had not intervened. For reviews involving at most three people, this training is less critical but it nevertheless can be useful.

There are several ways of providing comments. Some may come across as very antagonizing and aggressive. They invite the kind of response akin to, wait until your turn comes; I'll get you good. Others may subtly imply the message, scratch may back now and I'll scratch yours later. In both cases, peer reviews are counterproductive. Finally, a few peer reviews make it clear that the intent is to improve the product and to make future activities go smoother for everyone. The selection of participants is also important. Those who provide comments should be knowledgeable. It is much easier for an author to receive comments from someone who is recognized as an authority in his or her field.

The training referred to in this section is more an awareness than training proper. It typically requires less than half a day and focuses on the objectives and principles of peer reviews, what needs to be done to prepare for a peer review, what needs to be recorded, and how to conduct the review. We usually experienced some resistance when we introduced peer reviews which is inevitable. In one particular organization, people eventually came to see the benefit of peer reviews, so the obstacles were removed relatively quickly. Some developers went as far as developing a video to train peer review participants, in which some of the depictions of what not to do were hilarious. This free entertainment contributed in securing the adoption of peer reviews even more.

Assign Peer Review Leaders, Especially when There Are Many Reviewers

Training for peer review leaders is recognized as being something taken more seriously than training for peer review participants: 30 percent of organizations provide it. Peer review leaders not only lead and facilitate peer reviews, they organize them, and coordinate the participation of knowledgeable reviewers. In addition, they ensure that everyone has had time to look at the work product before the review is scheduled to take place. They also follow up on completed reviews and determine if another will be required. Peer review leaders collect data such as the number and type of identified defects, time spent by reviewers to prepare for the review, time spent conducting the review, time required to fix identified defects, and the size of the reviewed artifact in whatever measurement units are appropriate for that type of artifact.

Peer review leaders should also be trained, if only so they can fulfill their administrative tasks properly. They should also be made aware of facilitating techniques; these will actually be useful to them throughout their career. Ideally, peer review leaders should be objective and neutral. Quality assurance representatives or personnel assuming that role are therefore good candidates. There may be no need of peer review leaders when fewer than four individuals are involved, but given they take care of the administrative tasks associated with peer reviews, it may be a good idea to have them in each review, independent of the number of participants.

Ensure Peer Reviews Are in the Plan

Unplanned peer reviews are peer reviews that will probably not be conducted. That's effectively the lot of 65 percent of the organizations involved in IT development and maintenance, at least according to our sample.

After the Work Breakdown Structure (WBS) has been prepared, identify the work products to be reviewed, especially those that are liable to present some difficulty and are therefore vulnerable to defects. Estimate the effort required to conduct those reviews, prepare a schedule of reviews to be conducted, and negotiate for the participation with personnel from other groups. Keep in mind that peer reviews also provide a great way to train junior personnel. The objective may consist of training candidates being considered for project or application management by letting them attend peer reviews of requirements specifications or development plans in which managers are likely to participate. More often, the goal is to expose junior developers to components they will have to maintain and enhance later on.

In the course of planning peer reviews, it is also a good time for defining the approach that will be used to conduct them. The approach itself may be integrated into the plan or referenced by it. Generally, we observed that the existence of a documented peer review process, even if it applies only to a particular initiative, makes it much easier to implement peer reviews successfully. Reviewers and authors are then less inclined to take comments as a critique of personal abilities. They are simply following the process that the manager has dictated.

We witnessed peer review planning for an entirely different reason than the one most often invoked. In an initiative involving complex algorithms and real-time transactions, a manager was terrified of losing key individuals. The demand for that kind of expertise was high at the time because of the large number of contracts issued by the government and the relatively low number of experts available. That manager had trained four members of his staff over the course of almost a year in different aspects of the subsystem for which development was envisioned to start in the near future, and there were a few resignations over the past six months, which made him particularly edgy. He needed back-ups and he did not have any.

As development work started, he assigned his experts the responsibility of writing the detailed specifications for different components of the subsystem. On completion of the specification stage, he switched them around. Whoever wrote the specification for a specific component now had to develop the high-level design of a component for which someone else had written the specification. He proceeded in this round-robin fashion until integration. In essence, what he had done was to force peer reviews on his team. After each stage, whoever was taking on the next stage for a given component had to sit down with whoever had developed the artifacts for that component in the preceding stage, along with the manager who was orchestrating the whole exercise.

After three stages, his team members were knowledgeable about the entire subsystem. The learning curve at the beginning of each stage did have a dampening effect on the rate at which progress was achieved, but his subsystem was nevertheless the second one to successfully complete acceptance testing. The manager received a financial reward along with a certificate of recognition for the work he and his team had achieved.

Follow the Plan

The benefit of planning peer reviews is that it makes them official activities in an IT initiative. It then becomes more difficult to discard them and to change the plan without a valid reason. Several types of peer reviews are documented in software engineering references. There is first the technical review, which is most often mentioned in connection with the topic of requirements and design. It is somewhat akin to undergoing a review in front of an examination board after wanting to become a firefighter.

The term walkthrough also comes up. Some define a walkthrough as a gathering where an author (or authors, as there may be more than one for a given IT artifact) walks reviewers through his or her work product, explaining to them the approach he or she has adopted, while the reviewers ask questions and provide comments.

There are also references to inspections, which makes walkthroughs that more confusing because some use the term walkthrough to mean inspection and vice-versa. What has been described so far in this chapter comes close to the official definition of what an inspection is: a methodical examination of a work product by the author's peers to identify defects and areas where changes are needed.

Collegial reviews also constitute a form of peer reviews, during which the author is usually not present and simply receives comments from his or her peers, possibly through a moderator who acts as dispatcher. This is the preferred approach in the scientific community, and it works very well in that environment. After all, the public's confidence in scientists is much higher than in politicians; however, the scientists generally seek the truth and an understanding of how things work, where politicians are more likely to seek power, fame, and fortune, which makes them more than willing to compromise on the truth when it suits their ambitions. Collegial reviews may not be a good fit for everyone. Because there is no direct participation implies that comments are only provided in writing, possibly anonymously. Without direct interaction with the reviewers, written comments may sometimes appear offensive and abrasive for the author, if not downright condescending.

Buddy reviews have become more popular and are typically implemented in small teams (two to four people) working closely together in which each team member reviews the work of the others on a continuous basis. In more formal implementations of buddy reviews, one team member is formally assigned the responsibility (or the accountability if he or she decides to delegate the review to another team member) with the author, of guaranteeing the goodness of his or her work products.

The best type of review for an organization to conduct can easily turn into philosophical debates, and we have witnessed deliberations that were worthy of learned medieval theologians discussing how many angels could fit on the head of a pin. My personal recommendation, from observations made in a number of interventions in industry and in public administration, is not to get hung up in terminology. Use whatever suits you and the environment in which you operate. Whatever review you choose, make it formal. People take what is formal much more seriously and are more likely to be careful and conscientious during execution.

Another aspect worth discussing is whether peer reviews should only involve the author and his or her peers or if their immediate superiors can attend. We found that this was more an issue related to organizational culture than anything else. In some organizations, having anybody other than peers will influence the way the review runs its course. Reviewers may refrain from providing comments that could make the author look bad in front of his or her boss, where the author may feel obligated to fight tooth and nail to defend his or her position. In other cases, particularly in mature organizations where transparency is highly valued, it really does not matter and managers are encouraged to participate. The argument brought forward by the proponents of the non-participation of managers is that they may use what they see to rate the performance and salary raises of personnel under their supervision. The counter-argument is that managers will need to know at some point because they have to plan their subordinates' activities and review their accomplishments. Time invested in rework for work products that have been peer reviewed will necessarily become visible at some point, so the non-participation of managers may be a moot point anyway.

Another point of interest is how long a peer review should last. The rule of thumb is two hours, meaning that the artifact to review may need to be broken up into parts that can be reviewed in two hours or less. We have seen peer reviews lasting much longer. Productora de Software S.A. (PSL), for example, currently implements peer reviews that last up to 36 hours, that is almost a week. These reviews are conducted before proceeding to the incremental integration of product components.

Over half of the organizations involved in developing products drawing on Information Technology do not conduct peer reviews. What is more significant is that, as a result, those organizations will have to deal with 15 issues, on average, in each of the initiatives they have undertaken. This is the highest ratio derived as part of our analysis considering the high proportion of affected organizations.

Collect Data

The benefits achieved through peer reviews have been demonstrated repeatedly. The fact that they are not more widely implemented is indeed unfortunate. However, their value can be amplified if data is collected and recorded for future use. Examples of data to collect have briefly been discussed in the section dealing with peer review leaders.

The topic of measurements has been addressed before, but it is worth reiterating that without measurements, one cannot say for sure if improvements have been achieved. Regarding peer reviews, measurements can quantify the return on investment that peer reviews provide. Among the organizations that did conduct peer reviews, 25 percent did not collect data. However, among those that did, the collected data was limited for the most part to the defects that were uncovered. There was no way of deriving quantifiable benefits demonstrating that peer reviews were at least as efficient as testing.

One of the initiatives we looked at in which data was both collected and analyzed was precisely the return on investment that peer reviews provided. Compared to testing, it was found that peer reviews resulted in fewer defects being injected in the process of correcting those that had been identified. The reason appeared to be that peer reviews were conducted earlier than testing activities. Therefore, defects were more likely to be detected soon after they were introduced in the components undergoing peer reviews. In the case of testing, some of the defects were liable to have been injected early in the development life cycle. It was consequently more difficult to take into account all the ramifications that characterized a particular defect in light of the sometimes intricate functionality of a component. Some of these ramifications were elusive but were nevertheless real. In the course of correcting the defect, some of those ramifications were bound to be unnoticed, resulting in a higher defect injection rate.

Make Sure That Quality Assurance Is Part of the Process

The contribution that quality assurance representatives make in peer reviews was described in the section on peer review leaders. In addition to coordinating peer reviews, following up on completed ones, and collecting and analyzing peer review data, which must be given priority over all others, quality assurance's role is also to ensure that the peer review documented in the plan actually took place.

Having quality assurance delegates act as peer review leaders is an option. Their role is to see that the process defined for a given IT initiative, including the peer review process, is followed, and that all those concerned are aware of it. They should also be made aware of any changes that should be introduced, either to comply with the IT initiative or to correct deficiencies that may have been uncovered with the process itself.

In some cases, we have seen quality assurance representatives acting as reviewers in a peer review. There is some rationale to this, especially when the artifact being reviewed deals with quality assurance or calls on expertise that individual quality assurance specialists may have. We certainly do not suggest having them involved for any other purpose.

In one particular project, it was customary to have a quality assurance representative attend all peer reviews in the capacity of reviewer (not as peer review leader). In most cases, he or she could contribute very little, not being sufficiently knowledgeable in the topic addressed by the reviewed artifact. As a result, his or her comments were often trivial or meaningless. It was a waste of time and put the quality assurance function in a light that did not emphasize its value. Unfortunately, quality assurance was not highly valued in that organization; in fact, it had been set up as a showcase for the eyes of the customer only.

Chapter 11

Providing Services to Customers

Customers can take a lot of abuse, but they will turn away at the time an organization needs them the most.

Customer relations and customer service were areas where we did not witness a large number of deficiencies. Personnel at all levels in an organization, particularly those who are on the front line and regularly interface with customers, are acutely aware of what customers represent; they essentially pay their salary, and if they go away, everyone knows too well that there will be serious consequences. Even those who are not in direct contact with customers realize that.

In only a few instances did we observe a certain lack of concern toward customers. In most cases, it had to do with monopolies. However, even in these organizations, senior managers usually have to report to either individuals or other organizations that must compete to survive. A public agency may have a de facto monopoly on the services it provides, but it is ultimately accountable to elected officials who are well aware that they may be voted out of office if there is too much complaining on the part of their constituents. As a result, its budget may be put under review or worse, there may be a slow but inexorable tide to set up competing agencies or to allow private enterprise to get involved.

Nevertheless, there are a few practices that are worth discussing because in our assessments, they were rather poorly implemented. In a few cases, they were indeed the precursor of dire times.

Seek, Compile, and Review Feedback from Customers

In all the organizations we assessed, everyone was adamant about the fact that they listened to their customers. Yet only 55 percent did it in a somewhat systematic way. For all others, it was inconsistent and customers' comments, when they were collected, were barely looked at. This particularly affects information technology (IT) solution providers who tend to take their internal customers for granted. Being part of the same organization, they feel protected by the mere fact that their customers have to buy from them.

Organizations that develop IT products and services, and particularly those IT organizations that provide solutions and services to other parts of an organization, have been unusually lucky so far because they have benefited from an extremely tolerant customer base. In fact, this tolerance sometimes borders on self-deception. However, things have started to change, and we have noticed it over the years in our interventions. As in many other areas, customers are voting with their feet; instead of complaining, they simply look elsewhere. This is a process akin to watching grass grow because it is very slow, and few organizations take it seriously at the beginning; because it is slow, the natural tendency is to take it as a marginal response. Sometimes it is, but sometimes it isn't. In the case of Information Technology, it isn't, as demonstrated by the recent outsourcing trend.

The organizations that succeed make a conscious effort to stay very close to their customers, probing them and asking them how they can be of service to them. They know that customers are willing to pay a premium to get good service and a quick response, and if this is maintained, customers are unlikely to look elsewhere. Getting feedback from customers can be through surveys but nothing will replace direct contact. Surveys should be seen as a complementary way of acquiring more precise information on particular items. They can easily be misinterpreted if they are not modulated by information provided by personnel in the field. Organizations that manage to build a loyal customer base also discuss survey results with customers; they do more than acknowledge feedback with a vague and automated thank you response.

I conducted seminars in the early 1990s where my colleagues and I were telling both industry and government representatives that the IT industry, particularly the IT service industry, was going through a slow but major structural change. At the macroeconomic level, India, among other nations, had embarked on a nationwide improvement of its IT capability. Indian software companies were adopting the Capability Maturity Model (CMM) *en masse* and were making impressive gains in quality.

Rajiv Ghandi, before he was assassinated in 1991, had adopted policies with the intent of having India be to software what Japan was to consumer electronics and manufacturing. It seems that few organizations in the West paid attention to his message, being too busy trying to impose their solutions on their customers, that is, until the IT industry in the West suffered a meltdown in the first few years of the new millennium. Then, those customers, who had also been affected, started looking at ways to cut their costs. The few that had already explored alternative sources and plowed through new ground showed the way to the others. Yet many IT solutions providers could have avoided the debacle that ensued. In fact, there is still time to prevent it from worsening even further if IT organizations take bold steps and listen to what their customers have to say.

Analyze, Document, and Communicate Customers' Needs

In 12 percent of the organizations, this was hardly done at all, and it resulted in major problems for all of them that eventually affected their balance sheet. It was often the consequence of a communication breakdown in the organization itself. In one instance, account managers had a particularly poor track record at communicating to engineering what customers wanted. Conversely, sales personnel did not have a clue what engineering was working on. The engineering staff was left in the dark and therefore came up with solutions and enhancements that customers did not care about, not having been sold on the idea and having provided little input. From the application team's perspective, it was the responsibility of sales personnel to sell it, period.

In one case, sales personnel got wind of the new enhancements for an existing graphics solution, and presented them to customers in a way that was entirely different from what the reality was. When the application manager learned from his immediate supervisor what had been sold, he literally flew into a rage, claiming that this was simply unfeasible and that sales people were distorting everything. In our opinion, having been privy to the discussions, this was an unfair statement since sales had never been told in any detail what the enhancements were. On the other hand, sales personnel had known for a while what customers were looking for. They just did not bother letting engineering know. Both parties were equally guilty.

Engineering was simply told to get to work and deliver what had been sold. The product was hardly functional; sales presented it to one group of managers from the customer, and then told engineering what they had done. Engineering told them what they had presented was wrong, and sales simply called the managers in again, and told them the reverse of what they had told them a day earlier. Being sales people and well versed in storytelling when the need warranted it, they did it in a way that made sense if no one was really paying attention. A few people raised their eyebrows at this seemingly incoherent approach that appeared to contradict what they had been told earlier, but by the time they were ready to argue their point, the presentation was over and sales personnel were moving on to other topics.

This is quite different from another organization where application and account managers work closely together. Biweekly meetings are held during which application managers explain the progress achieved in their current work. Account managers provide feedback from customers based on the information sales and consulting personnel have provided in the course of their activities. Discussions then take place to reconcile viewpoints and to assess what can be done to meet what account managers feel should be addressed on a priority basis, and constraints that application managers are facing. Minutes are prepared and placed on the server, with a notice sent to everyone who may need to know.

In fact, the same practices described in Chapter 9 in connection with coordinating are applied. The main difference is instead of focusing on a single initiative, these meetings often span several applications. It is never as easy at it sounds, though. Crises do occur, and compromises have to be made constantly. For instance, an application manager may temporarily lose resources because another needs them urgently, or an account manager may have to announce to his customer that what he had promised earlier will not be ready in time. But overall, it does work and everyone feels empowered by the process.

Ensure That Information Provided by Customers Remains Private

Seventy-seven percent of organizations claim that they maintain the confidentiality of their customers' information. Yet only 50 percent have documented procedures to that effect, which makes one wonder how those who claim they do it actually ensure it is done.

Quality assurance specialists can hardly verify that customers' information is kept in confidence if they have nothing to verify against. All they can do is ask and the answer is unlikely to be an admission of guilt, so what's left is to poke around and accidentally fall on indications that there may be threads to follow, possibly leading to some evidence.

In our investigations, there was little doubt that government agencies take the issue much more seriously than private companies, especially small companies. For instance, I worked with a company that maintained memberships for several organizations. These memberships were composed of a few thousand members each, and the company was quite willing to sell its membership lists to whoever wanted to acquire them, as long as the buyers' requests sounded somewhat plausible. Members had never been asked if their identity and coordinates could be sent to third parties. The reasonableness of a request was essentially assessed by whoever processed it at the time it was received.

Compare this to a government agency where individuals wishing to change their address were invited to step into a private cubicle where an office clerk would record the change. When I asked why there was so much fuss for a simple change of address, I was told of individuals coming in and saying that they had just got out of a troubled relationship with their spouse. The last thing they wanted was to have their new address broadcast all over the neighborhood.

Excluding information related to national security, where procedures are extremely rigorous, organizations should adopt measures that will contribute to institutionalizing the handling of private and potentially sensitive information. As people are becoming more aware of having their coordinates like e-mail addresses being widely distributed in the public domain, the benefits of doing so greatly outweigh the cost of having to deal with the repercussion of leaked information, whether it is done intentionally or not.

Awareness is the key. Too often, the establishment of confidentiality and privacy policies is done in a way that appears to grant those who must handle private information a feeling of superiority. They have been trusted with information that nobody else has, and they are only too glad to make their colleagues know it. Yet the most trustworthy are those who claim to know so little that they give the impression that it's really not worth talking to them about anything remotely private.

Discretion is highly valued in business. The lack of discretion can certainly spoil a business relationship, and IT provides innumerable opportunities to do so by spreading information quickly and pervasively.

Chapter 12

Focusing on Processes

> People carry in their brains a share of their organization's knowledge, which is by far one of the most important assets of an IT organization.

The term knowledge capital was introduced in Chapter 1. Knowledge capital (or human capital) has become an area of interest in information technology (IT) over the last few years and several attempts have been made to quantify it.

Knowledge capital leaves the organization as people switch jobs or work elsewhere, unless it has been captured in one form or another by the organization before the people leave. Knowledge capital is not everything in itself, because it must be exploited. For instance, the technical knowledge necessary to produce a new application must be harnessed. The management knowledge to do so is also part of an organization's knowledge capital.

Establishing and maintaining knowledge capital in organizations that develop products and deploy services relying on Information Technology, essentially means focusing on capturing and making available to the rest of the organization the knowledge people acquired while performing the work for which they are being paid. This is the topic of this chapter.

As a reminder, process in the context of this chapter is defined as the way human resources, methods, procedures, and tools are integrated in order to obtain a desired outcome. It is the way of doing things, the knowledge that an organization acquires through its human capital.

With this chapter, we move to another dimension of applying Information Technology. Where previous chapters focused on managing requirements, planning work, tracking progress, assuring quality, releasing and controlling changes, subcontracting work, developing products, coordinating activities among stakeholders, conducting reviews and inspections, and providing customer service in individual IT initiatives, in this chapter, the organizational dimension comes into play. The knowledge that was acquired while performing the preceding activities in individual IT initiatives will now be consolidated, massaged, and documented so all IT initiatives will share a common way of carrying out these activities. This means the way requirements are managed, work is planned, tracked and subcontracted, quality is assured, releases are made, changes are controlled, products are developed, activities are coordinated, reviews and inspections are performed, and customer service is provided will be revisited to apply to the organization as a whole, and new processes will be defined as needed to reflect this new perspective.

As Blaise Pascal said over 350 years ago, "The last thing one discovers in composing a work is what comes first." Once the enhancement and maintenance processes, the basic IT development, have been enacted and sufficient experience has been gained, then a more coherent way of implementing them can be devised. The more experience is available at the onset, the more coherent the process will be.

Make It Clear for Everyone That Improving Is a Priority

Unless it is clear to everyone that knowledge must be shared within an organization, it will probably not happen, at least not at a level where it can make a difference. It is not that personnel are keeping what they have learned to themselves, it is simply not on their minds. With new task assignments and everything that comes up, sharing knowledge means going back in the past and consolidating what may have been learned then. For one to put his or her head to it while there is much work ahead, and the rewards that may come with completing that work, takes motivation that can only be provided by senior management.

It should therefore be explicitly stated that everyone must contribute to the pool of knowledge that characterizes the organization and makes it unique among all others. But that's not enough. This is only the push action. A pull action must also be implemented by assigning a corporate responsibility to someone to go around and compile that knowledge in whatever form it comes, to massage it in order to extract its essence, and to feed it back into the organization.

We have observed that in all organizations, if senior management is not strongly endorsing continuous improvement, it was either a flop or a mitigated success at best. We have seen one organization where this type of an initiative was sponsored by middle managers. This was in fact an incongruity because middle managers often constitute the main obstacle to changing the way of doing things. Changing is indubitably associated with uncertainty, which translates into risk, and ultimately into problems. A middle manager may have a lot to lose and little to gain by making changes. In any case, in the organization where middle managers were the driving force for improving, very little actually happened, and the initiative was barely surviving.

A statement made and periodically reiterated by senior management that improving the process is important will convey the message that not only is it something to work on, it is something that senior managers want to see happen. If that statement is visibly important to senior managers, it will be important to everyone in the organization. This type of organizational improvement comes only through capturing, consolidating, measuring, improving, and sharing knowledge.

To be frank, very few organizations focus on defining and improving the way they conduct activities related to their business without some external impetus. Organizations — and behind organizations there are people — are not so virtuous. They focus on process because their competitors are doing it, customers are demanding it, or things are starting to go so bad that something has to be done.

Another reason to focus on process and to issue a written commitment to that effect, is that changes at the basis of what is described in this chapter are quite fundamental, and take a long time to implement. Quick attempts to change direction usually fail. In fact, technological and business changes are easy compared to changes in social and cultural practices, and capturing and sharing knowledge entail this type of transformation.

In addition, it is difficult to prove beforehand that focusing on process will translate into an improvement and there will be resistance. All those factors make it likely that a program established with that objective will falter and eventually vanish unless it is supported by the organizational equivalent of a constitution, that is, something unlikely to change in the short-term.

Over three quarters of the organizations we worked with had not formulated any guiding principles along these lines. The result was not so much the problems that ensued as the opportunities that were lost.

Periodically Assess Your IT Development and Maintenance Process

Periodically perform an inventory of your knowledge capital in IT development and maintenance. To do this, there must be an established function in the organization to assume that responsibility. Process and risk assessments are one way to go about it. These consist of holding workshops with various organizational units, which may include surveys, interviews, documentation reviews, and presentations, to get an idea of what the process assets and liabilities are. Find out which individual IT initiatives did well and which did not. Once this is known, then priorities can be established. Compile that information and make it available or use it to derive additional process-related activities. Quality assurance specialists can play an important role by providing first-hand information on process deficiencies they noticed as part of their verification responsibilities.

According to our data less than 45 percent of IT organizations perform such assessments. Among the organizations, some use formal assessments such as Capability Maturity Model (CMM)- or Capability Maturity Model Integration (CMMI)-based appraisals. However, these are relatively expensive and not everyone can afford them. Others carry out self-assessments using the CMM, the CMMI, ISO 9001, Control Objectives for Information and Related Technology (COBIT), Information Technology Infrastructure Library (ITIL) and other models, and standards that have been developed over the years. Finally, some have developed their own models based on the practices they have implemented and fine-tuned as part of their IT development and maintenance activities.

The use of models is not essential, but it helps. Without a model, the risk is that there may be strong differences of opinion on what needs to be addressed first. Without some consensus, it will be difficult for the organization to stay focused and to move ahead. The credibility of those who carry out such assessments represents by far the biggest obstacle to overcome. The process group, as it is sometimes referred to, is vulnerable to the same potential barriers that affect quality assurance.

One organization opted to establish a process group after the market it was pursuing was dissatisfied with the overall quality (i.e. number of residual defects, delivery delays, high cost, and poor functionality) of its products. The organization quickly set up a team of two individuals who were given the mandate to develop a plan of action to implement in the short and medium terms. Unfortunately, the organization selected two members of the staff who exhibited a performance below average in past assignments. Putting them in charge of the process group was equivalent to giving them the rope with which they could hang themselves, which they did. In order to complete that task successfully, the best and brightest should have been selected, but they were too busy.

Prepare a Plan of Action

Fifty-three percent of organizations plan what needs to be done to improve their capability in developing IT products and deploying IT services.

Comparing this with 45 percent of organizations carrying out an inventory of their strengths and weaknesses, it means that relatively few organizations forge ahead without really knowing what they are trying to solve. The good news is that most organizations that plan their capability improvement do it on the basis of collected evidence.

Managers we talked to are uncomfortable about preparing a plan of action. It makes them feel that they are throwing money in a hole. From our observations, they are sometimes right because capability improvement plans often have a beginning but no end. There is indeed a risk that capability improvement initiatives will become an end unto themselves, calling on staff positions that mean little other than having so-called process experts offering their opinion and giving advice that will mostly be ignored. We have been privy to such plans and they provided little if any value.

The plans that have been successful were prepared by process specialists in very close coordination with personnel involved in real IT initiatives. In fact, resources to carry out the plan often came from those initiatives. Process specialists coordinated the work and helped capture the information, recording it in a form that was usable by as many people as possible, and disseminating it within the organization.

These plans also contained realistic work packages corresponding to process deliverables for which tasks of finite duration and resources were clearly described. Each work package also contained a training component and a burn-in period during which the deliverables were planned to be used on a trial basis to check their adequacy. Finally, trial results were analyzed and modifications were made as appropriate, possibly followed by more trials, until the deliverables were officially released into current practice. This approach closely mimics the approach for developing or enhancing an IT product component. The assessment essentially corresponds to a requirements elicitation phase applied to process definition and organizational capability improvement.

Implement the Plan to Define and Improve Organizational Processes

In order to improve an organizational process, that process must first be defined. That's usually the initial version of an improvement plan. We found it undesirable to take on an improvement task with too large a scope. It is unrealistic to want to concurrently improve the way requirements are managed, IT initiatives are planned and tracked, quality is assured, releases are made, changes are controlled, work is subcontracted, products are developed, activities are coordinated, reviews and inspections are conducted, and customer service is provided. In reality, either a few aspects of each area are worked on or only a few areas are selected. The idea is to pick the best features of past IT initiatives and to consolidate them into organizationwide standard processes.

For instance, one organization, after having performed an inventory of its strengths and weaknesses, found that the accuracy of its estimates left something to be desired. The discussions that took place during the assessment led to a possible cause: the number of changes that were made to requirements in the course of the project execution. Requirements change control and estimation were therefore the two areas selected for immediate improvement.

First, the way requirements were defined was looked at. Some measurements were available and helped quantify the problem. Customers had a poor understanding of the impact changes they were making had on projects. The process group worked with application managers to define a way to elicit requirements in a consistent manner across the organization, then to analyze the impact of changes. The organization presented this to its customers to ensure they would be willing to follow the processes. The planning process was then defined, with special attention given to estimation. After six months, sufficient experience was gained in the requirements and planning processes to release them officially.

The organization then moved on to other areas and at each stage, a new building block was obtained until over a period of two years, the organization defined most of the processes that needed to be followed from beginning to end. At that point, the organization's development life cycle took on a new meaning because tangible artifacts to which everyone related could be visualized, and that was now shared across organizational units. Two years seem like a long time, but we found that was not unusual and it sometimes took even longer.

Defining processes should be undertaken in collaboration with those who will have to apply them. The crystal tower syndrome, whereby the process group comes up with a process in isolation and releases it to the masses like Moses with the stone tablets should be avoided, unless the group is guided by some divine inspiration.

We have seen it happen on numerous occasions and it invited similar types of responses. The first type of response was very emotional; recipients literally went through the roof and told the process group without mincing any words, that the group could shove its process where it saw most fit. The second response was intellectual; the peasants for whom the process was intended turned out to be smarter than they looked. They logically argued why the process was not going to be useful to them and, for these very reasons, should not have to abide by it.

The third type was by far the worst. Development personnel showed great enthusiasm on being presented with the process group's magnum opus and were ever so grateful that someone had finally paid attention to what they were doing. They then got rid of it as soon as the process group departed, and upon being queried, they assured the group that this process made their job so much easier. It sometimes took up to a year for the process group to come to terms with the fact that its process had never been used.

Having worked extensively in Europe and North America, we also found it interesting how the approach to define process differed on both continents. Europeans, being more Cartesian, adopt a top-down approach where the process architecture is first established and subsequently pop-ulated, even if it sometimes results in something more or less efficient. North Americans tend to proceed from a bottom-up paradigm, coming up with process components and assembling them in a more or less coherent structure later on.

The argument has been presented to us several times that some processes can be bought off-the-shelf. We have been privy to some of them and without disputing the fact that for the most part, they were logical and made sense, we have not seen these processes implemented in an organization with much success. At times, parts of an off-the-shelf process were a good fit and were deployed with some success, but wall-to-wall processes are not easily transferable. The concepts and principles underlying a process are easily transferable, but not the detailed processes themselves. The only situation we envisioned where it could work is if an organization started from scratch with an off-the-shelf process. How-ever, we have not witnessed that as most organizations start small, grow, and develop their own way of doing things along the way.

Establish a Library of Process-Related Documentation

There can be more than one IT development and maintenance process in an organization. It often depends on the platforms and the technologies that are used. For instance, there may be a process for client-server applications, one for Web-based applications, another for real-time devel-opment, and one for management information systems.

In addition, and this is often neglected, there should probably be a process for initiatives that are in trouble. When the house is on fire, it is not the time to go out to the nearest hardware store to look for a fire extinguisher. Drastic measures need to be taken, but it does not necessarily mean that they should be improvised.

The process library contains process descriptions and templates, along with maps (or life cycles, because there may be more than one) that guide personnel in implementing the knowledge acquired by the organization as far as IT development and maintenance is concerned. It also contains guidelines and tailoring options that can be exercised as a function of project size and complexity. It is also strongly recommended to add particularly good and representative examples of artifacts that have been developed in the course of past initiatives to make it easier for the staff to understand what is expected of them.

In the past, this library used to be in the form of electronic copies of documents stored on servers or even on diskettes that personnel would use in their IT initiatives. With the advent of the Web, most organizations now have an Intranet where all these documents can easily be accessed by clicking on a URL, with guidelines on how to use them.

Developing a library does take time. In one financial institution, we spent well over a year doing so. As for any change, personnel were resisting the changes in work habits that such a library entailed. It meant that they would not have as much flexibility as before. After the library was set up and personnel got used to it, they told us that there was no way they would go back to their old ways. The library did contribute to making their life easier.

Over 55 percent of the organizations we assessed had not established a process library, and by the same token, guidelines on how to use processes. This is the cause of the highest number of issues that had to be dealt with later on as far as process improvement is concerned. Development teams keep reinventing the wheel (or at least part of it) in each new IT initiative. For senior management, the job is also more demanding because each initiative has its unique set of artifacts. It should be obvious that assessing progress and keeping a tab on how things are going is a challenge under such conditions.

Establish a Historical Measurements Repository

A historical measurements repository is commonly referred to as a process database, and it is used to estimate IT development, enhancements, and maintenance. The data stored in the process database comes from measurements made in individual IT initiatives, as discussed in Chapter 2, Chapter 4, Chapter 8, and Chapter 10.

This section focuses on compiling data, extracting useful ratios, deriving baselines, and helping development teams making use of data, which is essentially the role of the specialists who are part of the process group, either on a part-time or a full-time basis. Once the repository has been established and populated, the job of personnel assigned to the process group will consist of coordinating its use across the organization and of updating it with whatever fresh data is collected in current and future IT

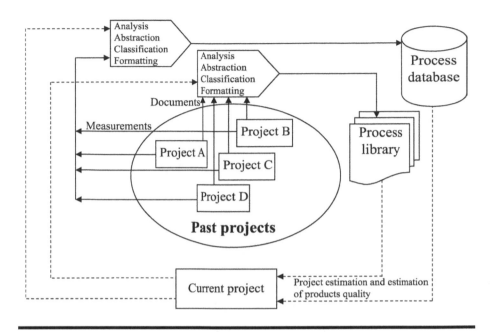

Figure 12-1 Use of the process database for estimating

initiatives. As time goes on, and more data becomes available, patterns are likely to emerge as a function of the organization's attributes, such as scope, team size, technology, and methodology used, that will make possible a finer characterization of the organization's capability. As an example, Productora de Software S.A. (PSL) currently maintains six baselines that are used to plan new projects; the appropriate baseline is selected based on a project's characteristics, and it is subsequently updated after the project has been completed and its data analyzed.

Establishing a usable process database is more difficult if there is no normalizing parameter. By normalizing, we typically mean size. This was discussed in detail in Chapter 3 in the section Start by Estimating Size.

One use of the process database is represented in Figure 12-1. Data normalized over the types of projects that an organization has undertaken can be used to estimate a new IT initiative. The normalization allows comparing data collected over several projects. If an iterative and incremental approach is adopted, the data could represent each increment of a project and provide a finer level of granularity.

Close to 60 percent of IT organizations have no data at the corporate level for estimating and tracking progress. Individual initiatives may take measurements; however, these may differ between each initiative, which makes comparison at an organizational level more difficult. In addition, those who have data do not systematically use it. Indeed, we came across

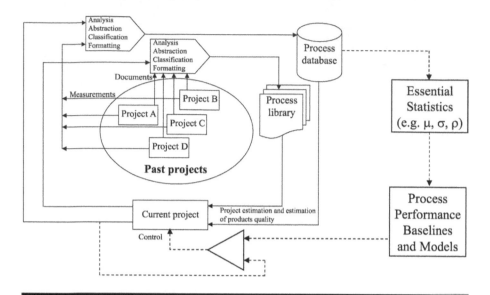

Figure 12-2   Use of a process database in execution control

several organizations that had accumulated a wealth of data over the years, but that data was not easily usable. The best one could do was to access a specific project file and extract data pertaining to that project only. Because it had not been reduced through analysis, and the data had not been normalized, no ratios were available and its use was limited to a qualitative examination to determine if estimates for another project made sense.

Figure 12-2 shows a more sophisticated use of the process database. The data is not only used for estimation, it is also used to control the execution of a project or an iteration in a project.

The same principle is applied for enhancements and maintenance.

For instance, at PSL, personnel assigned to the process group have an intimate knowledge of the data stored in the process database, how it was analyzed, and what use can be made of it in a new IT initiative. They help the application manager define what measurements should be taken and how to analyze them, possibly setting up control charts like those described in Annex A.

At times, the PSL process group personnel had to backtrack because as they analyzed collected data, they realized that it had not been properly categorized. In one particular instance, they had to re-categorize 3,000 bug reports, a painful exercise for those who had to go through it.

We once worked with an organization that had a lot of data at its disposal. Over the years, it had accumulated data for over 80 projects. The problem we faced was there was no quality assurance and some of that data was unreliable. Nevertheless, after analyzing it in detail, we managed to extract 34 projects on which we could rely.

Number of processing units criteria	Very simple	Simple	Medium	Complex	Very complex
Number of tables affected	1	2	3 or 4	5 to 7	8 or more
Number of fields affected	1 to 5	6 to 20	21 to 40	41 and more	Note 1
Number of validations	Note 2	Note 2	Note 2	Note 2	Note 2
Number of calculations	Note 2	Note 2	Note 2	Note 2	Note 2
Weight	1	2	**3.5**	6	10
Note 1:					
When this criteria is extreme for a given table, estimate on a case by case basis					
Note 2:					
Evaluate as a function of their complexity					
Effort distribution (Core)					
Functional analysis	0.4	3.0	5.0	8.0	12.0
Construction	0.4	2.0	5.0	12.0	18.0
Functional tests	0.2	1.0	3.0	5.0	7.0
Total	1.0	6.0	13.0	25.0	37.0

Figure 12-3   Size and effort estimation criteria

This organization had structured its IT development and maintenance in way that proved very beneficial. It had devised a standard Work Breakdown Structure (WBS) that governed the execution of all its initiatives. As shown in Figure 12-3, the core function of its WBS was centered on deliverables associated with three WBS elements, namely functional analysis, construction, and functional tests. Other WBS elements included project management, support, change requests, implementation, training, operations, and software quality assurance. Unfortunately, this is where things broke down. The data was not systematically collected with respect to these elements, and we had to ignore them in our analysis. Nevertheless, the core elements represented over 75 percent of the effort invested in a project, and they could therefore be used to characterize IT development and maintenance.

Figure 12-3 also shows the approach used to estimate size. The term processing unit was arbitrarily used for this purpose, which corresponded to a scale ranging from very simple (1) to very complex (10).

Each element at the lowest level of the WBS was estimated with this scale.

Figure 12-4 illustrates the normalization process for a sub-sample of five projects among the 34 that proved usable, and how we used it in analyzing data.

As can be seen in the shaded part of Figure 12-4, the total actual effort for those five projects was 715, 1,059, 347, 274, and 3,434 person-days, respectively. This data does not appear to provide any useful information

Normalized Effort = Core Effort divided by Total PU Count → (5.71)

No QA done - Unreliable data

CRITERIA	Weight	Project#1 units			Project#2 units			Project#3 units			Project#4 units			Project#5 units		
		Count	PU count	Normalized	Count	PU count	Normalized	Count	PU count	Normalized	Count	PU count	Normalized	Count	PU count	Normalized
Very simple	1	30	30		20	20		0	0		11	11		31	31	
Simple	2	6	12		38	76		10	20		13	26		54	108	
Medium	3.5	23	80.5		18	63		7	24.5		2	7		67	234.5	
Complex	6	6	36		11	66		2	12		1	6		33	198	
Very complex	10	2	20		1	10		2	20		1	10		3	30	
TOTAL		67	178.5		88	235		21	76.5		28	60		188	601.5	
EFFORT (person-days)																
Core		715		4.01	1059		4.51	347		4.54	274		4.57	3434		5.71
Project management		85		0.48	111		0.47	7		0.93	30		0.50	340		0.57
Support		150		0.84	286		1.22	114		1.49	26		0.43	928		1.54
Change requests				0.00	3		0.01	0		0.00	22		0.37	400		0.67
Implementation		48		0.27	127		0.54	58		0.76	29		0.48	155		0.26
Training				0.00	25		0.11			0.00			0.00			0.00
Procedures				0.00	93		0.40			0.00			0.00	103		0.17
SQA				0.00			0.00			0.00			0.00			0.00
TOTAL		998		5.59	1704		7.25	590		7.71	381		6.35	5360		8.91

Processing Unit (PU) count = Number of units *times* weight assigned to each unit based on size criteria

Figure 12-4   Analysis for a sample of 5 projects among 34

for estimation purposes. However, when the figures are divided by the total number of processing units for each project, the normalized effort, defined as the total effort divided by the total number of processing units, comes up to 4.01, 4.51, 4.54, 4.57, and 5.71, which shows some correlation.

For that organization, we analyzed the data for all 34 projects, and using the techniques described in Annex A, we concluded that its process was indeed under statistical control. The problem was that its projects experienced, on average, a 20 percent schedule overrun and their costs were 11 percent higher than what had initially been budgeted. This was a significant finding for senior managers who immediately initiated a program to implement corrective actions to reduce those variances. Once shown how they could apply simple techniques to control their IT development, they were then in a position not only to control individual projects, but also to quantitatively determine the capability of their organization.

The challenge for an organization is to come up with a weight scale (shown in Figure 12-3) that makes sense. The scale that one comes up with must be validated with existing data, using a representative number of projects, enhancements, work packages, or bug fixes. The sample size does not need to be extensive at first, because it is only needed to come up with a reasonable estimate for the scale. The scale may be different for work performed with different technologies (for instance, Web-based versus client-server). It can always be refined later as more data is acquired.

It is clear from this example that deriving such a scale, which is somewhat related to function points, is more complex than counting pages of documentation, USE cases, objects, or lines of code. This is why lines of code are more commonly used to estimate size, which, being an independent parameter, is then used to normalize all other measurements so they can meaningfully be used to compare and control IT initiatives.

Provide Training and Support as Processes Are Deployed

Process training is a topic that does not always receive the attention it deserves. Members of the process group are liable to get caught up in the development of processes and forget that what is very familiar to them is new to those who must apply them.

Our own observations in the field substantiate this statement: 55 percent of organizations develop processes and force-feed them to their staff, which more often than not results in resistance and resentment at having no say on how they should carry out their responsibilities. Consider conducting pilots of new processes (after they have been peer-reviewed) before deploying them throughout the organization, and as part of these pilots, develop training and ensure that support will be available during the trial period. You will get feedback on the training material and on the processes themselves, and you may gain useful allies when the time to deploy on a larger scale comes up.

People who have invested a lot of time in developing a new process may not take it lightly to see their masterpiece torn apart by those who test it. Yet, their comments are essential to a successful organizationwide deployment. In order to circumvent this response, organizations that have acquired a lot of experience in continuously improving their capability often have institutionalized a process to develop, maintain, and deploy processes.

It sounds recursive, but it is not. Indeed, having such a macro-process, in which training and support are essential components, helps ensure that personnel are familiar with the introduction of new processes and know their role in this activity, thereby alleviating the typical name "it we're against" it response to change.

Chapter 13

Training Personnel

He who knows nothing can only learn by failing, and unless he admits it, will go on failing in each new undertaking until he has exhausted all his assets.

Training was discussed throughout the preceding chapters in connection with specific topics, like requirements, planning, and contracting out. Training was also discussed in the context of individual projects, namely to ensure that the essential skills were available to carry out the tasks defined in these initiatives. As such, training was reactive.

As an organization starts defining and deploying coherent ways of developing and maintaining software applications across the organization, training does take on a new meaning. Economies of scale are investigated, and as the organization seeks to improve its capability, the efficiency of training provided to personnel is also looked at. In addition, there is now a more solid base on which training can stand; it is no longer provided solely from the standpoint of particular IT initiatives. Rather, it proceeds from a larger perspective, one that takes the whole organization into consideration. Training now becomes more proactive.

The importance of training also takes on a new dimension as it becomes more widely recognized. We have witnessed this change in organizations that undertook to improve and to pursue excellence. Personnel attending training were no longer feeling guilty of abandoning their colleagues, nor were they perceived as not having much to do if they had time to attend training sessions. Training was no longer an option; it became a requirement.

On average, lack of training was found to be the cause of 12.6 percent of all the problems experienced in the course of developing or maintaining information technology (IT) applications. This is the highest single cause of problems that plague software development and maintenance. Mistakes that are made are largely due to inadequate or inappropriate training. Indeed, people are usually not intent on creating havoc for themselves and for their organizations. Being unable to benefit from the experience others may have acquired, they just take a more arduous path that often leads to failures.

I worked in an organization where training was not highly valued. During a meeting with senior management, I brought up the issue that personnel did not all have the skills to carry out the tasks to which they had been assigned, and that time and money were being wasted as a result of constant rework. The response of a senior manager has remained vividly in my mind ever since: "If we train them, they will leave."

Well, they did eventually leave to the company across town that provided three months of training to new hires, and the turnover in that company was very low. After all, who would want to leave a place where one is given the opportunity to learn and where one's skills are considered an asset to everyone?

Convey the Importance of Training and How It Will Be Provided

Make it an incentive for personnel to attend training sessions and seminars, to participate in pilots, to exchange information with colleagues, and to populate the knowledge library that has been put in place as part of the endeavor to improve the organization's capability. This is the spark that ignites the pursuit of doing better; yet only 30 percent of the organizations we worked with had actually done something to that effect.

It is everyone's responsibility to learn and to improve. The organization can help by providing time and resources, but individuals must ultimately invest the effort. Nobody is reluctant to learn and improve if people feel they are not being exploited, that is, the organization is not only pushing them to improve for its own profit but also for their own personal benefit.

As soon as training is mentioned, the immediate response from personnel is to think about external courses provided in a classic classroom environment. However, the transfer of knowledge is most efficiently provided through coaching and apprenticeship. There certainly is a need for training in the classic understanding of the term for general managerial and technical topics, but the training we are talking about here has as an objective the dissemination of the knowledge capital that has been accumulated by the organization. Few, if any, external resources are in a position to do that. This kind of training, in our opinion, should be promoted a lot more than it is now. The catch is that internal resources are likely to be the ones who need to provide it, and it requires instructors and coaches who have experience or are themselves being trained in such avenues.

Wherever we have seen this approach implemented in an organization, we have also noticed a much stronger corporate fabric. People were usually proud to be part of that organization, they took more interest in making sure that the organization succeeded, which came out through the commitments they made to the initiative to which they had been assigned. It often turned out to be cheaper than acquiring external training and it contributed to building the organization's knowledge capital, whereby training material developed for that purpose became available to others. Even after individuals left the organization to work somewhere else, possibly motivated by personal interests or family constraints, they spoke highly of their past employment and often kept in touch with former colleagues.

We came across one organization that had been particularly successful at it. Even after 10 years, former employees enjoyed meeting on a regular basis, even if only once or twice a year. Of course, their new employers benefited from the skills they developed, but the message they passed to others was straightforward: their previous employer was among the best, and when they were in a position to do so, they tried to emulate it in their new environment. Ultimately, everyone in the community benefited.

Assign the Responsibility for Coordinating Training and Make a Plan

All organizations exhibiting a high capability level take training seriously. They simply know that it will save them a lot of hardship and that it is one of many ways to gain loyalty from their workforce, not to mention that in the long run, it will improve productivity and reduce the cost of their products and services.

In order to implement a sound training program, the training needs and skills to be imparted should first be known. This is the job of training coordinators, who can be part of the Human Resources department or integrated into the teams to which specific tasks have been assigned, or the job of managers in the organization specifically given that responsibility. Training coordinators typically participate with development teams in identifying skills that are needed to complete the work having been undertaken or work envisioned in the future. They also suggest or define profiles for positions in the teams (e.g. architect, manager, designer, or tester), measure the gaps that exist between the team's actual and desired profiles, and then pass the list of remedial actions to whoever must organize or procure the training. In some instances, they may organize the training themselves, especially when a skill needs to be acquired on short notice.

Some organizations maintain an inventory of skills at the organizational level that they subsequently map to the organizational chart, in a way somewhat similar to the mapping of the Work Breakdown Structure (WBS) described in Chapter 3 and represented in Figure 3-1. Intersections of the Organizational Skills Breakdown Structure with the Organizational Chart identify whether the skill is mandatory, desirable, optional, or not applicable with respect to the position. For instance, it may be that a task leader must have training in Earned Value management, whereas training in testing methodologies is desirable, training in quality assurance is optional, and technical writing skills are not applicable for this position. Another chart maps Training to the Human Resources Directory. Intersections of those two charts indicate whether an individual has received training, the date at which training was provided, and whether the training was successfully completed. Finally, mapping the Human Resources Directory to the Organizational Chart indicates the training a specific individual has received with respect to the position he or she assumes. Conversely, the same mapping also indicates the position a specific individual can assume given the training he or she has received.

Planning can then start.

A training plan not need to be overly complex. Once the individual in charge has compiled training needs submitted by training coordinators, gaps are easily identified, and a schedule can be prepared. The chart mapping Training to the Human Resources Directory can then be updated to include the date at which training is planned for personnel. Coupled with training arrangements specifying the vehicle through which training is to be provided, this essentially constitutes the training plan. Regrettably, we found that only 25 percent of the organizations we assessed had something close to this. As a result, 10 to 12 issues, mostly in the form of rework, had to be dealt with later on, which impacted both the work schedule and its cost.

Some organizations collect training needs in a way similar to what was described earlier, with the exception that skills are now inventoried for a specific IT initiative. This results in a Project Skills Breakdown Structure that can subsequently be mapped to the Project Chart. The mapping between the Human Resources Directory to the Project Chart specifies the training required for the staff assigned to the IT initiative, and may be passed to the organizational training coordinator in that format.

Productora de Software S.A. (PSL) plans its training in a somewhat similar way. The organizational training coordinator collects all training requests, prepares an organizational schedule that will satisfy as many people as possible, reserves the training facility and equipment, makes appropriate arrangements when external instructors are required, and ensures that training material is available, both for the instructor and the participants. Of course, it's never that easy. Unexpected events do happen and training has to be rescheduled for some individuals who were called on to resolve urgent matters. But overall, it works and it turns out to be very efficient.

Deliver and Track Planned Training

High-performance organizations also take every opportunity to convey the message that training is important, and that personnel undergoing training must strive to improve, not only to be more efficient but also to reach their own personal goals.

Internal resources should ideally provide most of the training using the most appropriate vehicles, such as formal and on-the-job knowledge transfer, coaching, seminars, and guided self-study. External training should be reserved for specific topics and specialized skills that cannot be acquired any other way. Even then, there should be an attempt on the part of those who have been trained in this fashion to transfer their newly acquired knowledge to others. Using internal resources to provide training does contribute to establishing a strong corporate culture, the topic of Chapter 15.

From our perspective as assessors, on-the-job and guided self-study constitutes training mechanisms that have been abused by many organizations. Guided self-study does not consist of dumping user manuals on the desk of an individual and telling him or her to read them during the weekend and then get to work. It requires a lot more involvement on the part of the mentor, who should prepare exercises and tests, and conduct reviews to check how the student internalized the material. This requires significant time and effort. Likewise, on-the-job training does not simply mean throwing an individual in the lions' pit to see how he or she will fare. As for guided self-study, it requires supervision and guidance, both of which demand commitment and work.

Deficiencies observed in connection with the training delivery constitute the highest source of training issues likely to degenerate into problems later on. The challenges we most often came across are a mismatch between training and work schedules, crises preventing those who were scheduled to attend training to effectively get trained, and training provided too early or too late. When training was provided too early, it was mostly forgotten when the time came for personnel to apply the knowledge they had received, and when it was provided too late, personnel had already taken the wrong path.

The minus side of using internal resources to deliver training is that not everyone has the skills and aptitude to both prepare the training material and to deliver training. In one particular organization, external resources are secured to help internal resources. Experienced instructors sit down with specialists and essentially pick their brains in order to capture the knowledge they have and to format it in a way conducive to being transferred to others. They also often deliver the training, while specialists sit in as observers and intervene as needed to provide details and examples.

In an organization where internal resources show some potential as instructors, the organization encouraged them to act as teaching assistants at the local university, where they develop their teaching skills and become qualified instructors. The training material developed internally is used to teach future software engineers, and instructors can identify those students who display particularly good abilities, who may then be offered a position in the organization at the end of their studies. That way, the organization has first pick and has had time to introduce future prospects to the environment in which they could eventually work.

Maintain and Regularly Review Personnel Training Records

Training people who have no talent is like beating a dead horse. Reviewing training records, performance reviews, and personal objectives will certainly help determine if an individual is well matched to his or her job assignment. Of course, this assumes that the individual was properly interviewed before being hired and has talent for something that represents some value to the organization.

The main purpose of maintaining training records is to make available to those who must manage IT initiatives the skill set characterizing the organization. Over 40 percent of the organizations we looked at did not maintain such a reference. In some cases, the reference was only maintained to satisfy government regulations or union agreements. The consequence is that when a new initiative starts, those who assume responsibility for it and who must select resources choose personnel they have worked with (they know their strengths and weaknesses, even though some others could prove a better fit), or individuals they have been told have performed well in the past. As a result, it is often the same ones who get selected repeatedly; those who never had the chance to prove themselves or to work in close collaboration with a manager are likely to be left out. This makes the organization less efficient since in general, its resources are underutilized where a small number are over utilized.

As an example, one organization had one particular individual always left out of important tasks. For the most part, he was assigned to non-essential work. Being rather shy and introverted, no one really noticed him and his skills and experience were unknown to most managers. Overall, his performance was rated as acceptable, but certainly nothing out of the ordinary. When product integration came up, the most experienced (and already well-known) resources were in short supply. At one point, the system being integrated had to be reconfigured in a hurry. This happened at the beginning of the midnight shift, and nobody knew the system well enough to undertake this reconfiguration. Everyone was getting ready to go home since there was no point in staying there for nothing. It turned out that this individual had studied the system extensively as part of the menial tasks he had been given. He had ample time to observe the most experienced individuals performing the very reconfiguration task now being on the critical path. He reconfigured the system and the shift could go on as planned. It was by no means an amazing feat, but his action did result in managers suddenly realizing that they had someone at their disposal who could do a lot more than what he had been assigned to.

This is precisely where a waiver becomes useful for inciting verification of personnel training records by supervisors and managers. This allows them to assess if individuals possess the knowledge and skills required to perform their designated roles, in addition to developing a better appreciation of the skills currently available. Waivers are used in less than 40 percent of organizations; yet, in the form of tests and checklists, they are very helpful to ensure that the right people are assigned to the right tasks. Too often, when resources are being urgently sought, a lot of hope is placed on the first few individuals who show up, to the point where those who are looking for human resources convince themselves, against their better judgment, that they need not look any further.

PSL administers tests to individuals who join a new initiative if they have not had extensive supervision in the task for which they are being considered. The existing members of the team also interview them, especially if they are new in the company, to ensure that they will fit in and their integration into the team will not cause unexpected difficulties.

Periodically Assess the Training Relevance and Quality

One of the most important tasks of the training coordinator is to get feedback from those who underwent training. Compiling that information indicates where improvements should be made and helps fine-tune training material.

We found that 40 percent of the organizations providing training did not bother to assess the quality of the training their personnel received. Among the 60 percent that did, fewer than 10 percent also collected feedback later to measure how useful the training had been and how it helped personnel perform their job. One aspect often neglected is probing supervisors and managers for their opinion on how trained personnel under their responsibility performed in light of the training they received. Supervisors and managers are asked what training should be considered in the future and what changes would improve overall productivity.

Training usually needs to evolve along the capability of an organization and in the direction toward which it is moving. These are topics in which senior managers should have a say, since they are the ones who impart this direction. Surprisingly, in close to 50 percent of the organizations we assessed, senior management had little or no visibility in training, other than approving its budget. Sometimes, the budget was not even considered until the time to cut expenses came up.

In one organization that displayed a particularly high capability, a review team was put together at the end of each fiscal year to look at training. The team first sits with senior managers to get their vision as to what the next fiscal year should look like, the initiatives that are likely to be undertaken, and the new technologies that are likely to be pursued. The team then reviews all training activities that have taken place in the past two years, the current skills inventory, and the gaps that still exist. Following this review, the team makes its recommendations to senior management, which become one of the inputs to planning for the next fiscal year.

Taking PSL as an example, the CEO is actively involved in training, not only in planning but also in preparing training material where senior management must provide input, and in delivering it to personnel. In fact, training offers one of the best opportunities to convey to staff the organization's values and what it stands for. The payback is enormous and literally permeates every corner of an organization.

Unfortunately, in most organizations, senior management rarely takes advantage of it.

Chapter 14

Managing IT Initiatives

> No IT initiative is ever a complete failure — it can always be
> used as a bad example.

Planning and tracking progress have already been discussed in Chapter
3 and Chapter 4. However, these topics were then presented in the context
of individual information technology (IT) initiatives, where the manager
of each was essentially defining how the work was going to proceed. It
could bear little resemblance to what other initiatives are using, although
in all likelihood, bits and pieces would be common to both.

This chapter assumes that the way to manage IT development and
maintenance has been defined throughout the organization by taking the
best out of individual IT initiatives and making this information available
to others in the form of a process-related documentation library and a
repository of historical measurements, as described in Chapter 12. For
instance, an estimation process that has been defined for a particular IT
initiative will be generalized, documented, supported by templates, procedures, and guidelines, and will become part of the organizational way
of managing IT development and maintenance work.

The main advantage this approach provides is lessons learned in each
IT initiative can now be shared, because they are managed the same way.
There may be differences stemming from particularities that each must
address; nevertheless, they have the same root. If there is anything that
differentiates a mature organization from an immature one, it is probably
this characteristic.

When we present this approach to software professionals, their first reaction is often to equate it to a centralized bureaucracy where they see themselves as apparatchiks who blindly follow established rules, whether they make sense or not. On the contrary, tailoring is allowed and encouraged, and more importantly, changes are constantly sought. But these changes are controlled and implemented in a structured way; they are not simply improvised and arbitrarily mandated by those who feel like doing things differently.

In this chapter, the focus is placed only on standardizing the way software management is carried out in an organization. In all organizations where a standard approach has been implemented to manage IT development and maintenance, everyone agrees that it has been a major improvement.

Mandate That Every IT Initiative Use a Management Approach Based on the Organizational Standard

Chapter 12 presented the establishment of an organizational development and maintenance process. The management aspect of that process is what we are talking about here. This is where everything starts, where successes are made and where failures take root. Close to 60 percent of organizations have no management process, or at least nothing that comes close to what was suggested in Chapter 12; the directive, when there is one, is often reduced to a statement to the effect that work must be managed... somehow.

For an organization, having a shared approach of managing IT development and maintenance is a huge step forward. The first thing that should be done, once this approach is sufficiently stable, is to enforce it so IT managers must make use of the assets namely, procedures, tools, templates, methods, and techniques that comprise this defined process. If it is not enforced, entropy will prevail and will result in uncontrolled tailoring. Eventually, the organization will slowly revert to the tower of Babel that characterized its former condition and everything will have to be rebuilt. Quality assurance has a particular role to play here, assuming the process-related documentation and the measurements repository are used, and feedback is collected to make them evolve.

Actually, moving from a state where work is managed differently in each IT initiative to a state where each IT initiative is managed the same way is not an easy transition. One would think that managers would jump at the timesaving opportunities that a common approach provides, but this does not take human nature into account. An IT manager who has for years defined how his or her IT initiative would proceed has (or feels he or she has) a lot of power and authority. In practice, the IT manager would likely have consulted with other managers, but ultimately, he or she makes the decisions. Having to follow a common approach takes a big chunk of that power away. Given the culture of individualism that permeates the way software has evolved for the past 30 years, this resistance should not be entirely surprising.

For instance, we have helped several organizations implement Earned Value management over the years as part of our risk management and organizational improvement services. It appears that commercial organizations have only discovered Earned Value management in the late 1990s but it has been around since the early 1960s. In addition, because some of the parameters associated with Earned Value management are already normalized (i.e. Schedule Performance Index (SPI), Cost Performance Index (CPI)), they can be used to statistically control projects, as explained in Annex A.

Earned Value management is probably one of the most logical approaches to managing work; yet the amount of effort we had to invest in the first organization where we undertook to deploy this method was way beyond what we initially expected. Everyone was against it. We eventually learned our lesson and the second time around, we secured the support of senior management who provided the stick, while we provided the carrot in the form of timely support all the way to cajoling and sweet-talking those who we had identified as opinion leaders. In any case, it was not easy and we felt a lot of empathy toward those who are trying to implement new techniques in their organizations, such as estimation with function points. Mandating the use of an organizational management approach means making it clear to IT managers that their initiative will not be accepted unless it follows the accepted standard, and rewarding those who contribute to its improvement.

Provide Tailoring Support and Training

No two IT initiatives are alike and thus the need to tailor the organizational standards to the needs of each initiative. Some organizations prepare guidelines that help perform this type of tailoring. Others tackle it by defining several standards that have already been pre-tailored to the needs of classes of initiatives. The tailoring is not complete, but it greatly reduces the effort that has to be invested by development team members. In the course of our work, 50 percent to 60 percent of organizations had defined organizational standards but did little with respect to tailoring. It resulted in situations that sometimes made little sense, like having team members spend time developing documents simply because the standards referred to them as being required, even though they served no useful purpose in a particular initiative.

In one extreme, the standards required that 100 person-days be invested on each new initiative before work associated with developing the application (i.e., requirements analysis) actually started, in order to prepare project documentation, which for the most part would be shelved shortly thereafter. The documentation consisted of impact analyses, case studies, cost-benefits analyses, budget authorization, resources allocation authorization, and material request documentation, among other required documents. Whether the initiative was a multi-year program or a two-month project, all these documents had to be prepared in accordance with organizational standards. For a one person-year initiative, almost half of it had to be dedicated to prepare this documentation. The consequence was that small initiatives were avoided, and where there was no choice, several were bundled together to make it worth the effort. Only large projects were undertaken, which made the development cost arbitrarily high. Some opportunities were lost because the development work they called for could not logically be packaged with anything else.

Granted, there is a fine line between tailoring and improvisation. This is the reason why process groups must have a say and be actively involved in providing support and training to development teams. Quality assurance must also have visibility, because it will be the last barrier preventing tailoring from deteriorating into chaos.

The most mature organizations train their managers and some insist that they be certified before taking on the responsibility of managing an IT initiative. This helps ensure that managers are knowledgeable about the tools to use, the methods to apply, the measurements to take, the procedures to follow, and the administrative tasks called for by the tailored standards in order to manage an IT initiative to a successful outcome. As such, training is deemed the best line of defense against rash and excessive deviations from the organization's accepted ways.

A minority of organizations (probably less than 5 percent) encourages improvisation. Initiatives that look like they have potential are assigned to small teams, with a small budget, and little control, if any. These teams are usually kept apart from the rest of the organization to prevent them from polluting the standards. If they manage to get to something that looks profitable, it is given to another group that will make it come to fruition, using the organizational standards.

We found that those who are attracted to that kind of work share a desire for freedom to do what they want, and an uncontrollable attraction to taking risks. Risk there is because in dire times, they are the first to be let go. However, due to their unconventional ways, they can sometimes make the difference between triumph and mediocrity for an organization.

Distribute the Tailored Process to Everyone in the Team

Team members can hardly be blamed for not adhering to a process that is not documented. Telling them in a kick-off meeting what the process is will help for a limited duration. As work progresses, events will occur that call for some decisions to be made and actions to be taken. By then, they will have forgotten about the process to follow. Without documentation, this will lead to deviations, which will eventually result in more events, more decisions and actions, and more deviations until a new improvised way will have found its way into the initiative. Most organizations opt to reference the process standards to follow in the plan of each IT initiative. Only tailoring options are normally documented. The plan, being available to everyone in the team, implies that team members can refer to documents to guide them in the performance of their tasks.

About one quarter of the organizations we worked with did not follow some sort of documented standards governing the management of their development and maintenance activities. Several did not have a wall-to-wall process, but they had components that were common across the organization. Project management was usually the first one to be standardized, where anything connected to technical topics came later. Indeed, most executives are well aware that management is the first topic on which to get a solid grip, in the sense that if things go wrong, problems usually find their source in the way the initiative was managed. The number of platforms liable to be supported in an organization and the amount of detail associated with technical process standards simply make adoption of the standards more difficult.

Unfortunately, little support is available to come up with a tailored process, which is probably why a significant number of organizations don't bother doing any tailoring. Only recently have tools become available to tailor comprehensive processes before undertaking IT initiatives. The approach usually adopted consists of referencing organizational standards located in the library of process-related documentation. This, from our observations, is quite acceptable if the standards are easy to apply and to tailor, and personnel have been trained in their use.

There are also cultural differences that make adherence to processes either easier or difficult. In assessments we performed in Germany and in Switzerland, we found relatively little process documentation; yet, we did not observe significant differences in the way standards were followed. It seemed that everyone understood them the same way, which was rather unusual from a North American perspective.

A friend of mine from France involved in defining standards made a rather amusing comment to that effect. His colleagues from France and Italy had happily been defining process standards in a conglomerate spanning Germany, Italy, France, and England. They themselves had no intention of strictly adhering to these standards, seeing them more as guidelines than standards. This friend was rather worried because as a program manager, he knew from experience that Germans would be following them to the letter, with the potentially huge costs that this implementation presented for his program.

Harmonize Performance and Needs

In all the assessments we performed, we observed that organizations having adopted a management standard are vulnerable to turn it into a bureaucracy if they do not periodically re-assess it. There is a natural tendency to follow what has been established if it has been in use for several years. Simply being around and surviving the erosive effect of time provides credentials of respectability and entrenched superiority. This is why some apparently solid corporations collapse like a house of cards when challenged by new and innovative enterprises.

We had the opportunity of following most of the IT organizations we assessed, either through subsequent appraisals or simply by providing additional risk and process implementation services. Those that managed to grow and prosper all have these things in common:

- Controlled changes in the way they manage their IT development and maintenance
- Harmonization of their performance, results with current and projected needs of the market, customers, and end-users

Controlling management processes has been addressed in Chapter 12 (Focusing on Processes) and in Chapter 5 (Assuring Quality). Harmonization is achieved through collective assessment of the progress in each IT initiative, the quality of the work products delivered so far, the team productivity, and any outstanding issues. For example, in order to adapt to its market, Productora de Software S.A. (PSL) holds regular meetings both at the organization level and at the project level. The Chief Executive Officer (CEO) makes it his priority to participate. Issues are discussed openly, without laying blame on anyone, and each team is encouraged to propose new approaches. This is supplemented by a defined way for each employee to make proposals to which the process group must respond in writing.

One way to achieve harmonization is by compiling lessons learned at the end of each phase of an IT initiative and disseminating them within the organization. Sixty percent of organizations prepare these reports;

unfortunately the majority of those that do it do so only because these reports are required to close a phase or a project, and do not invest the time and effort to make them into a useful by-product that would guide future undertakings. Yet, the availability of this information can prevent, on average, seven instances of lost time, rework, and other inefficiency in IT development and maintenance.

Measure the Effectiveness of the Organizational Management Approach

Good organizations take measurements and manage with numbers. This does not conflict with business acumen; it complements it. Only 40 percent of IT organizations actually spend any amount of time examining how effective their management process is. This deficiency does not result in a particularly high number of problems later (only 1.7 on average per initiative), but a qualitative assessment based on interviews with managers indicates that it has a significant impact on competitiveness.

The following are examples of data that can be collected, analyzed, and used to determine how effective organizational management standards are.

■ The actual effort and cost expended over time to manage software initiatives compared to what had been planned
■ The frequency, causes, and magnitude of re-planning efforts
■ The adverse impacts experienced in the course of development and maintenance compared to the estimated loss due to the risks to which the initiative has been exposed

It would be wrong to state that management effectiveness is generally not measured. In fact it is subjected to detailed analyses in terms of financial performance, and almost all the organizations we dealt with paid a lot of attention to their financial performance. The few that did not paid dearly for it.

An organization is limited in what it can do in terms of fine-tuning its management process by only looking at financial data. Financial results will certainly indicate that there is a problem somewhere, but it will not say where it is or how to resolve it. Large organizations are particularly vulnerable to this condition and we have observed it numerous times. The typical scenario is: financial statements do not look good for the current period, so the chief financial officer reduces the budget expenses. However, the organization is so large that knowing exactly where to cut is not trivial. The obvious solution is to cut everywhere. In other words, both the good and the bad initiatives are affected. This resolves the crisis for the time being, and then the whole cycle starts over again at some point in the future.

A manager we came across in one of our interventions had a lot of foresight in prevision of the budget cuts that would likely be coming at the end of the fiscal year. She set up her project to collect and analyze as much data as could reasonably be gathered, and she also conveyed to her team members the importance of doing so. Cuts were indeed as regular and precise as clockwork. When the fiscal year end came up and the predictable across-the-board budget reductions were announced, she requested that her project be spared based on the performance she had achieved, stating that she had already made the cuts where it counted, according to the data she had accumulated and the actions she had taken. She was successful at convincing senior management with the quantitative arguments she brought forward. Senior management offered the same opportunity to other managers, and no one had similar figures. Ultimately, hers was the only project that was not affected by the cuts.

At PSL, project teams meet regularly to look at collected data. Quality assurance personnel, who verify the data collection process, ascertain the data reliability. The process group is also involved in ensuing data reduction and archival to update the company's baselines, which characterize PSL's capability in terms of software development and maintenance. Control charts similar to those shown in Annex A are maintained and results are compared to the company's baselines to assess overall performance. Then, at least once a year, managers meet to set goals and to propose actions that will make the company more competitive.

Chapter 15

Building a Culture

> A cohesive organizational culture is a formidable wave that can be harnessed to accomplish the greatest feats.

When we started conducting assessments in the early 1990s, we used the Capability Maturity Model (CMM), which we tailored to make it fit to the organizations with which we were working. The cultural aspect of organizations intrigued us as potentially having a high impact on the capability of developing information technology (IT) products and services, and for that matter on the capability of any organization.

The potential high impact was solely based on experience and intuition, and we were at a loss as to how to measure an organization's culture. Through research and consulting with organizational psychologists, we derived a set of topics on which we collected information through surveys and interviews. The results we obtained were far more significant than what we had originally expected. When the likelihood of experiencing problems (LEP) was high in a given organization, and the contribution of organizational culture to this likelihood was also high, experience taught us that the implementation of remedial actions was going to be painful. In fact, all cases turned out to be very unpleasant.

Senior managers were far more defensive when we presented the appraisal findings pertaining to organizational culture, than when we presented findings on quality assurance or training, for example. We came to the conclusion that senior managers take these findings as failures on their part. They rightly feel that establishing desirable behavior patterns is their personal responsibility, and any deficiencies in this area puts their leadership capability into question.

Finding shortcomings related to planning work, tracking progress, releasing and controlling changes, or developing products in IT initiatives is like telling homeowners that the plumbing in their house has to be replaced or that the roof is leaking. It may require significant investment, but it can be fixed. Finding serious flaws related to organizational culture is like telling these homeowners that their house is built on contaminated ground. It would be cheaper to tear the house down and rebuild it somewhere else.

Implementing remedial actions in order to improve organizational culture is a tricky business. Organizational culture must be nurtured with great care and it matures slowly. It takes years to establish, and it can be destroyed quickly. In one of the outstanding organizations we came across, the CEO proceeded to merge his company with another that had more cash on hand to relieve temporary problems his company was going through at the time. Rumor has it that the CEO committed suicide shortly after when he realized that the merger had destroyed the culture he had taken so long to build. At GRafP Technologies, we have learned to diagnose organizational culture but we rarely act on it because of the risk of doing more harm than good. When we detect that there is something wrong in the organizational culture, we call on experts with whom we have worked for several years, and who have the experience and skills to take on the challenge.

In the early 1980s, I worked in a company that had developed a unique and cohesive corporate culture. People who joined were astonished at the way it operated and claimed they had never seen anything like it. As part of a project involving several divisions of that company, tension among personnel in one division had deteriorated to the point where it jeopardized successful system integration. Senior management called in organizational therapists to provide several five-day sessions to bring back harmony among groups and individuals. Senior management felt that if one division had problems, those problems would eventually propagate to other divisions like a contagious plague. I personally felt, along with my colleagues, that we certainly did not have challenges in our division, at least not to the extent where drastic measures were warranted; personnel relationships had not changed as far as we noticed. Nevertheless, our division was also slated to undergo the same shock treatment.

In a matter of one month, the organizational balance had been altered beyond repair. We went into this therapy as a homogenous unit and we came out as two separate entities. The company fabric had irremediably been modified, to the point where things were never the same after that. People aligned themselves along the two poles that the therapists had created, probably unconsciously (I give them the benefit of the doubt). They made some of the participants willingly divulge their inner self in front of others, as if they had been in a trance, where others resisted and either played the game or played dumb, whichever suited them.

Over the year that followed, the company slowly wasted away; those aligned along one pole felt awkward mixing with individuals from the other, which made them look elsewhere to pursue their career. After having closely observed well over 100 organizations, it seems that our culture may not have been as strong as I first thought. In fact, it probably did not have enough time to really take root.

Document and Communicate the Type of Behavior Valued by the Organization

Every new employee to an organization comes with his or her own baggage. The older the individual, the more difficult it will be for him or her to adapt. Some will fit right in, independent of their age and background; others never will. For instance, at Productora de Software S.A. (PSL), the hiring process is very demanding. The process consists of tests, interviews with the human resources manager, members of the team in which the candidate is envisioned to join, and the Chief Executive Officer (CEO). Nevertheless, PSL does sometimes make mistakes when new employees are hired. Some were let go or left on their own because they simply did not fit in.

We came across organizations where I would personally never work. Some had a very poor work environment; others were just different. I sometimes pitied those who had to earn their living by applying their skills in such a setting. Nevertheless, in all our appraisals, I always made it a point to ask people the one thing they would like to change in their workplace and its most important asset. This brings out a lot in the way they see their organization. Surprisingly, after talking to individuals about their workplace, I often found that an organization I had initially perceived as forbidding did present advantages, and one could get used to its shortcomings. The reverse was also true. Some workplaces looked very appealing at first, but when I dug in a little, it was not so pretty.

In the truly outstanding organizations we worked with, everyone had a clear understanding of what the organization's values were. There weren't very many organizations. Among the 40 that make up the sample on which this book is written, we saw only one that I can qualify as outstanding. The staff was relatively young, and the more senior personnel were rejuvenated by the presence of so many young people around and willingly joined in. In fact, the organization was more a meeting place than a workplace. Personnel stayed late and a significant number of employees came to work during the weekend, where this environment offered them the opportunity to meet colleagues and to go out at night. Most did not charge for their time, which actually created an unexpected problem, since it introduced a bias in the collected data used to plan future work. Managers had to rectify the situation by creating special cost accounts in which time invested during weekends, when the office was officially closed and overtime could not be paid, would go in a pool that the company would use to fund parties and company outings.

This way of operating became deeply engrained in the way people interacted, and the company had become more a family to its employees than a place to work. In fact, the environment had ultimately shaped the organization's administration, and produced an unusually strong effect on new employees. It turned out that some individuals were immediately well suited to the organization's values; some had to be drawn into the culture where the separation between family and work was fuzzy; a few others, who wished to maintain a clear demarcation, never made it and usually left when a favorable opportunity came up.

If I look at the 100 or so organizations where our interventions were sufficiently extensive to warrant a reliable characterization of their culture, only three get an outstanding rating. If the anthropological observation that 4 percent of individuals in a population apparently have the leadership qualities that make them stand above everyone else also applies to the population of organizations, then we would have expected to find at most four outstanding organizations.

Overall, 47 percent of organizations described what the organization stands for, characterized its culture, identified points to pay attention to, and established broad guidelines that personnel at all levels can instantiate in their own environment, in light of their role and the responsibilities they have been assigned. Yet there is no doubt in our minds that a strong organizational culture provides the fabric that brings seemingly different people together to accomplish great things. Most of all, personnel look at senior management, and sometimes at the most senior manager, to provide the role model on which they can align their own social and organizational behavior. Therefore, it is not enough for senior management to document what they wish to see in terms of organizational behavior, they also have to lead by example. This can be extremely demanding for a leader who may feel that he or she must never appear weak or indecisive in front of the staff, and may feel self-conscious about his or her presence in a group. Of course, this does not need to be so. The born leaders we had the chance to meet simply did not seem to care about what others thought of them; they were so passionate about their mission that everything else was of secondary importance.

I often asked the CEO of PSL about his secret. My objective was to model the way he built his company and export it. He always gave me the same answer, phrased more or less the same way: principles, hard work, and dedication. Never compromise your principles, and once you have set your objectives, invest everything you have in the attempt to achieve them. Then, take every opportunity to communicate these principles to your subordinates, always do more than what you ask them to do, and try to instill in them the urge to learn, and to constantly improve. His own principles were basic: work hard, study, ask for help only after you cannot find a solution yourself, tell the truth, and most importantly, respect your colleagues, and refrain from any form of violence.

Hold Frequent Meetings between Management and Personnel

The common theme in organizations we rated either outstanding or excellent was that management and practitioners met frequently. Both formal and informal meetings were held. In fact, managers and practitioners often intermingled in informal settings for lunch, after work, or during working hours to discuss the topic of the day. It was more than just an open door policy on the part of management; managers were actually seeking interaction with practitioners and vice-versa.

Meetings between management and practitioners are held in 60 percent of the organizations. The value of these meetings depend on their objective and on how they are conducted. This limitation happens to be one that is most problematic in an organization as far as organizational culture is concerned. As in any activity that involves people, communication is most critical. Where managers met infrequently with practitioners, we observed a cleavage that encouraged turf building and the establishment of silos that eventually became major obstacles to improvement.

Holding meetings does require a will to resist complacency. It is easier to pretend that everything is well and everyone can take care of his or her own challenges. We had to work with organizations where we saw personnel slowly lose the ability to synchronize their actions and reactions in response to external stimuli. As time went on, the organization became a set of groupuscules working out of phase without any apparent common objective. One may think that this type of degeneration is not possible, but it is necessary to understand that it usually happens over a long period of time. Personnel slowly fall into this modus operandi, which at first appears to present some benefits.

The worst case we witnessed happened in a department within a large organization, and as such, it could remain unnoticed for quite a while. It was revealing to listen to people talk about how their department had been in the past, how dynamic it was and of the successes personnel had achieved together. Yet, when we asked if they did not feel an urge to recreate this environment, we saw resignation and fatality. The good old times had passed, and personnel became accustomed to their organization, as they knew it now. It all started by a reduction in regular meetings between management and personnel, mostly because of a department manager who preferred to lead by proxy rather than in person. As this manager reduced meetings to the bare minimum, so did the other managers, and eventually personnel, seeing that there was no need to interact on a regular basis, took advantage of the free time they had acquired. These people were honest, and for the most part, did not defraud the organization of the time they spent at the workplace. They just started to concern themselves with their own little pet projects, which did not lead to anything useful because they lacked the goals and inspiration that only a mix of personalities and minds can bring to an undertaking of any sort.

The average age was around 55, and the department probably needed an influx of new blood to rejuvenate it. A few joined the department but not in a sufficient number to change it. Many of those left shortly after joining because they did not get the challenges that fit their temperament. A few remained and were simply molded into it.

Share Goals and Results Achieved by the Organization with Personnel

Make personnel feel like they have a role to play in achieving the goals that have been set for the organization, and that they are contributing to the results that have been achieved; good or bad. If the results are good, personnel should share the rewards; if the results are bad, personnel should have a say on what could be done to remedy the situation.

In all the organizations we assessed, personnel were in strong agreement that financial rewards are not necessarily what is important to them. A letter issued by senior management recognizing the effort that the team has made to meet its goals or a mention in the organization's newsletter may be all that is needed. Sharing goals and results is a subset of topics that can be addressed in meetings between management and practitioners discussed in the previous section.

In PSL, there is very little financial reward. Yet the dedication of personnel is truly outstanding. The CEO is omnipresent in all company activities and keeps repeating the same message to his troops. Personnel meet weekly (sometimes more often) in a large meeting room, in a small cafe across the street, or in a discotheque next to the company's premises. Not only are personnel dedicated to the success of the company, they are also devoted to improving the city where the company is located and bettering the country. To a North American, I must admit that it sounds suspicious, and initially, I had the feeling that I was the target of a monumental set-up. However, after having conducted two comprehensive assessments in this organization, including multiple interviews spanning well over 50 percent of the staff, I had to accept the fact that there was no set-up, nor was there any intention of devising one.

Our only disappointment was that our initial goal of exporting PSL's way of doing things to other parts of the world looks remote. Organizational culture has grown from within in this company and as such, it appears unlikely to be transplantable.

Define and Deploy Logical and Flexible Operating Procedures

Procedures that are too lax are either ignored or misinterpreted. Procedures that are too prescriptive prevent personnel from using their judgment and incites them to protect their back. Procedures in place should ideally allow the most qualified personnel in a given area to make the decisions dealing with specific issues in that area. This will help ensure, among other things, that issues are resolved quickly and that the actions taken are the most practical ones.

Having the right procedures in place is easier said than done. Initially, the natural tendency is to leave a lot of freedom to personnel. After each blunder, the same natural tendency is to tighten the framework in such a way as to prevent this event from reoccurring, instead of providing guidelines and examples, and relying on individuals to use their common sense. As a result, the exact event is unlikely to reoccur, but people will be so focused on following the new ruling that they will forget about all other conditions that offer opportunities to get things wrong. From blunder to blunder, from restriction to restriction, the framework slowly turns into a cage. This scenario has actually been observed in about one third of organizations we surveyed.

We noticed that this syndrome particularly affects large organizations, which usually also covers government organizations. I was involved in an assessment where managers had specifically told me that creativity was not one of the attributes they wanted personnel to have, because those afflicted by it did not follow the rules. The result, as far as I have been able to conclude, was a sclerotic operation in which only the most daring showed any initiative.

In another organization, the senior manager wanted to turn her organization around and give it a more entrepreneurial spirit. She decreed that from now on, every individual had to treat the section to which he or she belonged as if it were a start-up company. When I met her, she was very enthusiastic about the idea and the early successes that she achieved with one of her subordinates elated her. I personally felt that she was being unrealistic, knowing many of the individuals there, and having the intuition that not all of them had the skills to act like entrepreneurs. There were no procedures or guidelines describing how to go about reaching this commendable goal, or for that matter, the role each individual could play in doing so, and no assessment as to whether everyone was able to accomplish it. I did express my concerns to her as diplomatically as possible, because I did not wish to spoil her dream. I saw her again a year later, and she had become extremely disenchanted with her subordinates, putting them down in front of strangers. She felt that they had let her down, and they had not taken up the challenge and the opportunity she offered them.

Chapter 16

The Reality of Information Technology Initiatives

The price to pay for not anticipating problems is to run into difficulties over and aver again.

This chapter presents the data collected in 40 comprehensive assessments conducted in organizations involved in developing products and deploying services relying on Software Engineering and Information Technology (SE&IT). These assessments spanned three continents: Europe, North America, and South America. The size of the assessed organizations ranged from 10 software professionals to 750, with an average of 113.5, a standard deviation of 237 and a median of 55.

Results Overview

Twenty-three of these 40 assessments were performed in private industry; 17 were performed in government organizations. Out of the 23 private enterprises, 10 were developing and selling products and the remaining 13 were providing software development and maintenance services, either internally or to other organizations. This breakdown is shown in Figure 16-1.

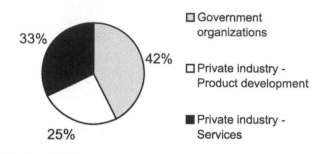

Figure 16-1   Distribution of assessed organizations

Three essential parameters are used to characterize the state of information technology (IT) projects for each assessed organization: the Risk Mitigation Capacity (RMC), the Risk Perception Level (RPL) and the Likelihood of Experiencing Problems (LEP). As described in detail in Chapter 17, RMC corresponds to the practices and mechanisms that are in place to prevent problems from occurring. In the context of software development and maintenance, and given the selected IT framework and the scope defined for the assessments, this is equivalent to the process capability i.e. the capability of integrating human resources, methods, procedures, and tools in order to develop an IT system that satisfies the needs for which it was undertaken, on budget and on schedule.

RPL essentially corresponds to the vulnerability of experiencing problems, as perceived by personnel. High-maturity organizations usually have a lower RPL than low-maturity organizations, with the exception of organizations involved in lines of work that are inherently high-risk. This stems from low-maturity organizations always being on the lookout for disasters to happen. High-maturity organizations can usually be less stressed out, because their process is more likely to provide an early warning of undesirable events. To some extent, RPL depends on personnel experience and knowledge. RPL also depends on the process capacity because an organization exhibiting a mature process is less likely to have to rely on the ability of its personnel to anticipate problems than an organization exhibiting a less mature process, since the high-maturity organization is more likely to have the integrated mechanisms required to generate an early warning of upcoming problems. In fact, such a process may compensate for the lack of experienced personnel. An organization may decide to hire very talented and experienced people (more expensive) and rely on them to develop the system with the help of a process reduced to its minimum (less expensive), or it can decide to implement a process characterized by a high level of maturity (more expensive) and hire less experienced people (less expensive). A cost-effective compromise may be to hire a few talented and experienced people and make them develop

Table 16-1   Summary of Assessment Results

Parameter	Average	Standard Deviation
Risk mitigation capacity	61.0%	11.0%
Risk perception level	37.7%	10.5%
Likelihood of experiencing problems	33.0%	11.6%

and implement a highly mature process that captures their knowledge and experience, which less experienced people can subsequently apply.

LEP is the probability that risks will materialize. In software development and maintenance, given the scope of the model used for conducting the assessments, this is equivalent to the probability that serious problems will occur in terms of cost overruns, schedule slippages, and products or services that do not satisfy the needs for which they were undertaken, to the point of jeopardizing the project or making it a failure.

It is usually desirable for an organization to exhibit a RPL significantly higher than its LEP, in order to provide a reasonable safety margin. When this is the case, there is a good chance that problems that are not detected or addressed by the process will likely be detected and addressed by personnel. However, a large difference between the RPL and the LEP is usually not desirable. When the RPL is much larger than the LEP, this indicates an over reliance on personnel's abilities. Conversely, a RPL significantly lower than the LEP indicates some complacency that usually ends in disaster. The average value of each of these three parameters, for all assessments combined, is shown in Table 16-1.

A RMC of 61 percent means that on average, 61 percent of the key practices at maturity level 2 and maturity level 3 of the Capability Maturity Model (CMM) (see Chapter 17 for a brief description of the CMM), plus those associated with Organizational Culture and Customer Service, are implemented. This percentage takes into account that some key practices have more risk mitigation potential than others do. A RPL of 37.7 percent means that on average, personnel feel that their initiative has a 37.7 percent chance of experiencing serious problems. Finally, a LEP equal to 33 percent indicates that on average, an IT initiative has a 33 percent probability of experiencing serious schedule, budget, or functionality problems. Expressed in terms of frequency, 33 percent of IT initiatives can expect to experience serious schedule, budget, or functionality problems, possibly to the extent of turning them into failures. This 33 percent value seems to confirm the finding of the Standish Group International documented in the report *Chaos — Application Project and Failure* published in 1995, to the effect that 31 percent of IT projects are cancelled before completion.

Table 16-2 Assessment Results for Government Organizations and Private Industry

Parameter	Government Organizations		Private Industry	
	Average	Standard Deviation	Average	Standard Deviation
Risk mitigation capacity	63.1%	11.1%	59.4%	10.9%
Risk perception level	34.4%	10.9%	40.1%	9.7%
Likelihood of experiencing problems	33.4%	10.3%	32.7%	12.6%

Government versus Private Industry — Services versus Product Development — Small versus Large

Table 16-2, Table 16-3, and Table 16-4 provide a more detailed breakdown of the data shown in Table 16-1.

Table 16-2 shows the three essential parameters for government organizations versus private industry; Table 16-3 shows the three parameters for private industry developing and selling products versus private industry providing software development and maintenance services; and Table 16-4 shows the three parameters for organizations having fewer software professionals than the median (i.e. 55) versus those having more.

Table 16-2 indicates that there is not much difference between the LEP in IT initiatives undertaken by government organizations versus those undertaken by private industry (0.7 percent lower in private industry). However, what is more significant is that the RMC is slightly higher in government organizations (63.1 percent) than in private industry (59.4 percent). Conversely, software professionals' awareness of what could go wrong and, as a result, their ability to take whatever action is appropriate, is higher in private industry (40.1 percent) than in government organizations (34.4 percent).

On a qualitative basis, we did find that government organizations have a better software process than private industry, but the flexibility of the work environment and the free flow of information are not as good as in private industry. The better process in government organizations may be because centralized systems (mainframes) are still fairly common (see Chapter 1 - The Old Software Ghosts That Haunt Us, regarding the two classes of programmers), whereas initiative and performance, which are more likely to be promoted and rewarded in private industry, lead to a greater amount of flexibility and better communication.

Table 16-3   Assessment Results for Enterprises Providing Services and Enterprises Developing Products

Parameter	Private Industry — Product Development		Private Industry — Services	
	Average	*Standard Deviation*	*Average*	*Standard Deviation*
Risk mitigation capacity	60.5%	10.9%	58.7%	10.8%
Risk perception level	35.7%	6.1%	43.8%	10.4%
Likelihood of experiencing problems	35.7%	14.6%	29.9%	9.9%

Table 16-4   Assessment Results for Small and Large Organizations

Parameter	Smaller Organizations (fewer than 55 software professionals)		Larger Organizations (more than 55 software professionals)	
	Average	*Standard Deviation*	*Average*	*Standard Deviation*
Risk mitigation capacity	59.2%	8.2%	62.8%	13.2%
Risk perception level	40.3%	9.8%	35.0%	10.7%
Likelihood of experiencing problems	33.1%	9.1%	33.0%	13.9%

When comparing private industry providing services and private industry developing products, the results shown in Table 16-3 indicate that the private industry providing services has a capacity slightly lower than the private industry developing products (58.7 percent versus 60.5 percent), but their risk perception is significantly higher (43.8 percent versus 35.7 percent). As a result of their lower LEP, enterprises providing services are more likely to be on schedule and on budget. The explanation of this is not clear but we surmise that software professionals in services are more likely to interact with a broader sample of people and must deal with a more varied number of situations, which makes them more apt to recognize when a condition may lead to an undesirable outcome.

Table 16-4 compares organizations that have fewer than 55 software professionals with those that have more than 55. It turns out that they are both characterized by the same probability of experiencing schedule, budget, and functionality problems. The smaller organizations exhibit a greater awareness of their vulnerability to experience difficulties (higher RPL), and they also have a lower RMC than the larger organizations, because they rarely have access to the resources that are available to the larger organizations.

Critical Value of Problems Likelihood

The compilation and analysis of the data collected through these assessments pointed out another finding of interest. The critical threshold associated with the LEP appears to be approximately 40 percent, that is, an initiative or an organization cannot sustain such a LEP for any significant duration relative to the planned or current activities. Out of the 40 assessments conducted, 25 percent exceeded this value and in all cases, major difficulties were observed during the 12 to 18 months that followed. Initiatives were indeed canceled, with the resulting losses or missed opportunities that this entailed. Some organizations declared bankruptcy, and others went through a very difficult period. In some cases, the high likelihood of problems was only a symptom of deeper problems, somewhat akin to looking in a living room and finding a mess because its occupants were trying to salvage what they could out of a house on fire.

Based on the concepts presented in Chapter 17, a LEP equal to 50 percent would correspond to an initiative or an organization operating at random, and if such were the case, it would be wishful thinking to expect any successful outcome over a significant period of time. Nobody can expect to get rich playing at the casino; one may get lucky over a short period of time but over a longer period, he or she will lose out.

This 40 percent critical LEP threshold has also been observed in the financial industry (venture capital) where it was noted that in a portfolio of 10 investments, a portfolio manager would tolerate four investments out of 10 not generating a profit. Anything higher than this ratio will result in restructuring the portfolio in order not to exceed the 40 percent limit, because this would result in a certain loss.

Detailed Results

The results shown in the previous section are analyzed in more detail in this section. We will see that a project or an organization can be characterized quite accurately in terms of its RPL profile, its RMC profile, the LEP profile, as well as other parameters, much in the same way a submarine can be characterized by the noise spectral distribution of its equipment picked up by underwater noise detectors.

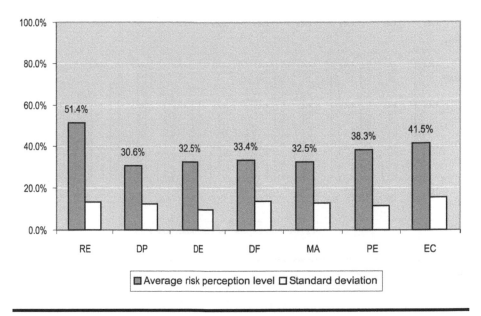

Figure 16-2   Risk perception level in key risk areas

Table 16-5   Legend Used in
Connection with Key Risk Areas

Acronym	Key Risk Area
RE	Requirements
DP	Design, Code, and Test
DE	Development Environment
DF	Development Framework
MA	Management
PE	Personnel
EC	External Constraints

Risk Perception in Key Risk Areas

Figure 16-2 shows the distribution of the RPL, for all assessments, in the seven key risk areas defined in Table 17-1 of Chapter 17. The legend shown in Table 16-5 is used in the graph of Figure 16-2.

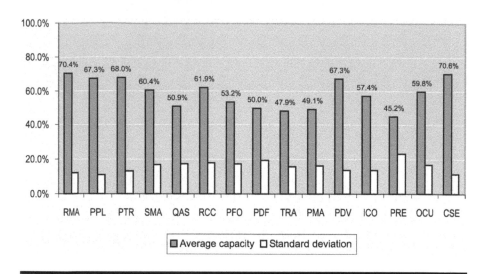

Figure 16-3   Risk mitigation capacity of key process areas

As seen in the graph, software professionals' perception of the vulnerability of their project is highest in the Requirements, Personnel, and External Constraints key risk areas, and surprisingly, it is the lowest in the Design, Code, and Test key risk area, a field in which they should be most proficient. It appears that software professionals are over confident when dealing with technical issues and are particularly careful when dealing with issues with which they are likely to be less familiar.

Risk Mitigation Capacity in Key Process Areas

Figure 16-3 shows the RMC, for all assessments, of the 15 process areas defined in Table 17-2 of Chapter 17. The legend shown in Table 16-6 is used in the graph of Figure 16-3.

Noticeable dips characterize the mitigation capacity profiles in Quality Assurance, Process Focus, Process Definition, Training, Project Management, and Peer Reviews.

Quality Assurance is often regarded in IT as an end of the road, career wise. This is an unfortunate situation as Quality Assurance has been crucial in producing high yields in the manufacturing areas, which, in turn, contributed in reducing costs.

Process, in the sense of assigning responsibilities for establishing and defining efficient and effective ways of integrating human resources, tools, methods, and procedures to come up with better quality products and services at low cost, is still wanting. In Information Technology, the

Table 16-6 Legend Used in Connection with the Risk-Mitigating Process Areas

Acronym	Risk-Mitigating Process Area
RMA	Requirements Management
PPL	Project Planning
PTR	Project Tracking
SMA	Subcontract Management
QAS	Quality Assurance
RCC	Release and Change Control
PFO	Process Focus
PDF	Process Definition
TRA	Training
PMA	Project Management
PDV	Product Development
ICO	Intergroup Coordination
PRE	Peer Reviews
OCU	Organizational Culture
CSE	Customer Service

product is all-important, and little consideration is given on how to get there and how to address problems when they come up. Improvisation is the key.

Training, when available, is ad-hoc and provided on demand without too much attention given to satisfying the long-term needs of organizations.

Project planning and project tracking are relatively well mastered but their integration into a coherent management approach to manage projects is still widely deficient.

Peer Reviews, which has the lowest observed capacity, is sorely lacking in software development and maintenance. Given that in most scientific areas and in fields such as publishing, which shares common characteristics with writing plans, specifications, and code, Peer Reviews are institutionalized, this is somewhat surprising. In fact, where they are implemented, they are usually the first to be abandoned when the pressure to deliver increases.

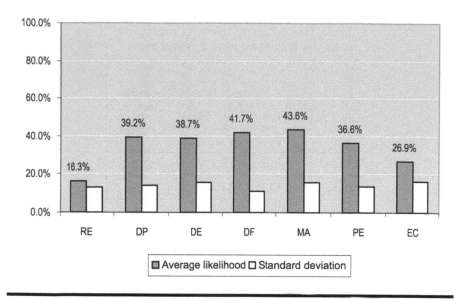

Figure 16-4   Likelihood of experiencing problems in key risk areas

Likelihood of Experiencing Problems in Key Risk Areas

Figure 16-4 shows the LEP in the seven aforementioned key risk areas.

Management comes out as the area most likely to experience problems, closely followed by the Development Framework, Design, Code, and Test, Development Environment and Personnel areas. Chapter 2 to Chapter 15 provide more qualitative details observed in various organizations that will help understand this data. The graph stresses that the LEP in the Requirements area is low. To a certain extent, the consequences of these problems were also taken into account. In fact, we did notice in the course of the assessments that this area is well monitored and software professionals are very well aware of the impact that requirements have on their projects. Likewise, the LEP in areas where project teams have little control (External Constraints) is also relatively low. In fact, given the relatively high RPL associated with this area, more attention seemed to be paid to the external factors liable to affect projects than to the internal ones.

Likelihood of Experiencing Problems in Key Risk Mitigating Process Areas

Figure 16-5 shows the LEP for all assessments, due to deficiencies observed in the 15 aforementioned key risk mitigating process areas. This essentially

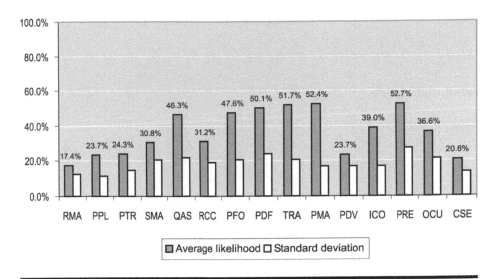

Figure 16-5   Likelihood of experiencing problems due to deficiencies in key risk-mitigating process areas

corresponds to the areas where problems are most likely to take their source. As can be noticed by comparing Figure 16-3 and Figure 16-5, the LEP is related to the RMC. The higher the capacity in a process area, the lower the likelihood that this area contributes to problems experienced in a project or in an organization. The likelihood profile shown in Figure 16-5 also indicates how well, on average, the RMC is matched to the risks an initiative or an organization is facing.

The contribution of the Requirements Management process area to the overall LEP is relatively small. In fact, one finding of interest that came out of the analysis of collected data is that it is not so much the lack of process to manage requirements that contribute to problems IT initiatives are experiencing, as the lack of peer reviews (PRE). The lack of peer reviews translates into a lack of understanding of requirements, and the poor coordination and communication (ICO) between groups participating in these initiatives.

Deficiencies in Project Management and in Peer Reviews contribute the most to the LEP. We also found that Organizational Culture had a major impact, not so much on the LEP but on the success of implementing remedial actions. In all projects and organizations where the contribution of Organizational Culture was high (higher than or equal to the LEP calculated for the assessed entity), major difficulties were experienced when attempts were made to rectify the situation. In light of the assessment results and the qualitative observations made during these assessments, Organizational Culture would probably warrant its own appraisal model.

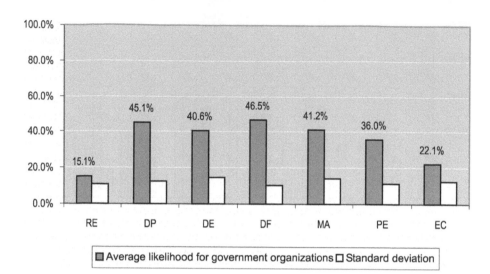

Figure 16-6 **Likelihood of experiencing problems in key risk areas for government organizations**

Likelihood of Experiencing Problems — Government versus Private Industry

It is instructive to compare the likelihood that government organizations and private industry have of experiencing problems in IT projects.

Figure 16-6 and Figure 16-7 show the LEP in the key risk areas for government organizations and private industry, respectively; Figure 16-8 and Figure 16-9 show the LEP due to deficiencies observed in key risk mitigating process areas for government organizations and private industry.

The probability of experiencing problems in the Design, Code, and Test, Development Environment, and Development Framework key risk areas is significantly higher in government organizations than in private industry. This is so even though on average, government organizations have shown to have a more mature process than private industry, as substantiated by their lower LEP due to deficiencies in Project Management (compare Project Management process area in Figure 16-8 and Figure 16-9). The risk mitigation potential of the government organizations' process is not as high as it could be because of the lesser amount of flexibility they have to tailor it and to make it evolve with changing needs. This lower flexibility is also evident when comparing the higher LEP in government organizations in connection with Process Focus (54.8 percent versus 41.9 percent) and Process Definition (55.3 percent versus 46.5 percent).

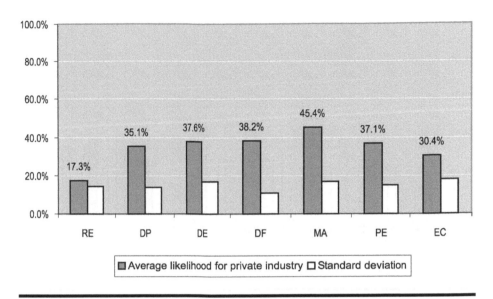

Figure 16-7   Likelihood of experiencing problems in key risk areas for private industry

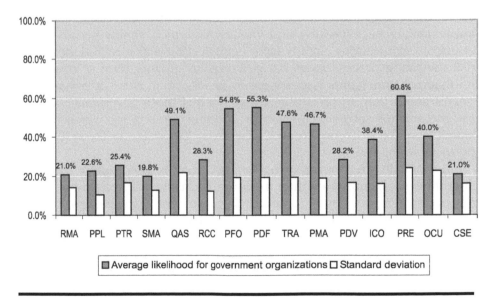

Figure 16-8   Likelihood of experiencing problems due to deficiencies in key risk-mitigating process areas for government organizations

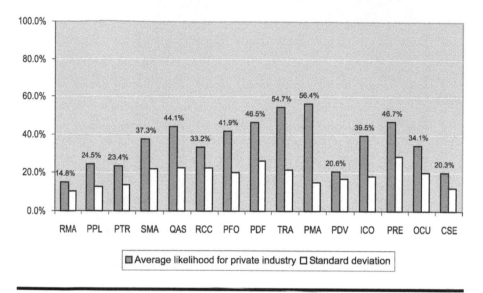

Figure 16-9   Likelihood of experiencing problems due to deficiencies in key risk-mitigating process areas for private industry

To a certain extent, the lower LEP in private industry in Quality Assurance and Peer Reviews also contribute to ensuring that information gained on the process it applies and on the results it provides is used to improve its efficiency and effectiveness. We did observe that overall, government organizations are more reluctant than private industry in implementing Peer Reviews and Quality Assurance, simply because government organizations already have enough control as it is, and these two risk mitigating process areas are perceived as another form of control.

External Constraints also appear to be less of an issue in government organizations than in private industry. Not that those government organizations are not subjected to factors affecting projects for which project teams have little or no control. They are, but these factors are more predictable than in private industry.

The LEP in the Management key risk area is also slightly lower in government organizations than in private industry. The reason for this is that management is more diluted in government organizations than in private industry. In private industry, management has more decisional power than in government organizations and if a bad decision is made, it is more likely to have negative consequences. This is reflected in the LEP due to deficiencies in the Project Management process area, which in government organizations can rely on a more uniform implementation than in private industry.

Focusing specifically on the LEP due to observed deficiencies in key risk mitigating process areas, Figure 16-8 shows that training is less of an issue in government organizations than in private industry. Subcontract Management and Release and Change Control contribute less to the LEP in government organizations than in private industry. Our qualitative observations corroborate this finding; these key process areas are better suited to prevent the occurrence of problems than in private industry. The subcontract selection and management process is much more mature in government organizations, mainly because of their vulnerability to being criticized by the media. Organizational Culture is more likely to be a concern in government organizations. This goes in line with the observation that management is more inspiring in private industry than in government organizations; focused management is more likely to translate into a cohesive and purposeful organizational culture, even if its is more likely to be improvised in private industry than in government organizations.

Although not pronounced, Project Planning is less likely to contribute to the problems with which government organizations have to deal in IT initiatives, whereas Project Tracking is less likely to contribute to the problems with which private industry has to deal. In other words, government organizations are better at planning than private industry, but private industry is better at executing the work.

We observed very little variation in Customer Service between government organizations and private industry. In the field of Information Technology, customers in government organizations are usually those that place an order to develop or modify an information system (usually another government department). Because customers are often co-located with the organization carrying out this development, the understanding of the system is less prone to interpretation since ambiguities can be resolved faster and more efficiently. In terms of customer service, this amply compensates for the weaknesses government organizations may have compared to private industry in paying more attention to customers.

Likelihood of Experiencing Problems — Small versus Large Organizations

Comparing small organizations with large organizations also provides useful information. In the assessments we performed, small organizations were those having fewer than 55 software professionals; large organizations were those having more than 55. The collected data confirmed several opinions and hypotheses we had, but some unexpected findings showed up.

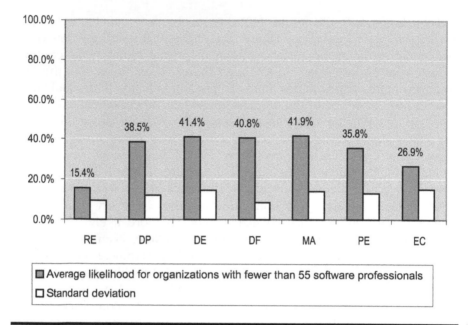

Figure 16-10   Likelihood of experiencing problems in key risk areas for small organizations (< 55 software professionals)

Figure 16-10 and Figure 16-11 show the LEP profile in the key risk areas for both types of organizations.

The most significant differences lie in the Development Environment and the Management key risk areas. As could be expected, the LEP in the Development Environment key risk area in small organizations (41.4 percent) is higher than in large organizations (35.8 percent). The small organizations have fewer resources and this translates into being more challenging for them. The gap increases for organizations having fewer than 25 software professionals (43.2 percent) versus organizations having more than 100 (35.5 percent).

As for the LEP in the Management key risk area, it is slightly lower in small organizations (41.9 percent) than in large organizations (45.3 percent). However, when organizations with fewer than 25 software professional and those with more than 100 were considered, the gap is reduced (40.4 percent versus 42.3 percent, respectively). The larger organizations benefit from a better infrastructure that compensates for the reduced management complexity characterizing smaller organizations.

The LEP due to deficiencies observed in key risk mitigating process areas is more meaningful, particularly for organizations with fewer than 25 software professionals and those with more than 100, as shown in Figure 16-12 and Figure 16-13, in which the differences are more accentuated.

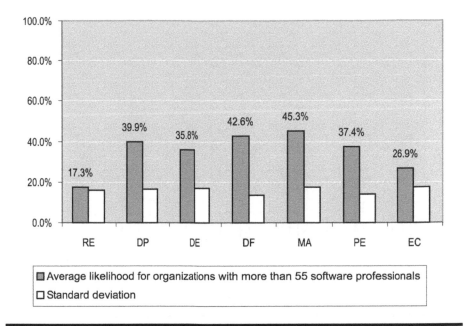

Figure 16-11   Likelihood of experiencing problems in key risk areas for large organizations (> 55 software professionals)

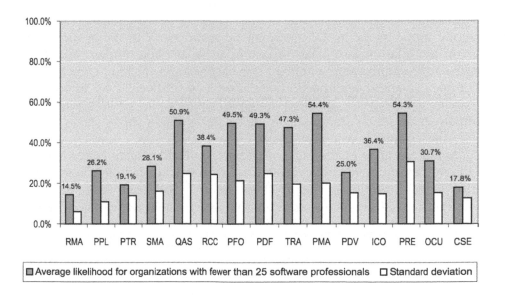

Figure 16-12   Likelihood of experiencing problems due to deficiencies in key risk-mitigating process areas for small organizations (< 25 software professionals)

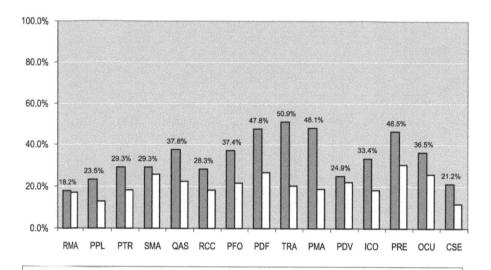

Figure 16-13   Likelihood of experiencing problems due to deficiencies in key risk-mitigating process areas for large organizations (> 100 software professionals)

For instance, deficiencies in the Project Planning risk mitigating process area contributes more to the LEP in small organizations than in large organizations. Conversely, the Project Tracking process area contributes significantly less to the LEP in small organizations. This is not surprising given that planning requires resources (time, budget, human resources) that small organizations often do not have. Project tracking is much less complex in these organizations because it is relatively easy for project managers to have a detailed understanding of the project status, as initiatives are much more likely to be smaller and to involve fewer people, thereby facilitating communication.

Again, because of the lack of resources affecting small organizations, Quality Assurance, Peer Reviews, and Release and Change Control contribute more to the problems they have to deal with than in larger organizations. Likewise, Process Focus and to a lesser extent, Process Definition contribute more to the likelihood of problems in small organizations. This, in turn, translates into a less coherent Project Management process area in these organizations. As a matter of fact, project management was observed as being largely improvised in small organizations, but taking into account that Project Tracking was less of a contributing factor in the LEP than in larger organizations, the result was often the same.

Not surprisingly, Organizational Culture is less of an issue in small organizations. This makes the implementation of changes easier. Customer

Service is also slightly less problematic in small organizations, where the number of customers is likely to be smaller.

Additional Characterization Parameters

Additional parameters can be used to obtain more information on IT projects and organizations. These parameters are the Software Quality Index (SQI), the number of Potential Instances of Problems (PIP) and the number of Potential Failure Modes (PFM).

Software Quality Index

The SQI provides a practical scale of the products and services quality that can be expected from IT initiatives. It is calculated with the following expression:

$$SQI = \log_e [1+(RMC/(RPL \times LEP))]$$

where RMC is the risk mitigation capacity, RPL is the risk perception level and LEP is the likelihood of experiencing problems.

One can expect sustained quality products and services from organizations that are characterized by a high mitigation capacity and a low likelihood of problems. The RPL does play a role, but for a given mitigation capacity, a low RPL will result in a higher LEP, and a high RPL will result in a lower LEP. Therefore, multiplying these two parameters will result in a number whose value essentially depends on how well the RMC is matched to the risks facing the organization. In any case, one can expect that a high RPL is likely to result in good quality products or services; the questions are can this quality be sustained, and how much dependence is there on the individuals who are assigned to the project?

The ratio RMC/(RPL × LEP) theoretically ranges from 0 to infinity. In practice, it ranges from one to five. Anything lower than one is dreadful and anything over five is terrific. To reflect this range of values, the SQI numeric scale is translated into an alphabetic scale similar to college report grades, with the help of the following expressions:

$$0 < SQI < 1 \quad E$$
$$1 < SQI < 2 \quad D$$
$$2 < SQI < 3 \quad C$$
$$3 < SQI < 4 \quad B$$
$$4 < SQI < 5 \quad A$$
$$5 < SQI \quad\quad A+$$

Table 16-7 Software Quality Index

Organizations	Software Quality Index
All	1.77
Government	1.87
Private industry	1.71
Smaller (<55 software professionals)	1.69
Larger (>55 software professionals)	1.86

Table 16-7 shows the SQI for government organizations, private industry, small organizations (fewer than 55 software professionals) and large organizations (more than 55 software professionals). As can be seen, despite all their failings and when everything has been taken into account, the SQI is higher for government organizations than for private industry (notwithstanding the fact that the average grade is D for all groupings). Likewise, the SQI is higher for large organizations than for small ones.

While the SQI is a parameter that helps assess an IT initiative for an organization involved in developing products and services using Information Technology, one must remember that it is not equivalent to the LEP, which focuses on the probability of failure if no corrective actions are implemented. For instance, a product or a service may be characterized as high quality, but it may not be readily available and as a result, the project may be considered a failure. This is precisely where the RPL makes the difference, and is more likely to be reflected in the LEP than in SQI.

Potential Instances of Problems

The PIP parameter provides an indication of the number of problems that arise on average in a given key risk area. In the assessments that we conducted, this parameter was calculated by counting the number of risk occurrences resulting from inadequate risk mitigation, averaging it over all monitored risks, and dividing the resulting value by the number of assessed organizations. In the analysis performed on the collected data, this parameter only took into account the number or potential problems, not their importance.

The total number of PIPs averaged over all assessments is equal to 17.8, and their distribution is shown in Figure 16-14. No marked differences were observed between government organizations and private industry, and between small and large organizations.

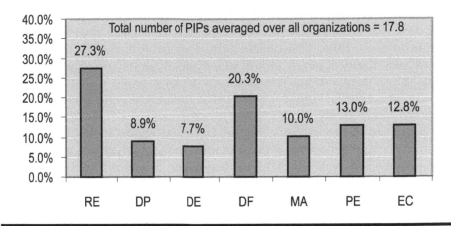

Figure 16-14   Distribution of PIPs averaged over all organizations

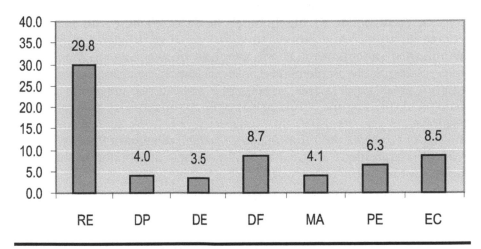

Figure 16-15   Effort invested in resolving PIPs

Not surprisingly, the number of PIPs is the highest in the Requirements and Development Framework key risk areas. In the Requirements key risk area, these PIPs do not all translate into actual problems because of the existence of risk mitigation mechanisms. It is therefore instructive to divide the number of PIPs by the LEP for a given key risk area. This provides an idea of the effort invested in resolving them, and indirectly, how much attention is given to risks occurring in each key risk area.

As shown in Figure 16-15, the effort invested in order to resolve PIPs is the highest in the Requirements risk key area.

No difference is made between effort invested to prevent problems and effort invested to correct them. What is also significant is that very little effort is devoted to resolving problems in the Development Framework key risk area despite the fact that it is associated with a relatively large number of PIPs. This observation does confirm that in Information Technology, the product is all-important and the way to get there is often given little consideration. The build-up of knowledge capital in the IT industry is sorely lacking compared, for instance, to the semiconductor industry, which partly explains the much larger cost reduction that has been achieved in this industry. Figure 16-14 and Figure 16-15 also indicate that the Management and Personnel key risk areas do not receive the level of attention proportional to the number of potential problems that characterize them.

Potential Failure Modes

The PFM parameter is the equivalent of PIPs for risk mitigating process areas. It corresponds to the number of ways a failure can occur, on average, in a given key process area as a result of deficiencies in implementing that process area. It was obtained by counting the number of times inadequately implemented risk mitigation mechanisms occurred within a given process area, averaging it over all risk mitigation mechanisms, and dividing the resulting value by the number of assessed organizations. As for the PIPs, this parameter only took into account the number or PFM, not their importance. The total number of PFMs averaged over all organizations is equal to 24.7 and their distribution is shown in Figure 16-16.

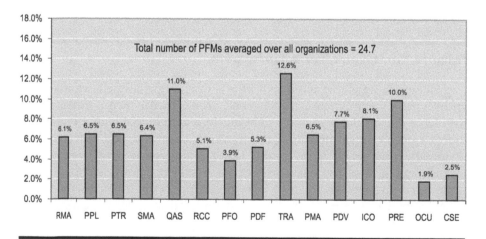

Figure 16-16   Distribution of PFMs averaged over all organizations

The three key risk mitigating process areas that stand out in terms of failure modes are Quality Assurance, Training, and Peer Reviews. Therefore, in Information Technology, what provides the most opportunities for risks to materialize into problems is the lack of skills and knowledge necessary to manage, plan, and carry out the work, the lack of attention paid to verify that the work is performed in accordance with the mandated approach, the lack of attention paid to verify that resulting products and services satisfy the specifications that describe them, and the lack of peer reviews, inspections, walkthroughs, etc. Quality Assurance, Training, and Peer Reviews are indeed interrelated. If more peer reviews were conducted, this would translate into a better sharing of knowledge and understanding of the products and services that are being developed. If better quality assurance was provided, more problems could be prevented and the number and frequency of peer reviews could be adjusted accordingly. If better training were provided, this would help personnel recognize the value of quality assurance and peer reviews, and in applying them more efficiently. The same three process areas come out with similar distributions, whether government organizations, private industry, small organizations, or large organizations are considered.

The effort invested in taking action on these PFMs is calculated by dividing the number of PFMs by the LEP, for each key process area, as illustrated in Figure 16-17.

It is evident from this graph that Training, Quality Assurance, and Peer Reviews do not receive the attention they deserve. Implementing adequate mechanisms to define and implement adequate processes (Process Focus

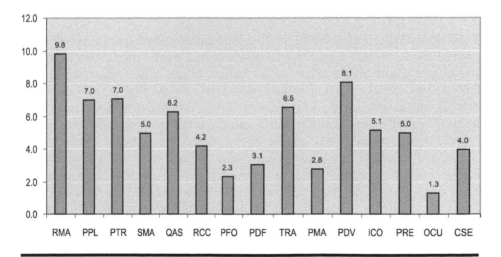

Figure 16-17   Effort invested in taking action on PFMs

and Process Definition) and to manage projects in a coherent and uniform way (Project Management) receive little attention, which may partly explain why Quality Assurance and Peer Reviews are not taken care of.

Requirements Management and Product Development get the most attention, and Customer Service receives adequate consideration given the number of PFMs that characterize it.

Organizational Culture does not receive a lot of attention but it does not generate a lot of failure modes either. As mentioned earlier, the main issue with this process area is the failure modes that are associated with it can be problematic and can require a long time to rectify, because they entail cultural changes, as the name implies. To use an analogy, PFMs related to any other process areas are equivalent to finding one's lack of house maintenance has led to leaks in the roof, which now has to be replaced. PFMs related to Organizational Culture is like observing that as a result of deficient soil analyses, one's house has been built on contaminated land, and it may be cheaper to write it off and build another house somewhere else.

Some Specifics

Chapter 2 to Chapter 15 provide a detailed qualitative discussion of the findings that resulted from the analysis of the 40 assessments. Nevertheless, four examples will be presented in order to illustrate how quantitative characterization of organizations can be achieved.

The Road to Success

This organization, a division of a large company, had over 100 software professionals at the time of the assessment and is presented as an example of what a good organization looks like. It is not a perfect organization. But it does deliver what it says it will, it is very profitable, and one can expect quality products and services from it. And yes, it is more expensive to buy from this organization than from the other two presented hereafter.

This organization's RMC, RPL, LEP, and SQI are listed in Table 16-8.

Its RMC is high at 81.8 percent. Nevertheless, its staff's awareness of what could go wrong, its RPL, remains relatively high at 28.5 percent. This organization has had failures and is on guard. Yet its development costs are kept to a reasonable value because its staff can rely on a mature risk mitigation process. Typically, one project out of 10 will experience serious problems in terms of schedule, budget, products, or services that do not adequately satisfy their requirements.

Table 16-8   Essential Parameters for the Organization on the Road to Success

Parameter	Value
Risk mitigation capacity	81.8%
Risk perception level	28.5%
Likelihood of experiencing problems	10.7%
Software Quality Index	3.3 (B)

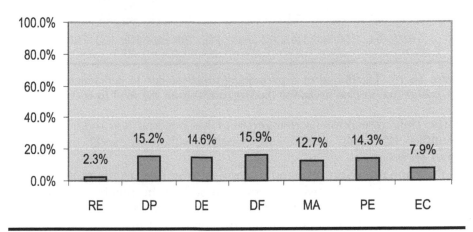

Figure 16-18   Likelihood of experiencing problems in key risk areas for the organization on the road to success

This organization's LEP in key risk areas is shown in Figure 16-18 and its LEP resulting from deficiencies observed in key risk mitigating process areas is shown in Figure 16-19.

It is interesting to note the relatively high values of LEP in the Design, Code, and Test, and in the Development Framework key risk areas. In fact, we observed that despite its process maturity, the organization had difficulty in adapting its process to the latest technologies. It was a challenge to undertake projects making use of these technologies and some bureaucracy had crept in over the years. This is reflected in deficiencies observed in the Process Focus, Training, and Project Management key process areas. The organization's relatively high value of LEP in Organizational Culture and Intergroup Coordination (these two areas are often linked) also made it that much more challenging to bring about the needed changes. However, we had the opportunity to follow the evolution of this organization after the assessment and changes were made that go

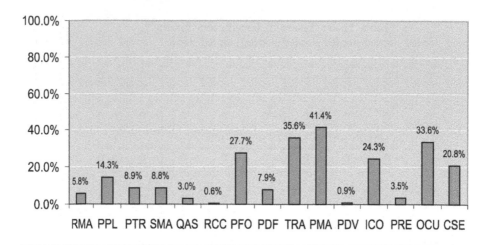

Figure 16-19   Likelihood of experiencing problems due to deficiencies in key risk-mitigating process areas for the organization on the road to success

in the right direction. Its management has become less rigid and more flexibility has been introduced, which resulted in better interactions between groups.

PIPs and the effort invested to resolve these can also be quite descriptive.* Figure 16-20 shows areas proportional to the number of PIPs and areas proportional to the effort invested to resolve them. As can be seen, there is a good match between the two. Indeed, it makes sense to invest more effort in resolving areas that are plagued by more problems, which is what this organization does. It is also noticeable that a lot of effort goes into resolving issues associated with Requirements because of the severe consequences they may have if left unattended.

Likewise, Figure 16-21 shows areas proportional to the number of PFMs and areas proportional to the effort invested in taking action on these PFMs. The match is not so good in this case. Notice however the effort invested in Quality Assurance and in Release and Change Control, two process areas deemed essential for this organization, as it had to keep up a certification of quality for its products and services in order to be in business, and to maintain several versions of its products used by a large number of customers. In one case, a customer, having requested a modification to a product version seven years older than the most current version, had his wish granted without any hassle.

---

* In the figures representing PIPs and the effort invested to resolve them, what is important is the ratio between the number of issues and the effort invested to resolve them. The vertical scale is different from organization to organization. The same concept applies to PFMs.

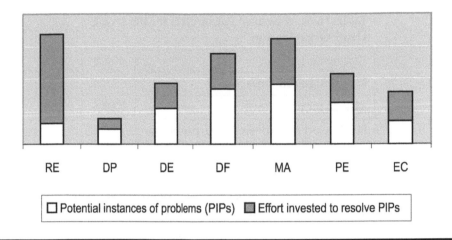

Figure 16-20   PIPs and effort invested to resolve them

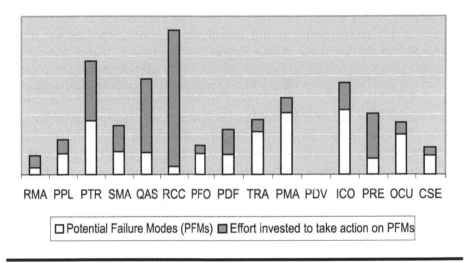

Figure 16-21   PFMs and effort invested in taking action on them

Figure 16-21 points out the necessity to do something about Intergroup Coordination and Organizational Culture.

The Living Dead

The example provided under this theme was selected to illustrate an organization fighting for its survival. The organization employed 250 software professionals at the time of the assessment and had been forced, a few years earlier, to suddenly compete in an area where it previously

Table 16-9   Essential Parameters for the Living Dead Organization

Parameter	Value
Risk mitigation capacity	57.6%
Risk perception level	32.9%
Likelihood of experiencing problems	45.5%
Software Quality Index	1.6 (D)

had a virtual monopoly. The adaptation had been rather painful. Several key members left the organization as a result of the uncertain future it offered.

The organization's RMC, RPL, LEP, and SQI are listed in Table 16-9.

Given the organization's mitigation capacity, awareness of potential problems should have been higher and it appears that this organization was waiting for a miracle. Its LEP, at 45.5 percent, indicated that serious problems were to be forthcoming if nothing was done. The results of the assessment were not very well received by the board of directors, who believed that their organization was much better off than what the picture presented to them provided. Practitioners and middle management received it very well and considered that it truly represented the actual situation. This is rather unusual, as most often, senior management and practitioners are eager to change the way things are done (senior management want to increase revenues and profits; the practitioners want to work more normal hours), whereas middle management is more likely to be the obstacle.

One of the projects the organization had undertaken was essential and was included in the assessment. According to the assessment results, the chances of completing it successfully were very slim. Indeed, one year after the assessment had been completed, the project had to be written off. The organization had to incur the loss of time and money that had been invested, but more importantly, the opportunity that the project offered in terms of recovery potential was also lost. As of the writing of this book, the organization was still alive but it was struggling. The biggest obstacle, by far, has been the recognition by senior management that things are not going well and the willingness to listen to personnel who have first-hand knowledge of the problems the organization is facing. Only senior management has the power to act, and action will not take place until these two conditions have been satisfied.

The LEP plotted against key risk areas and the LEP plotted against key risk mitigating areas is shown in Figure 16-22 and Figure 16-23.

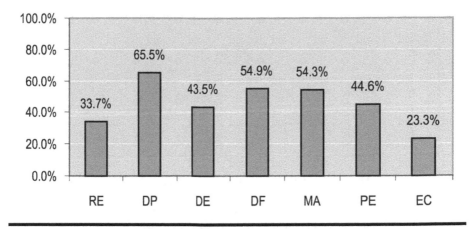

Figure 16-22   Likelihood of experiencing problems in key risk areas for the living dead organization

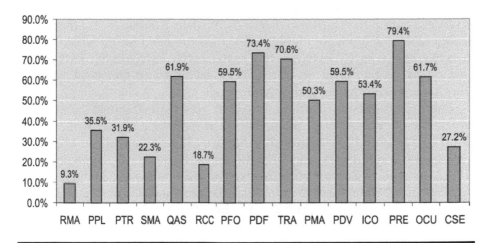

Figure 16-23   Likelihood of experiencing problems due to deficiencies in key risk-mitigating process areas for the living dead organization

The Design, Code, and Test, Development Framework, and Management key risk areas are the areas most vulnerable to experiencing problems. In fact, the organization was used to carrying out relatively small projects (usually no larger than 100 person-months). Over the preceding years, it had initiated larger, multimillion-dollar projects to increase its revenues and was stretching itself thin, which explains these levels. The other key risk areas have a smaller LEP, but they are nevertheless significant and constitute a sign of the challenges facing the organization.

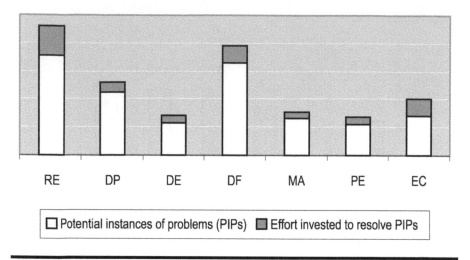

Figure 16-24   PIPs and effort invested to resolve them

The LEP resulting from deficiencies in key risk-mitigating process areas is not encouraging. The Process Focus, Process Definition, Training, and Product Development are all high and stress the need for the organization to revise the way it develops and maintains its systems, in addition to training its staff in applying them. Peer Reviews and Quality Assurance were largely improvised if they were done at all.

The most worrisome finding, however, was Organizational Culture, for which the likelihood of problems stood at over 61 percent. With such a level, it is doubtful that senior management will be more open to bridge the communication gap with practitioners and middle management. The work atmosphere was not very good and during our assessment, it became obvious that practitioners and middle managers alike feared senior management and would not propose anything that could be perceived as a rebuke by senior management. In this organization, the move has to come from senior management, and unfortunately, there was not much hope of this happening without a replacement of individuals. In fact, two years after we performed the assessment, the entire Board of Directors was replaced. It appears that the organization is on the way to recovery but several years of hard work are likely to be required before it can be achieved.

PIPs and the effort invested to prevent or to resolve them are eloquent. The large number of PIPs in the Development Framework is also seen as an indication that its knowledge capital is eroding. Management seemed to have recognized this and had invested a token effort to prevent it from deteriorating further. It is also interesting to notice that in Figure 16-24, a significant amount of energy, proportionately speaking, was invested in

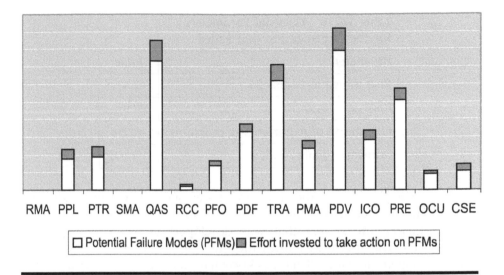

RMA PPL PTR SMA QAS RCC PFO PDF TRA PMA PDV ICO PRE OCU CSE

☐ Potential Failure Modes (PFMs) ▣ Effort invested to take action on PFMs

Figure 16-25   PFMs and effort invested in taking action on them

addressing the External Constraints key risk area, namely trying to regain a lost monopoly, which is no longer an option for the organization and where little can be done anyway. Graphs such as the one shown in Figure 16-24 are typical of organizations exhibiting low RMC. Having few measurements, if any, they tend to spread their resources uniformly across problem categories instead of investing their resources proportionately to the number of issues they face in each.

The situation is similar with PFMs and the effort invested in taking remedial action, as shown in Figure 16-25. In comparison with the organization on the road to success presented earlier, a token effort is invested and given the state of this organization, a lot more is needed. Furthermore, from our observations, the invested effort was more reactive than proactive, in the sense that it was focused on containing crises.

The Failure

This organization provides an example of a large project that failed, resulting in a loss of close to $60 million U.S.

Several factors contributed to the failure. One was a new development environment being used with which few people were thoroughly familiar. Two different divisions were involved in the project and were continually trying to pull the rug their way. People from both divisions were working alongside each other and even though the working relationship was good between practitioners, the tense relationship at higher levels did affect the project. Midway through the initiative, senior managers felt that something

Table 16-10   Essential Parameters for the Organization that Failed

Parameter	Value
Risk mitigation capacity	62.4%
Risk perception level	22.9%
Likelihood of experiencing problems	48.2%
Software Quality Index	1.9 (D)

was not going right and the assessment was seen as a way to identify appropriate corrective actions.

In addition, the system that was developed as part of the project changed the way personnel from the customer sites would be carrying out their regular activities. This was known from the beginning and proper mechanisms had been implemented to describe current methods and to elicit requirements in order to ensure that the transition would be as smooth as possible. A pilot site was selected where the system would be fine tuned before deployment. This, however, did not take into account turf battles going on at the pilot site; among these, conflicts between managers who felt that the new system was going to alter their influence within their own organization, not to mention prima donnas who insisted that their requirements had priority over everything else.

The RMC, the RPL, the LEP and the SQI characterizing the organization are listed in Table 16-10.

The RMC was higher than average, and so was the SQI. However, the perception level of the risks facing the project was unusually low and indicated that a certain amount of complacency had crept in over time, which ultimately resulted in a LEP equal to 48.2 percent. This value largely exceeded the critical threshold associated with the likelihood of problems empirically set at 40 percent.

The LEP in key risk areas is shown in Figure 16-26. The LEP resulting from deficiencies observed in key risk-mitigating process areas is shown in Figure 16-27.

Figure 16-26 stresses the problems experienced in connection with the Development Environment key risk area, along with the difficulties associated with the lack of experienced personnel and those encountered in the Management key risk area. The high likelihood of problems in the External Constraints key risk area is a reflection of the situation at the customer site. There was nothing the project team could do about it, and unfortunately, given the rivalry between the two divisions that assumed

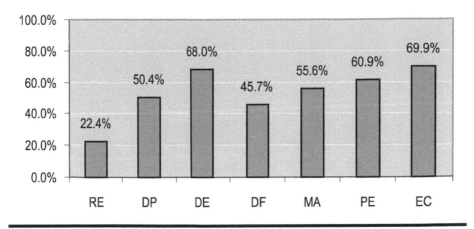

Figure 16-26 Likelihood of experiencing problems in key risk areas for the organization that failed

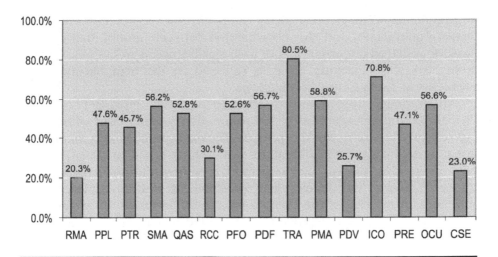

Figure 16-27 Likelihood of experiencing problems due to deficiencies in key risk-mitigating process areas for the organization that failed

the responsibility of developing the system, more energy was spent in internal feuds than in ironing out obstacles.

As to the risk-mitigating process areas, everything is high. It turned out that the organization was overly relying on its process to develop the system and was ignoring crises in the making. For instance, project planning and project tracking were relatively well mastered and the risk

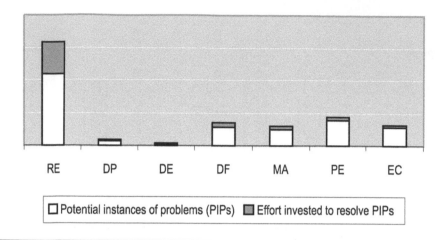

Figure 16-28   PIPs and effort invested to resolve them

anticipated in these areas was very low. On the other hand, these processes did not take into account the underground mess that was developing. Requirements were given a lot of attention, but the communication of these requirements and the coordination between groups that had to develop a shared understanding of their significance in order to implement them was sorely lacking. This is reflected in the high likelihood of problems in Intergroup Coordination.

An academic approach was adopted regarding Process Focus and Process Definition. Again, these led to a relatively mature way of integrating resources to carry out the project. The main problem was that it was not a good fit given the difficulties with which it had to deal. Training was an issue in the sense that project personnel did not have a good understanding of the development environment and they did not have sufficient knowledge of the operational context in which the system was ultimately going to be deployed. This created major problems in implementing changes proposed by customer representatives that were subsequently found to be in conflict with other aspects that had to be taken into account.

The PIPs and PFMs, along with the effort invested in resolving and taking action on them, respectively, are shown in Figure 16-28 and Figure 16-29.

Figure 16-28 stresses that a lot of effort was invested in dealing with requirements but very little on other key risk areas, particularly in the Management, Personnel, External Constraints, and Development Environment areas. In Development Environment, one problem was standing out, namely, the lack of proficiency of project personnel with it. Yet little if anything was done to rectify the situation. The academic approach of

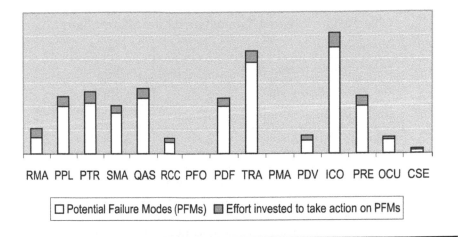

RMA PPL PTR SMA QAS RCC PFO PDF TRA PMA PDV ICO PRE OCU CSE

☐ Potential Failure Modes (PFMs)   ▣ Effort invested to take action on PFMs

Figure 16-29   PFMs and effort invested in taking action on them

investing in the analysis and the definition of precise requirements was blindly adopted without any regard to other equally important aspects.

As can be seen in Figure 16-29, effort was uniformly invested across all risk mitigating process areas. Recommendations that were presented to senior management included a significant investment in Training, Peer Reviews, Quality Assurance, and Intergroup Coordination. The Intergroup Coordination essentially consisted of initiating a team building blitz and involved senior managers to hold awareness sessions at all levels in the organization and at the customer site. Effort in Quality Assurance focused on establishing a function that would keep a flow of essential information going among senior management, the project team, the two divisions involved in the project, and the customer.

When this diagnosis was presented to senior management, it was well received. People at that level agreed that the organization was facing an uphill battle. The recommendations, however, were seen as creating too much of a change that would result in disturbing the way the project was actually being carried out. The investment was also seen as too risky given the available budget. A token effort was invested in Quality Assurance and in Intergroup Coordination, but it was too little too late. Eighteen months later, crises had reached a level that made cancellation of the project unavoidable. The incurred loss represented too much pressure for the organization, which filed for bankruptcy soon after.

The Success Story

Ever since we started applying the concepts described in this chapter, we have been searching for the Holy Grail. This would be an organization

Table 16-11   Essential Parameters for the Success Story

Parameter	Value
Risk mitigation capacity	99.2%
Risk perception level	If > 2%
Likelihood of experiencing problems	< 1%
Software Quality Index	> 6.5 (A+)

having devised an optimal set of monitoring and mitigation mechanisms, consuming resources at a rate lower than its capacity to provide them, and making it operate at an arbitrarily low LEP. We came to believe that this was a theoretical limit and we would never find an organization that came close to achieving it.

In 2002, we were involved in assessing an organization that exemplified what we thought was possible. We came upon it by chance, through a colleague involved in conducting International Organization for Standardization (ISO) audits. This colleague, being familiar with the business GRafP Technologies was in, told me that it would be worth for us to look at that organization. Of all places, it was located in Medellín, Colombia. I had never been there and all I knew about Colombia was what I read in the newspapers, which mainly consisted of bad news, drug dealing, crime, and kidnappings. In other words, nothing that would make me enthusiastic about a business trip there.

Nevertheless, curiosity prevailed and we found ourselves conducting an assessment in this organization, Productora de Software S.A. (PSL). It confirmed that I had to be more critical of what I read in the newspapers. Like any other large city, there are delinquents in Medellín and one has to be careful. However, one also has to be careful anywhere or in any situation with which one lacks familiarity. Risk management has taught me that. After nine trips, I had not seen any criminal activities; I know they exist like I know they exist in New York, Toronto, and Paris. The people there were no different from people in other locations and Medellín turned out to be very nice and friendly. I could drink water from the tap, which I rarely do in any country in South and Central America.

Table 16-11 summarizes the assessment results. The SQI of 6.5 is particularly noticeable, given that practically all the organizations we had assessed fell between the range of zero and five (keeping in mind that this is a logarithmic scale).

Table 16-11 shows that as long as the staff's perception of the organization's vulnerability to problems is kept over 2 percent, the likelihood of experiencing serious problems in the projects in terms of cost overruns, schedule slippages, and products or services that do not satisfy the needs for which they were undertaken, will be less than 1 percent. In fact, at PSL, in order for the LEP to reach a value of 9 percent (roughly one in 11 projects experiencing serious difficulties), the RPL would have to decrease to less than 1 percent, which is very unlikely. Indeed, for risk perception to go down to such a low level, PSL personnel would have to display a lack of awareness that is difficult to imagine (in a group of 100 people, only one individual would have to correctly identify the possibility of facing serious problems).

It appears that PSL has succeeded in defining and implementing a near optimal process in light of the environment in which it operates.

If PSL had been located in North America, one can surmise its success would have been the topic of countless management journals and the company would be much larger, given the material and human resources available to North American organizations. The lingering uncertainty is if PSL had been located in North America, would it have achieved that level of success, given the influence that the environment can have on the evolution of an organization? It could be imagined that without the environment and the challenges Medellín provided, the organization would never have evolved the way it did.

One aspect that makes PSL particularly interesting is the impact of the organizational culture on establishing its drive to achieve excellence. For instance, personnel exhibit an unusually strong team spirit and share the vision of what the company stands for. People who have left PSL remain in contact with their former co-workers and participate in the company's sponsored activities. That culture promotes learning, sharing of information, social responsibility, and continuous improvement at all levels (personal, professional, technical). During the assessment, one observation came up over and over again: finding a way to help personnel improve at the personal level, to contribute more to PSL, Medellín, and Colombia, and to make the company's dream come true.

PSL was well summed up in a particularly eloquent way by a project manager during the assessment: "Initially, PSL was the reflection of its General Manager; now, the General Manager is the reflection of PSL."

Chapter 17

On Probabilistic Risk Identification, Mapping, and Evaluation

> The worst problems are those that have not been anticipated
> and for which there are no measures that can be called upon
> to mitigate their impact.

The method used to collect the data on which this book is based was derived from the work we undertook in Probabilistic Risk Identification, Mapping (to mitigation mechanisms that are currently in place), and Evaluation (PRIME). The general concepts developed as part of conducting this work are explained in this chapter. Because of the nature of the theme this chapter addresses, it is a little more theoretical than the rest of the book. The reader who wants get to the heart of the matter can read Chapter 16 without incurring any loss in ability to comprehend the assessment results.

This chapter starts by introducing general concepts on risk, particularly in terms of losses and opportunities. It then moves on to describe how these general concepts have been applied to Information Technology (IT) and to gathering the information that can be of practical use to software managers and practitioners alike.

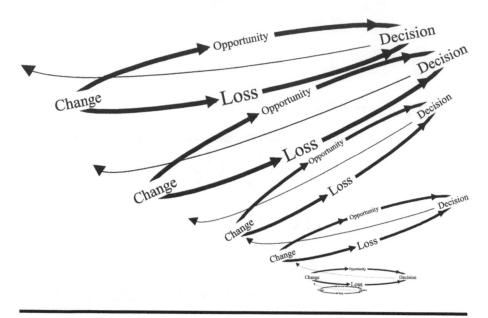

Figure 17-1 **Loss versus opportunity**

The Complexity of Preventing Losses and Making the Most of Opportunities

Any change translates into a loss or an opportunity. Each of these demands that a decision be made which, in turn, will generate more changes, as shown in Figure 17-1. This can lead to an avalanche effect (usually destructive) or it can be channeled to have a constructive outcome.

If one looks at any entity, whether it is an organization, a project, a system, or an individual, at least three main axes should be taken into account when attempting to prevent losses. The three main axes are the human resource(s) associated with this entity, the tools, equipment, and technology used in (or by) this entity, and the mission that this entity is pursuing (or the function it is performing). Assume that 10 changes can occur along each axis over a given period of time, each being associated with a loss or offering an opportunity. If there were four ways to prevent the loss from occurring and four ways to take advantage of the opportunity, one would theoretically have to go through all possible outcomes when any one of these changes occurs, and examine the entire number of combinations of two items drawn from among 300, which is expressed mathematically as $C_{300}^2 = 300 \times 299 \div 2 = 44,850$, before making an optimal decision. Given that, at times, several changes may occur over a period of one day, this is not an easy task, as depicted in Figure 17-2 for only

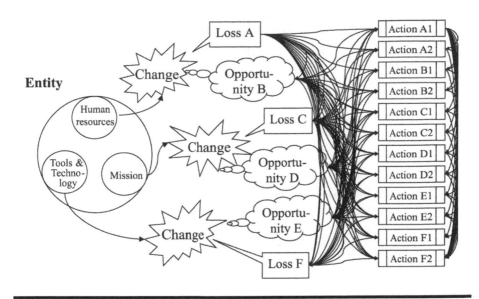

Figure 17-2 The complexity of preventing losses and exploiting opportunities

one change per axis. Statements such as the one made by Napoleon Bonaparte, to the effect that all he wanted from his generals is that they be lucky, are therefore not entirely surprising.

In theory, it is conceivable to imagine a system that can identify the risks to which an entity is exposed with the help of suitable sensors, map the risks that have been identified in this fashion to the entity's readiness to deal with them, and then devise the most appropriate countermeasures to prevent these risks from materializing. In fact, this type of control mechanism had already been built when the entity consisted of a physical system whose behavior could be modeled and predicted under specific conditions. The difficulty starts when the entity is very complex and its behavior cannot be accurately predicted, particularly if this entity interacts with other equally complex entities. For instance, initiatives undertaken by people are all but excluded because of the unpredictable behavior of human executors.

For example, in 1994, an Airbus A300 crashed at Japan's Nagoya airport, resulting in the death of 264 people. From what is known about it, the inexperience of the co-pilot combined with the A300's automatic flight control systems were at the root of the crash. The plane was being flown by hand and prior to landing, the autopilot somehow put the plane into go-around mode. The result was that the co-pilot continued to attempt to land the plane by pitching the nose down while the autopilot was trying to pitch the nose up to perform the go-around flight procedure. Other flight control systems, either automatic or activated by the pilots,

Figure 17-3   PRIME

jumped in to prevent the plane from stalling, which, in effect, just made things worse.

PRIME

The approach developed by GRafP Technologies is based on fuzzy relationships established between monitored risks and mitigation mechanisms. Assuming that specific categories of sensors are available to detect and to monitor certain types of undesirable conditions (risks), and specific classes of mechanisms are available to mitigate their deterioration into crises (risk mitigation), the approach essentially consists of calculating the likelihood of experiencing problems (LEP) to which an entity is exposed for each risk area, and each class of risk mitigation mechanisms. The likelihood of experiencing a problem P, given the probability that its occurrence is higher than the risk r monitored by sensors, and the status m of mitigation mechanisms in the entity under observation, $Pr(P>r|m)$, is based on fuzzy logic and the exponential cumulative probability distribution function. This function is effectively the one most commonly used to determine the probability of failure for large, complex systems, in which the failure modes are so elaborate that a very large number of paths leading to deterioration involving different failure scenarios are operable simultaneously.

An example is shown in Figure 17-4, in which a system is used to assess the survivability of a cruiser to possible threats given information provided by intelligence gathering units and the status of her equipment and combat-readiness.

Other applications include calculating the odds that a candidate applying for a job will effectively turn out to be a good performer in the organization where he or she is applying. Given that the success of an

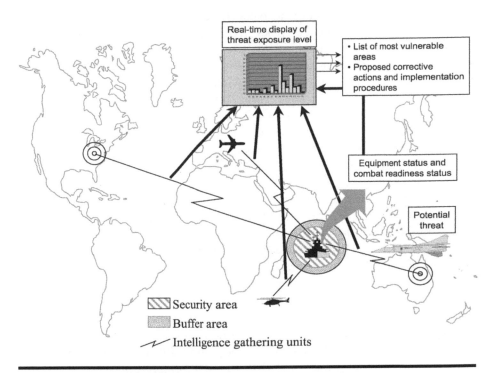

Figure 17-4   Risk mitigation applied to threat assessment and reduction

organization is closely linked to the ability of its human resources to fully exploit their potential while fulfilling the organization's objectives, this is an area where such an application would have major implications.

More recently, the potential of the PRIME approach has been assessed to determine the feasibility of applying it to a personal process aimed at harmonizing one's abilities with one's ambitions, based on the use of validated models. In theory, it is possible to calculate the LEP assumed by the entity under observation, by integrating the first moment of the variable r, that is:

$$LEP = \int_0^1 r \tfrac{d}{dr}\big(1 - \Pr(P > r \mid m)\big)\, dr$$

where r and m are linked through a set of fuzzy relationships and $\Pr(P > r \mid m)$ is based on an exponential distribution.

With this approach, as the risk sensing level approaches one, the LEP approaches zero. In theory, this should be true even when the risk mitigation capacity (RMC) is very low. The interpretation of this result is that as the quality of monitoring risks increases, ad-hoc corrective actions will prevent the monitored risks from materializing. Therefore, even though few mitigation mechanisms are implemented, their effectiveness is perfectly known and allows sensors to map a risk profile perfectly matched to the entity's mitigation capacity.

Conversely, as the risk sensing level approaches zero, the LEP approaches one. In theory, this should be true even when the RMC is very high. The interpretation given to explain this result is that as the quality of monitoring risks decreases, the mitigation capacity becomes poorly matched to the risk profile, and the first glitch of any significance that occurs will wreak havoc in the entity under observation. Therefore, even though many mitigation mechanisms are in place, they may not be the right ones, that is, the ones that allow effective risk mitigation, and problems are bound to occur.

Let me explain this with a simple car driving analogy. Assume for a moment that I live in the northeastern United States. It is wintertime and there is freezing rain (a rather frequent occurrence in that part of the world). Assume also that I am an inexperienced driver who just received his driver's license six months earlier. Knowing that I do not have a lot of experience driving, let alone driving in such weather conditions, I rightly deduce that the best way of not getting into an accident is to stay home. My risk perception level (RPL) is 100 percent and as a result, the probability of having an accident is zero. Now let's also presume that I must go out. Keeping in mind my lack of experience, I may choose to call a cab and thus transfer the risks I am facing to someone who, in all likelihood, has more experience than I. Unfortunately, I am running out of luck! There are no cabs. I am alone, and I must resign myself to driving. I therefore set out to carefully plan my itinerary, choosing roads that I know will not be heavily traveled. I take the car out and I drive at low speed, taking care to let drivers behind go by me. My probability of getting into an accident is no longer zero, but it is still small. I have now been driving for the last half hour and nothing has happened. I surmise that I was worrying about nothing and I accelerate in order to get to my destination faster. As a result, my RPL has decreased and I am increasing the likelihood of having an accident given my limited driving abilities. Indeed, my car hits a patch of black ice and starts swerving; I am unable to control it and I end up in the ditch.

The reverse is also true. Assume that I have 30 years of driving experience, in all kinds of weather conditions. I even managed to survive in Rome without a scratch to my car. A little bit of freezing rain will not stop me from going out. I therefore take the car out of the garage and off I go. My RPL is rather low, but for now, it is adequately compensated by my excellent driving abilities. The car starts swerving but I quickly get it back under control. It so happens that I am now driving behind a driver who only has six months of driving experience. I proceed to overtake him just as he loses control of his car and I end up in the ditch right behind him.

The essence of this thesis is that, no matter how modest our personal means are to limit the risks associated with a given undertaking, a greater perception of such risks will undoubtedly minimize our likelihood to encounter difficulties. This has been observed by psychologists working with children; little girls have fewer accidents than little boys because they exhibit better risk perception. A higher capacity to minimize such risks further decreases this likelihood to encounter difficulties.

The preceding paragraphs explain the relationship between a risk sensing suite intrinsically linked to the risk mitigation suite, or in other words, a biased relationship. The same principles expounded in the foregoing paragraphs are applicable in the case of an unbiased relationship, for instance an experienced driver sitting next to the inexperienced one and monitoring his or her moves. The experienced driver will have an excellent perception of the risks involved, and as a result, will be able to detect when the inexperienced driver does not perceive them well, which contributes to a greater accident likelihood. This situation also had to be taken into account. The way in which a high risk sensing level can influence our likelihood to cope with undesirable outcomes turned out to be as important an aspect of the PRIME approach as the set of risk mitigation mechanisms that allow one to reduce the probability of such undesirable outcomes. The car driving analogy provided one example. Here is another.

The northeastern United States and eastern Canada suffered a major ice storm a few years ago. Some areas did not have electricity for a duration exceeding one month (not a particularly pleasant experience in 30 degrees below zero). Diesel generators were selling like little hot cakes. In the fall following the storm, there was another brisk sale of generators as people wanted to be ready in case of another storm, even though this kind of weather glitch happens rarely.

The RPL of people who acquired generators had increased significantly due to their experience during the previous winter. This increase can be explained with a Bayesian approach as follows. Assume that the meteorologists tell us that an ice storm of this magnitude occurs once over a period of 1000 years with a 99.5 percent probability, P[Ice storm=1 in 1000 years]=0.995, and that it occurs once over a period of 10 years with a probability of 0.5 percent, P[Ice storms=1 in 10 years]=0.005. The first statement is equivalent to a frequency of occurrence equal to 10^{-3} and the second to a frequency of occurrence equal to 10^{-1}. This is the distribution of such an ice storm before it has happened, which the public would accept, not having anything else to go by.

After the ice storm, we can find the distribution after it has happened, which made the RPL of the public go up significantly. Denoting by the term IS98 the fact that an ice storm occurred in 1998, by event E the fact that an ice storm occurs once every 1000 years (i.e., at a frequency of 10^{-3}), and by event É the fact that an ice storm occurs once every 10 years (i.e. at a frequency of 10^{-1}), we have, assuming that E and É are mutually exclusive:*

$$P[E] = 0.001$$

$$P[\bar{E}] = 0.1$$

$$P[IS98 \mid E] = 0.995$$

$$P[IS98 \mid \bar{E}] = 0.005$$

$$P[IS98] = P[IS98 \cap (E \cup \bar{E})]$$

$$P[IS98] = P[(IS98 \cap E) \cup (IS98 \cap \bar{E})]$$

$$P[IS98] = P[IS98 \cap E] \cup P[IS98 \cap \bar{E}]]$$

which can also be written as

$$P[IS98] = P[IS98, E] + P[IS98, \bar{E}]$$

where

$$P[IS98, E] = P[E] \cdot P[IS98 \mid E]$$

and

$$P[IS98, \bar{E}] = P[\bar{E}] \cdot P[IS98 \mid \bar{E}]$$

---

* The probability of event A and event B occurring is denoted by the expression P[A∩B] or P[A,B]. The probability of event B occurring, given that event A has also occurred, is given by the expression P[B|A], and the laws of probability tell us that P[A,B] = P[A]·P[B|A], where · is the multiplication symbol. The probability of event A or event B occurring is denoted by the expression P[A∪B], which is equal to P[A] ∪ P[B] or P[A] + P[B].

Then the distribution of ice storms, as perceived by the public after an ice storm had occurred in 1998 is:

$$P[\bar{E} \mid IS98] = P[\bar{E}, IS98]/P[IS98]$$

$$P[\bar{E} \mid IS98] = P[\bar{E}] \cdot P[IS98 \mid \bar{E}]/P[IS98]$$

$$P[\bar{E} \mid IS98] = P[\bar{E}] \cdot P[IS98 \mid \bar{E}]/\{P[E] \cdot P[IS98 \mid E] + P[\bar{E}] \cdot P[IS98 \mid \bar{E}]\}$$

$$P[\bar{E} \mid IS98] = 0.1 \cdot 0.005/(0.001 \cdot 0.995 + 0.1 \cdot 0.005) = 33.445\%$$

Comparing the 33.4 percent value distribution with the 0.5 percent value, the public perception that an ice storm of this magnitude can happen once every ten years has increased almost 67 times after it had happened in 1998.

In any case, since this type of severe ice storm is indeed very rare, risk mitigation models are more likely to propose the acquisition of salt to melt the ice on the pavement rather than to promote the acquisition of diesel generators. Therefore, such a move can be viewed as one of the *ad hoc* corrective actions mentioned earlier. Even though it does not change the probability that another major ice storm will occur, it certainly increases the capacity of the people who made such an acquisition to deal with the situation should there be another similar natural disaster. It is therefore obvious that anyone who underwent difficult weather conditions was much more apt at countering the 1998 ice storm than other people.

Therefore, to summarize, an entity with a high RMC is not necessarily successful because it may have to overcome unexpected difficulties resulting from the high LEP it faces, where an entity with a low RMC is not necessarily inefficient because this capacity may be well matched to the risks to which it is exposed. However, the assumption can be made to the effect that an entity with a high RMC is more likely to be successful than one with a low RMC, simply because the high RMC must operate within a high and very narrow margin of risk sensing level to maintain its likelihood of undesirable outcomes to a low value.

It should nevertheless be theoretically possible for an entity to exhibit a mitigation capacity, whatever this capacity may be, that is near perfectly matched to the risks it faces, in the sense that the set of mitigation mechanisms, along with the risk sensing suite, minimize the probability that the risks will materialize. Therefore, it should be possible, at least in principle, to devise a set of mitigation mechanisms and monitoring sensors whereby an entity operates at an arbitrarily low LEP as long as the resources consumption rate of this set of mechanisms and sensors is lower than the entity's capacity to provide it. To continue with the preceding analogy, it is wishful thinking to provide the inexperienced driver with a battle tank, with the hope that he will not have an accident under freezing rain conditions, if his driving abilities are not also improved. It will only increase the damage he is likely to cause, if not to himself, then to others. The optimal set of mitigation mechanisms and monitoring sensors is initially unknown. Furthermore, it must be assumed that such a combination is not static but is system-dependent and time-dependent, and will have to be modified as the context in which the entity operates evolves.

All the same, it should be obvious to everyone that the simple act of preparing oneself makes it easier to cope with a thorny situation once it occurs. Indeed, devising mitigation mechanisms based on erroneous risk perception, which in turn arises out of some unjustified fears and therefore lack of experience, may have strange consequences. For example, having decided to find shelter from a possible nuclear war, a couple from British Columbia went to live in the Falkland Islands on the eve of the war between Great Britain and Argentina. The same principle applies to people who insist on having guns at home without proper training and safekeeping. They are likely to be harmed during a robbery, see children injured because of their finding and playing with them, and contribute to the overall crime level by having the guns stolen.

Application to Information Technology

The concepts presented in the preceding section were subsequently applied to the field of Information Technology, particularly to software development and maintenance activities. In order to do so, there was first a need to identify the framework to use to compute the RPL and the RMC.

Selecting the IT Framework

Extensive research was invested in identifying an appropriate risk model for IT. The types of risks vary widely as a function of the type of product or service being investigated. Our objective was to remain at a relatively high level, in the sense that we did not wish to focus on a particular industry or on a specific sector in which IT is applied.

Establishing a parallel with the car driving analogy described in the last section, the objective of applying the PRIME approach was to calculate the chances that, having chosen to undertake a trip, the driver will not get there on time (the driver got lost along the way), that the driver will not have enough resources to complete the trip (e.g., the car ran out of gas or was wrecked), or that if the driver completes the trip without major incidents, the driver will not get to the right place. The impact resulting from the occurrence of any or all of these conditions is, of course, that the trip is a failure.

Given the current state of the software practice, as summarized in Chapter 1, this amounted to computing the likelihood of IT initiatives to experience cost overruns, schedule slippages, and deployment of products or services that do not satisfy the needs for which they were undertaken in the first place. For an IT initiative, it can be expected that if the delivery date keeps being postponed, the sponsor is liable to cancel the project and to seek another solution. If the costs keep increasing, the sponsor is liable to get tired of putting money into a black hole and to reduce his or her losses by canceling the project. If the resulting product or service does not do enough of what it is supposed to do, it is subject to being abandoned shortly after having been delivered. In other words, the project is a failure.

In addition, identifying the following information presented a particular interest: risks that had not been properly anticipated, those that had been anticipated but for which no solutions were at hand when they occurred, and risk mitigation solutions that had not properly been implemented or which proved to be deficient.

Having defined the scope, it then became easier to select an appropriate framework. With respect to the RPL, we finally opted for the Taxonomy-Based Risk Identification, developed at the Software Engineering Institute (SEI). For the RMC, we selected the Capability Maturity Model (CMM), which was also developed at the SEI. Other models were available but this one is relatively well known; it is well documented, and has been used for several years, and there is plenty of support available to put it into practice.

Some assumptions had to be made regarding these models, particularly the CMM. For instance, we had to assume that the CMM was an optimal model, in the sense that if it were perfectly applied, it would reduce the LEP to zero. We know it is not true, but in order to use this approach, we did not have the choice. However, there is international consensus that the CMM is a good model if not an optimal one. Finally, in order to use a terminology consistent with the Taxonomy-Based Risk Identification (shortened to risk taxonomy) and the CMM, the expressions risk sensors and risk mitigation mechanisms were replaced with RPL and RMC, respectively. These expressions, in particular, reflected the fact that the main actors in this field are people and not gauges and sensors.

The following paragraphs briefly describe the CMM and the Taxonomy-Based Risk Identification.

The CMM

The CMM provides organizations involved in software development and maintenance with guidance on how to gain control of their process and how to evolve toward a culture of software engineering and management excellence. The term software process is defined as the way human resources, methods, procedures, and tools are integrated in order to develop a software application. The CMM does not distinguish between development and maintenance; it assumes that once a project is initiated, in order to implement several modifications and change requests (or to implement a single, major one), it effectively becomes a development project. By focusing on a limited set of activities and working to achieve them, a project or an organization can steadily improve its software process to enable continuous and lasting gains in its ability to improve the quality of its products and services.

The CMM follows the premise that improvement is based on many small, evolutionary steps rather than revolutionary innovations. In the model, these evolutionary steps are distributed over five maturity levels numbered 1 to 5 that lay successive foundations for improvement. These five maturity levels define an ordinal scale for measuring the maturity of a project or an organization in terms of process capability.

The five maturity levels are listed below:

- Initial: At maturity level 1, the process is informal and largely improvised, and performance is unpredictable. Few processes are defined, and success depends on individual effort.
- Repeatable: At maturity level 2, a process is defined within the scope of each undertaking (task, work package, enhancement, project). The focus is placed on stabilizing the approach used to carry out the work associated with each individual undertaking. This approach may substantially differ for each undertaking.
- Defined: At maturity level 3, an organizational process is in place and consequently, the emphasis is directed at defining a process from the best practices implemented in connection with past and current undertakings. The resulting process is then adapted to the needs of each new undertaking, and at establishing and using a database in which the data gathered as part of performing the work is consolidated for use in connection with future work.
- Managed: At maturity level 4, the process defined at maturity level 3 is instrumented, quantified, and characterized statistically, and the focus is placed on controlling the process outputs with respect to statistical parameters. When enough information has been gathered on the process, its outputs can be monitored in order to

determine whether they are under control, in the sense that the measurements that characterize them fall within the allocated ranges for the categories of undertakings in the organization.

■ Optimizing: At maturity level 5, the quantitative data is used to improve the process by tightening the control parameters established at maturity level 4, in order to improve productivity and to reduce costs. The causes of random variations observed with collected measurements are investigated in order to determine if they can be removed or reduced, either through innovative ideas or through new technologies, which would result in more accurate planning, more efficient execution, better applications, and a more capable process. Continuous improvement becomes a way of life in order to satisfy the business objectives of the organization.

Each maturity level provides a layer in the foundation for improvement and comprises 18 Key Process Areas (KPA). Each KPA is associated with two to four process goals which, when satisfied, contribute to increase process capability. In order to determine if a goal has been achieved, each KPA is made up of key practices, along with sub-practices and explanatory notes. For example, the Requirements Management KPA, at maturity level 2, is made up of two goals and 12 key practices.

In North America, the adoption of the CMM as the cornerstone of the software process has become the norm in the software community, particularly in the aerospace and banking sectors.

The Taxonomy-Based Risk Identification

The risk taxonomy is a comprehensive classification of undesirable situations that are most often encountered in the course of developing or maintaining software applications. It encompasses the entire software development life cycle and can be used to identify the issues that are most likely to cause trouble in a project or, for that matter, to determine the recurring problems that hinder projects in an organization involved in developing software applications.

This taxonomy is structured along three classes. Each class is made up of elements and each element, in turn, is characterized by attributes. The three classes of this risk taxonomy are: Product Engineering, Development Environment, and Program Constraints. For example, the Program Constraints class is made up of three elements: Resources, Contract, and Program Interfaces. The Resources element is further characterized with the help of the following attributes: Schedule, Staff, Budget, and Facilities. Situations liable to deteriorate into problems are subsequently listed in the taxonomy as a function of the attribute that best applies to them.

The risk taxonomy has not received as much attention as the CMM, because it is more recent. In addition, human nature is such that the term risk makes people cringe. Risk management is too often perceived as unproductive activities, even if it is one of the disciplines that contributes the most to the success of a project. However, managing risks also means being able to determine how much to invest in something that may never happen or that may have little impact if it does, which in itself is not an easy task. People also tend to believe that they do manage their risks, even though they do it intuitively. The problem is that some people are very good at it while others are not and could learn by adhering to a more methodical approach.

We have all heard stories about people who made a fortune without having completed high school. Unfortunately, this is often anecdotal. Either these people had a natural business savvy that few other individuals possessed or they happened to be at the right place at the right time, and were quick and clever enough to take advantage of the situation. It does not tell us about the thousands of others who, during the same period, failed miserably because they did not have that flair or happened to be just plain unlucky, and could have succeeded if they had better managed their risks.

In any case, it is worth quoting Andrew Grove, CEO of Intel Corporation, a company that has had a major impact on IT, in his book *Only the Paranoid Survive*: "Sooner or later, something fundamental will change in your business." The Wallace Corporation is a good example: it won the prestigious Malcom Baldridge Award in 1990 and declared bankruptcy in 1991.

Tailoring the IT Framework

After having identified appropriate models, the second step in applying PRIME to IT consisted of tailoring these models (i.e., the CMM and the risk taxonomy).

The CMM, in particular, proved to be well adapted to large organizations, particularly those involved in defense and aerospace. As the assessments we were anticipating were targeting a broader range of organizations, some having only 10 software engineers, programmers, or computer scientists, others hundreds, the model had to be tailored to take this aspect into consideration. The choice of the CMM proved to be a good one as the SEI itself stresses that the CMM is a model (as opposed to a standard), and therefore needs tailoring to be used properly. The tailoring activity also had to take into account that some organizations were likely to be involved in developing management information systems, whereas others would be involved in developing industrial or engineering applications. Even though the tasks are often the same, their designation varies considerably from one field to another.

As mentioned in Chapter 16, software has yet to be structured into a full engineering discipline, and there currently exists a significant rivalry between software engineers and computer scientists. The assessments we conducted emphasized the differences that characterize the software practice, as many software professionals are neither engineers nor scientists. The terminology to use in the course of tailoring was at times a delicate issue.

The initial tailoring was performed with the participation of one government organization, one organization developing industrial applications, and a third developing commercial software.

With respect to the risk taxonomy, tailoring involved flattening the structure to seven key risk areas: Requirements, Design, Code, and Test, Development Environment, Development Framework, Management, Personnel, and External Constraints. This led to a regrouping of the situations liable to cause problems in a project in order to be able to collect more information under each key risk area. Each situation described in the risk taxonomy was reviewed and the terminology used to describe it was adapted to make it understandable by personnel from all three organizations. The result was a list of 163 situations deemed the most relevant to software development and maintenance.

With respect to the CMM, a similar approach was taken. Each KPA described in the CMM, and each key practice was reviewed and the terminology used to describe these practices was adapted to make them understandable by personnel from all three organizations. In addition, given the scope of computing the likelihood of problems to which projects are exposed in terms of cost overruns, schedule slippages, and products or services that do not satisfy the needs for which they were undertaken, it was deemed appropriate to focus on KPAs at maturity level 2 and maturity level 3. Indeed, maturity level 4 and maturity level 5 focus on quality and competitiveness, and exceed this pre-defined scope. Furthermore, there are not many maturity level 4 and maturity level 5 organizations (over 80 percent of all assessed organizations have been rated at maturity level 1, maturity level 2, or maturity level 3) and it is unlikely that most organizations we anticipated assessing would be in a position to provide relevant information on the key practices at these maturity levels.

Excluding maturity level 4 and maturity level 5 resulted in a total of 13 KPAs to investigate. As part of the discussions that took place with the three organizations participating in the tailoring activities, it was also decided to include two additional non-CMM KPAs, Organizational Culture and Customer Service. To be sure, it was felt that Organizational Culture had a significant impact on software process capability, even though we did not have anything to rely on other than our personal experience in dealing with various types of organizations to support this claim. As for Customer Service (which includes customer service and customer relations), there was a wide consensus that, given the importance of the customers in the development of any product or service and the scope agreed on, it had to be included. Following this, key practices were individually tailored to fit as many organizations involved in as many fields as possible. The result was a list of 259 risk mitigating practices deemed the most relevant to software development and maintenance.

Table 17-1 summarizes the final key risk areas used to calculate the RPL. Within each key risk area, a varying number of situations are documented and contribute to identifying and quantifying the potential difficulties facing the project.

Table 17-2 summarizes the final set of KPAs used to calculate the RMC. Within each area, a varying number of key practices are documented and contribute in qualifying and quantifying the process used to carry out the project. It is worth noting that some of the process areas were renamed compared to their CMM designation. For example, the designation Software Configuration Management, a CMM KPA at maturity level 2, was changed to Release and Change Control to make it clear for people involved in developing management information systems. Likewise, the designation Software Product Engineering, a CMM KPA at maturity level 3, was changed to Product Development in order to avoid ruffling the feathers of computer scientists for whom the development of software products is not necessarily an engineering activity.

Implementing the IT Framework

After having identified and tailored an appropriate IT framework, the final step consisted in defining how this framework would be applied in the field to collect information needed to evaluate the likelihood of problems in IT initiatives. Unlike physical systems, the entities under investigation had people as both sensors and mitigation actuators. It was therefore not possible to dream up some combination of sensors and gauges to read the information and automatically feed it to processing units to be analyzed.

Two basic approaches were possible: checklists and surveys. In the first approach, an audit team would use checklists to perform on-site verifications of projects. In the second approach, project personnel would complete the surveys, and this would be complemented with interviews

Table 17-1   Key Risk Areas

Key Risk Area	Description
Requirements	The purpose of this key risk area consists of eliciting potential problems related to end-product requirements dealing with both the quality of the requirements specification and the difficulty of implementing a system that satisfies these requirements, from either the perspective of in-house development or subcontracted development.
Design, Code and Test	The purpose of this key risk area consists of eliciting potential problems related to the software development effort itself, from the requirements, through the design, code, and unit test, and up to the integration and acceptance tests.
Development Environment	The purpose of this key risk area consists of eliciting potential problems related to the development environment used to carry out the project. This development environment is typically made up, among other items, of project management tools, compilers, simulators, test equipment, and test software, etc.
Development Framework	The purpose of this key risk area consists of eliciting potential problems related to the development framework in which the project is taking place, that is the procedures, methods, and tools that are called upon to carry out the project and, in turn, to satisfy the customer's requirements.
Management	The purpose of this key risk area consists of eliciting potential problems related to the project management approach and, at a more general level as far as the project is affected by it, the management approach of the organization in which the project takes place.
Personnel	The purpose of this key risk area consists of eliciting potential problems related to personnel of the organization directly or indirectly involved in carrying out the project. These personnel issues typically include skills, responsibilities, the way people work together, etc.
External Constraints	The purpose of this key risk area consists of eliciting potential problems related to factors affecting the project for which the project team has little or no control. On the other hand, senior management of the organization in which the project takes place may have the influence and the authority to resolve or help resolve some of these issues.

Table 17-2   Risk-Mitigating Key Process Areas

Key Process Area	Description
Requirements Management	The purpose of this area consists of establishing a common understanding, between the party issuing the requirements (e.g., the customer, the marketing department, the program management office, etc.) and the project team, of the requirements that will be addressed by the project.
Project Planning	The purpose of this area consists of establishing reasonable plans for carrying out the project.
Project Tracking	The purpose of this area consists of establishing adequate visibility into actual progress achieved in the project so that management can take effective actions when the performance deviates significantly from the plans.
Subcontract Management	The purpose of this area consists of selecting qualified subcontractors and managing them effectively.
Quality Assurance	The purpose of this area consists of providing management and the customer, as appropriate, with suitable visibility into both the process being used by the project and the products being developed.
Release and Change Control	The purpose of this area consists of establishing and maintaining the integrity of the products resulting from the development or maintenance effort throughout the entire software life cycle.
Process Focus	The purpose of this area consists of establishing the responsibility for software process activities undertaken to improve the overall software process capability of a project, if its size warrants it, or of the organization in which the project takes place.
Process Definition	The purpose of this area consists of developing and maintaining a software development and maintenance process that improves performance in and across projects, and provides a basis for cumulative, long-term benefits to the organization.
Training	The purpose of this area consists of developing the skills and the knowledge of individuals so that they can effectively and efficiently carry out the tasks to which they have been assigned.

Table 17-2   Risk-Mitigating Key Process Areas (continued)

Key Process Area	Description
Project Management	The purpose of this area consists of integrating the project planning and project tracking activities into a coherent, defined process that is a tailored version of the standard process described in the Process Definition process area.
Product Development	The purpose of this area consists of consistently performing a well-defined engineering process that integrates all the development and maintenance activities to effectively and efficiently produce correct and reliable software.
Intergroup Coordination	The purpose of this area consists of establishing a means for software development personnel to participate actively with other personnel so the project is in a better position to satisfy effectively and efficiently the customer's needs.
Peer Reviews	The purpose of this area consists of identifying and removing defects from the work products early and efficiently, in addition to developing a better understanding of these products and of the defects that can be prevented.
Organizational Culture	The purpose of this area consists of establishing a set of collective values that will evolve with time and that may be harnessed to sustain changes introduced in the project or in the organization.
Customer Service	The purpose of this area consists of providing quality products and services to the customers and end-users in the course of the development and maintenance effort, along with the support they need to operate the delivered system.

and documentation reviews to allow an evaluation team to gain better knowledge of the project, and to be able to correctly interpret the information collected trough the surveys.

The checklists seemed attractive and offered the possibility of facilitating data collection. We were concerned that people might want to depict an optimistic picture, either deliberately or unconsciously. Not knowing which approach to use, we adopted the safest line of attack. We used both checklists and surveys, and carried out a comparative analysis of the

Figure 17-5   Framework implementation flow

results obtained with each. It turned out that the approach based on surveys proved to be more reliable than the approach based on checklists. When project staff completed the surveys, they tended to be more critical than when checklists were completed by external auditors.

We decided to use the approach based on surveys in the course of the 40 assessments that were subsequently conducted, with the exception of a few cases where it turned out that the approach based on checklists was more practical.

The framework implementation flow is shown in Figure 17-5. The first activity usually consisted of selecting the initiative(s) and work packages that would be part of the assessment, and selecting personnel involved in carrying them out to provide information on risks and risk mitigation. Once this selection was made, the surveys were reviewed and additional tailoring was performed where needed.

The next activity consisted of asking personnel to complete the surveys. Typically, managers, directors, and group leaders were asked to complete the survey dealing with risks. The intent was to determine the perception of people who had management responsibility and a good overview of both the project and the organization in which the project was undertaken. In other words, the risk survey respondents were selected to have a broad perspective on things but not necessarily a deep one. Typically, these people were able to complete the entire survey.

Practitioners were asked to complete the risk mitigation survey, with the aim of determining the capacity of mitigating risks in the project. Practitioners were asked to do this to determine how things really are in the trenches. Practitioners were selected because they have a detailed perspective on how work is performed but not necessarily a broad one. These people were typically not able to complete all areas addressed by the survey. For instance, practitioners who are assigned to product development activities are usually not in a position to provide significant information on process development or on project tracking topics. Therefore, the risk mitigation survey was broken down into mini-surveys (one per KPA), which were then assigned to the practitioners most likely to have the information required to complete them. The idea was to collect enough mini-surveys to have an adequate coverage of the areas addressed by the survey as a whole.

We were not so naïve as to believe that if the surveys were submitted to respondents, they would duly be returned to us. In fact, we tried it as a matter of curiosity and what we had predicted happened. We got about 10 percent of them back. In order to avoid this situation, we organized one or more sessions during which respondents completed the survey (or mini-survey) they had been assigned. No respondents left the room until his or her survey had been completed except in case of an emergency. This also had the advantage that if any questions came up, we were there to answer them and to provide clarifications as needed.

The completed surveys were collected and the information was analyzed with the help of a software application specifically developed for that purpose. The result of this analysis consisted of a RPL profile, a RMC profile, and a profile of the LEP, combined with detailed findings in the form of potential (or concrete) problems facing the project (or the organization) and deficient mitigation mechanisms.

We interpreted the results based on the information we had gathered during interviews and documentation reviews. The result was validated with respondents, changes were made to the raw data when appropriate, and a final analysis was performed. Forty assessments were conducted in this manner and the results are presented in the preceding chapters.

Annex A

A Crash Course in Statistical Process Control

> One sure way to improve is by measuring, understanding, controlling, and reducing variations; the other is by expecting the unexpected.

Statistical process control was first introduced in the early 1930s by Walter A. Shewhart of Bell Telephone Laboratories. It was eagerly used for a short time, then it lost some of its appeal during the Second World War, when industry's first priority was to produce a lot of goods and where due consideration was not always given to quality.

Edward W. Deming resurrected statistical process control in Japan after the War. Indeed, Japan provided an ideal world for introducing new concepts or dusting off old ones because everything had to be rebuilt and the Japanese were willing to try anything. It was immensely successful, particularly in the automotive industry, and it has since been reintroduced in North America.

The following is not an exhaustive description of statistical process control. Several textbooks cover it in greater detail. Our purpose is to give readers enough information to start using it immediately, because it can truly help an organization in processing the data it collects as part of developing its information technology (IT) applications.

Unconsciously, everyone does statistical process control. For instance, assume that I just traded in my old car for a new one. I now have to get used to a whole new set of noises, or more likely, the absence of noises I was accustomed to.

Assume that I have been driving my new car for a few thousand kilometers, and I feel that the engine is sluggish. I then go to the garage and the mechanic fine-tunes it. I drive for another couple of thousand kilometers, and I start hearing a rattling noise in the frame. I go back to the garage and the mechanic tightens a few screws that had come loose.

Essentially, by going to the garage, I have removed special causes of variation; in other words, non-random causes of noise.

I have now been driving my car for 10 thousand or so kilometers, and I am now used to the noises my new car should make and the ones it should not make. Practically, I have achieved statistical process control in the form of qualitative memories and feelings that I have registered in my brain. If I start my car one morning and I hear a new noise, this will generate an alarm in my brain telling me that something may be wrong. I may decide to go the garage right away to have it checked out or I may drive some more to see if this is a special cause of variation and discard the noise as a singularity.

Once special causes of variation have been eliminated, the remaining variations known as common causes of variation are essentially random. The process is then said to be under statistical control.

To continue with the car analogy, that time has now arrived to change the tires. I decide to buy high-quality Michelin tires. All of a sudden, I notice that ride comfort has improved significantly and that I can handle my car much better while driving. I must get used to new parameters in terms of handling and ride comfort. In fact, I am discarding the old control limits and generating new ones, which I will use from now on.

The essential difference between continuous process improvements is that the changes in control limits are accidental. I happened to replace my tires with top-of-the-line Michelin tires and I noticed the difference after the fact. Had I implemented continuous process improvement, I would have had as a goal to improve ride comfort and car handling characteristics, and I would have actively researched ways to achieve this, possibly by investigating the effect of replacing the tires.

Quantitatively Managing Processes

The technique most frequently used to statistically characterize a process is the control chart. Several types of diagrams are available and the most common one is the X chart. To develop an X chart, it is necessary to have from 20 to 25 data points. However, if this number of data points is not available, use whatever you have at your disposal.

In a first step, the average is calculated from available data (for instance, the ratio Actual duration/Planned duration (Ad/Pd) of a task). Note that by dividing the actual duration of a task by its planned duration, we normalized it. Normalization is essential in using control charts. This is why size estimation is so important; size becomes the normalizing parameter acting as the divisor of other estimated or actual parameters, so we will be talking in terms of work-days per function point, defects per source line of code, time duration per tick, whatever the definition of a tick is in the organization that uses it. In a second step, the standard deviation is calculated in order to determine the limits within which most tasks are envisioned to be completed.

The following graphs show the use of the control chart technique to determine these control limits. In Figure A-1, a set of data points representing the ratio Ad/Pd of several completed tasks is processed in order to calculate the upper and lower control limits characterizing the existing process capacity. As shown in Figure A-2, one data point exceeds the upper control limit (cell no. B8 in Figure A-1). This point is likely due to a particular event (and therefore not due to normal random fluctuations experienced in any physical process).

The reason one data point exceeding the upper control limit is treated as a non-random event is that control limits are established at $\pm 3\sigma$ from the average denoted by μ. Assuming a normal distribution of the data, the probability that an event will fall outside of these limits is equal to 0.27 percent, and at such a low value, it can reasonably be assumed that the event was not a random occurrence but was due to a particular cause.

For instance, assume that the average ratio μ of Ad/Pd for completed tasks is 0.996 and the standard deviation σ is 0.0479. Defining the upper control limit as $\mu + 3\sigma = 1.14$ and the lower control limit as $\mu - 3\sigma = 0.852$, the probability that a data point will exceed either the upper control limit or the lower control limit, as shown in Figure A-3, can be calculated with the help of the following Excel function:

$$\text{NORMDIST } (1.14, 0.996, 0.0479, \text{TRUE})$$
$$- \text{NORMDIST}(0.852, 0.996, 0.0479, \text{TRUE}) = 0.9973$$

This assumes that data points are distributed along a Gaussian probability density function, but this hypothesis is usually valid, even if individual tasks do not follow a Gaussian distribution, since the sum of random variables, independently of their individual distribution, will tend to behave like a Gaussian distribution.

In addition to exceeding control limits, other conditions are examined in order to determine which data points to eliminate in order to statistically characterize the process. These conditions are listed below and

B	C	D	E	F
Cell No	Actual/Planned duration	Average	Upper Control Limit	Lower Control Limit
B3	0.99	1.03315789	1.537345621	0.528970169
B4	0.98	1.03315789	1.537345621	0.528970169
B5	1.02	1.03315789	1.537345621	0.528970169
B6	1.01	1.03315789	1.537345621	0.528970169
B7	0.9	1.03315789	1.537345621	0.528970169
B8	1.7	1.03315789	1.537345621	0.528970169
B9	0.97	1.03315789	1.537345621	0.528970169
B10	1.02	1.03315789	1.537345621	0.528970169
B11	1.04	1.03315789	1.537345621	0.528970169
B12	1.01	1.03315789	1.537345621	0.528970169
B13	0.91	1.03315789	1.537345621	0.528970169
B14	0.94	1.03315789	1.537345621	0.528970169
B15	0.97	1.03315789	1.537345621	0.528970169
B16	1.07	1.03315789	1.537345621	0.528970169
B17	1.08	1.03315789	1.537345621	0.528970169
B18	1.03	1.03315789	1.537345621	0.528970169
B19	0.98	1.03315789	1.537345621	0.528970169
B20	1	1.03315789	1.537345621	0.528970169
B21	1.01	1.03315789	1.537345621	0.528970169

1.0332 Average	Calculated with the AVERAGE(C3:C21) Excel function
0.1681 Standard deviation	Calculated with the SQRT(VAR(C3:C21)) Excel function
1.5373 Upper Control Limit	Average + 3 standard deviations
0.529 Lower Control Limit	Average - 3 standard deviations

Figure A-1 Step 1 of calculating control limits

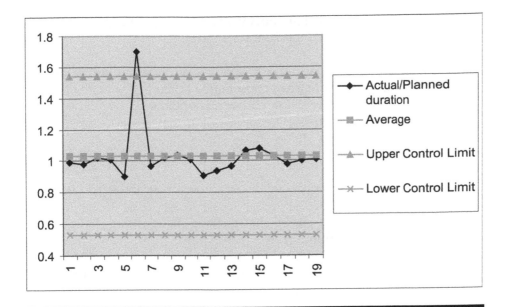

Figure A-2   Step 2 of calculating control limits

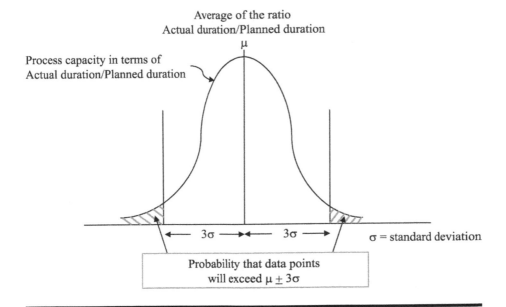

Figure A-3   Justification of 3σ control limits

are established by identifying the events for which the probability of occurrence is less than 0.27 percent ($\mu \pm 3\sigma$):

1. Seven or more consecutive points above or below the average
2. Seven or more increasing consecutive points
3. Seven or more decreasing consecutive points
4. Ten among 11 consecutive data points that are above or below the average
5. Two among three consecutive data points that are $\pm 2\sigma$ above or below the average
6. Four among five consecutive data points that are $\pm 1\sigma$ above or below the average
7. Sequences of data points that show a pattern, thus indicating a non-random distribution

When plotting data points in the diagram, it is also important to retain their time relationship, in order to be able to identify improvement or deterioration along the time axis. If one of the above conditions is observed in connection with a set of data points, this set is removed and the calculation of control limits is repeated (cell no. B8 is removed in Figure A-1, as shown in Figure A-4 in which all lower cells have been shifted up).

Once control limits have been established, a new control chart is created, in which these control limits are plotted. This chart will then be used to statistically control the current task. Data collected during execution of the current task over a period of time is plotted on this new diagram and compared to these control limits. If one of the above conditions is observed, including one data point exceeding the upper or lower control limits, this indicates a potential loss of control of the process. As a result, the project to which the task belongs may not meet its quality objectives (quality here is defined in general terms, since it may refer to the number of defects, time to market, reliability, etc.).

Note that a process that is under statistical control does not necessarily mean that it is a good process. A bad process can also be under statistical control; n this case, applying the process results in consistently bad products.

It is also important to stress the importance of Quality Assurance in statistical process control. If the process is not rigorously followed, it will be impossible to characterize it statistically. In this case, it can be anticipated that special causes of variation (i.e., non-random) will continuously be detected, resulting in a chronically out-of-control process.

The original control chart that has been used to establish upper and lower control limits is nevertheless retained and updated after the current task is completed, because it represents the evolution of the process

B Cell No	C Actual/Planned duration	D Average	E Upper Control Limit	F Lower Control Limit
B3	0.99	0.99611111	1.139853119	0.852369104
B4	0.98	0.99611111	1.139853119	0.852369104
B5	1.02	0.99611111	1.139853119	0.852369104
B6	1.01	0.99611111	1.139853119	0.852369104
B7	0.9	0.99611111	1.139853119	0.852369104
B8	0.97	0.99611111	1.139853119	0.852369104
B9	1.02	0.99611111	1.139853119	0.852369104
B10	1.04	0.99611111	1.139853119	0.852369104
B11	1.01	0.99611111	1.139853119	0.852369104
B12	0.91	0.99611111	1.139853119	0.852369104
B13	0.94	0.99611111	1.139853119	0.852369104
B14	0.97	0.99611111	1.139853119	0.852369104
B15	1.07	0.99611111	1.139853119	0.852369104
B16	1.08	0.99611111	1.139853119	0.852369104
B17	1.03	0.99611111	1.139853119	0.852369104
B18	0.98	0.99611111	1.139853119	0.852369104
B19	1	0.99611111	1.139853119	0.852369104
B20	1.01	0.99611111	1.139853119	0.852369104

0.99611	Average	Calculated with the AVERAGE(C3:C20) Excel function
0.04791	Standard deviation	Calculated with the SQRT(VAR(C3:C20)) Excel function
1.13985	Upper Control Limit	Average + 3 standard deviations
0.85237	Lower Control Limit	Average - 3 standard deviations

Figure A-4   Step 3 of calculating control limits

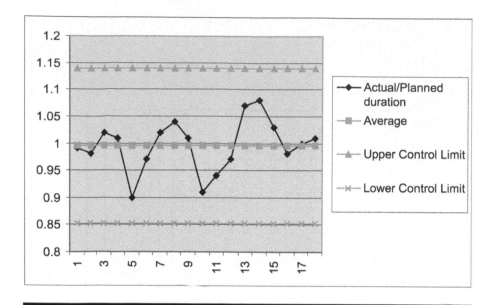

Figure A-5   Step 4 of calculating control limits

capacity of the organization for this kind of task. The control limits are recalculated only when a desirable permanent change has occurred. This calculation is made with only the most recent data points, which will have been analyzed to identify what caused this improvement (see Figure A-5).

Note also that the formulas used to calculate control limits vary as a function of the type of collected data samples (for instance, samples collected on an assembly line). However, these formulas all rely on the ± 3σ principle. For example, the calculation of upper and lower control limits is often expressed in terms of variables such as n, d2, D3, and D4 in statistical control theory. The difference comes from the fact that the range between the largest and the smallest value of a set of data points is used to estimate the standard deviation of that set of data points. Calculations made with these formulas are usually more accurate than calculations made with the Excel function SQRT(VAR( )), because the standard deviation estimation leads to a more precise value, especially when the number of samples is small. As a result, the control limits established with these formulas will be tighter than those established with the Excel function SQRT(VAR( )), and out-of-control conditions are more likely to be detected.

For the purpose of comparing calculations, Figure A-6 shows the control limits calculated with n, d2, D3, and D4, where n=2 (adjacent data points), d2 = 1.128, D3 = 0, and D4 = 3.268. As can be seen, the resulting control limits are tighter than those shown in Figure A-2.

B	C	D	E	F	G	H	I	J
Cell No	Ad/Pd	Av(Ad/Pd)	UCL(Ad/Pd)	LCL(Ad/Pd)	Delta	Av(Delta)	UCL(Delta)	LCL(Delta)
B3	0.99	1.03315789	1.260699266	0.805616524	0.01	0.085556	0.279596	0
B4	0.98	1.03315789	1.260699266	0.805616524	0.04	0.085556	0.279596	0
B5	1.02	1.03315789	1.260699266	0.805616524	0.01	0.085556	0.279596	0
B6	1.01	1.03315789	1.260699266	0.805616524	0.11	0.085556	0.279596	0
B7	0.9	1.03315789	1.260699266	0.805616524	0.8	0.085556	0.279596	0
B8	1.7	1.03315789	1.260699266	0.805616524	0.07	0.085556	0.279596	0
B9	0.97	1.03315789	1.260699266	0.805616524	0.05	0.085556	0.279596	0
B10	1.02	1.03315789	1.260699266	0.805616524	0.02	0.085556	0.279596	0
B11	1.04	1.03315789	1.260699266	0.805616524	0.03	0.085556	0.279596	0
B12	1.01	1.03315789	1.260699266	0.805616524	0.1	0.085556	0.279596	0
B13	0.91	1.03315789	1.260699266	0.805616524	0.03	0.085556	0.279596	0
B14	0.94	1.03315789	1.260699266	0.805616524	0.03	0.085556	0.279596	0
B15	0.97	1.03315789	1.260699266	0.805616524	0.1	0.085556	0.279596	0
B16	1.07	1.03315789	1.260699266	0.805616524	0.01	0.085556	0.279596	0
B17	1.08	1.03315789	1.260699266	0.805616524	0.05	0.085556	0.279596	0
B18	1.03	1.03315789	1.260699266	0.805616524	0.05	0.085556	0.279596	0
B19	0.98	1.03315789	1.260699266	0.805616524	0.02	0.085556	0.279596	0
B20	1	1.03315789	1.260699266	0.805616524	0.01	0.085556	0.279596	0
B21	1.01	1.03315789	1.260699266	0.805616524		0.085556	0.279596	0

1.0332 Delta (difference) between two adjacent ratios calculated with the ABS((x+1)-(x)) Excel function
1.0332 Average of Actual duration/Planned duration = Av(Ad/Ap) calculated with the AVERAGE(C3:C21) function
0.0856 Average of adjacent variations = Av(Delta) calculated with the AVERAGE(G4:G21) function
1.2607 Upper control limit for Ad/Pd = UCL(Ad/Pd) calculatged with the expression Av(Ad/Pd)+3*Av(Delta)/1.128
0.8056 Lower control limit for Ad/Pd = LCL(Ad/Pd) calculatged with the expression Av(Ad/Pd)-3*Av(Delta)/1.128
0.2796 Upper control limit for Delta = UCL(Delta) calculated with the expression 3.268*Av(Delta)
0 Lower control limit for Delta = LCL(Delta) set to 0 (cannot be less than 0)

(a)

Figure A-6 More precise calculation of control limits

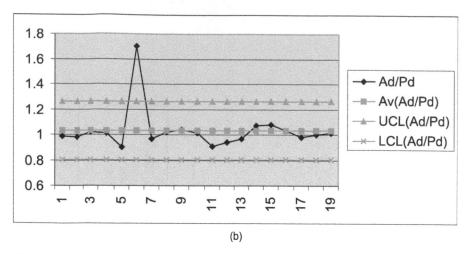

(b)

Figure A-6 (continued)

Quantitatively Managing Quality

In the preceding section, two concepts were presented: statistical characterization of the existing process and the collection of data to verify that a task currently in progress is compliant with that process.

This section focuses on establishing acceptable control limits for a given task.

In order to do this, the quality resulting from following the organizational process is examined in terms of reliability, productivity, availability, time to market, etc. The results of this examination are then translated into quality objectives. For instance, maybe the issue at hand is in order to be profitable, the ratio Ad/Pd must be less than 1.05 and higher than 0.95. If the ratio is higher than 1.05, additional resources required to complete the project will translate into a deficit. On the other hand, if the ratio is lower than 0.95, some of the planned resources will be unnecessary but their cost will still need to be borne by the organization. Additional quality goals can be defined as appropriate.

Going back to the example provided in the preceding section, it was established that a task for which quality objectives, expressed in terms of Ad/Pd, were set to be lower than 1.14 and higher than 0.852 had a probability of 99.73 percent of being met with the existing process. If quality objectives are now set so the ratio Ad/Pd must be lower than 1.05 and 0.95, the probability that they will be achieved with the existing process can be calculated as follows, with the NORMDIST Excel function:

$$\text{NORMDIST } (1.05, 0.996, 0.0479, \text{TRUE})$$
$$- \text{NORMDIST}(0.95, 0.996, 0.0479, \text{TRUE}) = 0.702$$

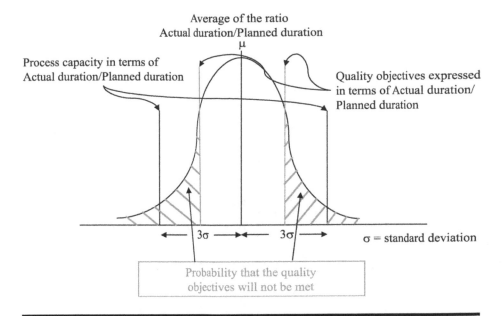

Average of the ratio
Actual duration/Planned duration
μ

Process capacity in terms of
Actual duration/Planned duration

Quality objectives expressed
in terms of Actual duration/
Planned duration

3σ ◄►◄ 3σ ►

σ = standard deviation

Probability that the quality
objectives will not be met

Figure A-7   Assessment of the risk assumed with defined quality objectives

This situation is represented in Figure A-7.

The task has a 70.2 percent chance of meeting these objectives by following the existing organizational process. We have determined at GRafP Technologies, as part of extensive surveys, that the critical value is 60 percent. That is, any undertaking for which the chances of success are less that 60 percent is likely to fail, in the sense that it will not satisfy its quality objectives. With 70.2 percent, it is therefore relevant to closely track the task because the safety margin is relatively low.

At times, it is possible that some quality objectives cannot be expressed as a function of the parameters currently used to characterize the existing process. In this case, specific parameters will need to be defined for the task. Since these parameters are not used to characterize the existing process, control limits have not been calculated based on completed similar tasks with respect to the current task, which would normally be statistically controlled.

For instance, assume that the ratio Ad/Pd is not a parameter for which data has been collected in the past, but that it is required to satisfy quality objectives for a given task. Control limits will therefore need to be established as the task is being executed. In addition, these limits will change as new data is collected for this parameter and plotted in its control chart. An estimation of these limits allows determining the risk to which the task is exposed as this task is executed, as well as identifying

Cell	B Ad/Pd	C Av(Ad/Pd)	D UCL(Ad/Pd)	E LCL(Ad/Pd)	F Delta	G Av(Delta)	H UCL(Delta)	I LCL(Delta)	J
B3	0.99	1.07375	1.487883739	0.65961626			0.508874286	0	
B4	0.98	1.07375	1.487883739	0.65961626	0.01	0.155714286	0.508874286	0	
B5	1.02	1.07375	1.487883739	0.65961626	0.04	0.155714286	0.508874286	0	
B6	1.01	1.07375	1.487883739	0.65961626	0.01	0.155714286	0.508874286	0	
B7	0.9	1.07375	1.487883739	0.65961626	0.11	0.155714286	0.508874286	0	
B8	1.7	1.07375	1.487883739	0.65961626	0.8	0.155714286	0.508874286	0	
B9	0.97	1.07375	1.487883739	0.65961626	0.07	0.155714286	0.508874286	0	
B10	1.02	1.07375	1.487883739	0.65961626	0.05	0.155714286	0.508874286	0	

Delta (difference) between two adjacent ratios calculated with the ABS((x+1)-(x)) Excel function

1.07375 Average of Actual duration/Planned duration = Av(Ad/Ap) calculated with the AVERAGE(C3:C10) function

0.15571 Average of adjacent variations = Av(Delta) calculated with the AVERAGE(G4:G10) function

1.48788 Upper control limit for Ad/Pd = UCL(Ad/Pd) calculatged with the expression Av(Ad/Pd)+3*Av(Delta)/1.128

0.65962 Lower control limit for Ad/Pd = LCL(Ad/Pd) calculatged with the expression Av(Ad/Pd)-3*Av(Delta)/1.128

0.50887 Upper control limit for Delta = UCL(Delta) calculated with the expression 3.268*Av(Delta)

0 Lower control limit for Delta = LCL(Delta) set to 0 (cannot be less than 0)

Figure A-8 Step 1 of calculating control limits

the situations likely to cause a loss of control of the process applied to perform the task.

Figure A-8 and Figure A-9 present this approach for a task in which eight measurements have been collected so far. As shown in Figure A-8, one data point exceeds the upper control limit. Eliminating it and repeating the calculation, results shown in Figure A-10 and Figure A-11, are obtained (in this case, process specialists would also look into what caused this point to exceed its threshold). As no more data points exceed the control limits, plots shown in Figure A-10 and Figure A-11 characterize the capacity of the existing process for the ratio Ad/Pd. Otherwise, affected data points would have been removed and the calculations would have been repeated.

An estimation of the capacity of the existing process leads to an average ratio Ad/Pd equal to 0.984 and tasks undertaken by the organization have a 99.73 percent chance of achieving a ratio lower than 1.113 and higher than 0.856.

The control chart used in this case calls on the more precise formulas to establish the control limits. It essentially consists of plotting the ratios Ad/Pd collected while the task is in progress and the absolute value of the difference between adjacent Ad/Pd ratios. This results in an estimation of the capacity of the existing process, by assuming that the task adheres to this process.

If quality objectives are such that the ratio Ad/Pd must be lower than 1.05 and higher than 0.95, the probability that the task will achieve them with the existing process is calculated to be 72.5 percent, with the help of the following Excel function:

NORMDIST (1.05, 0.984, (1.113-0.984)/3, TRUE)
– NORMDIST(0.95, 0.984, (0.984-0.856)/3, TRUE)

Note that in this case, because the baseline is established as data is collected, the upper and lower control limits keep changing as new data points are obtained. As more data becomes available, the capacity of the existing process and the likelihood of achieving quality objectives become more precise.

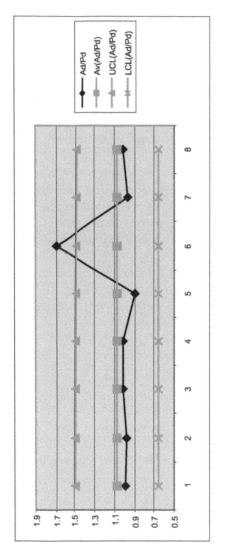

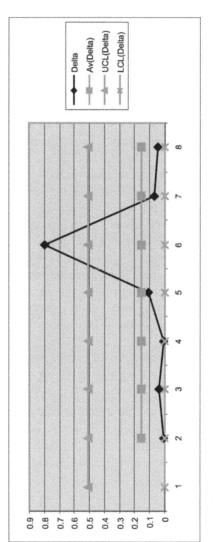

Figure A-9 Step 2 of calculating control limits

B Cell	C Ad/Pd	D Av(Ad/Pd)	E UCL(Ad/Pd)	F LCL(Ad/Pd)	G Delta	H Av(Delta)	I UCL(Delta)	J LCL(Delta)
B3	0.99	0.9842857	1.112831814	0.85573961			0.157953333	0
B4	0.98	0.9842857	1.112831814	0.85573961	0.01	0.048333333	0.157953333	0
B5	1.02	0.9842857	1.112831814	0.85573961	0.04	0.048333333	0.157953333	0
B6	1.01	0.9842857	1.112831814	0.85573961	0.01	0.048333333	0.157953333	0
B7	0.9	0.9842857	1.112831814	0.85573961	0.11	0.048333333	0.157953333	0
B8	0.97	0.9842857	1.112831814	0.85573961	0.07	0.048333333	0.157953333	0
B9	1.02	0.9842857	1.112831814	0.85573961	0.05	0.048333333	0.157953333	0

Delta (difference) between two adjacent ratios calculated with the ABS((x+1)-(x)) Excel function

0.98429 Average of Actual duration/Planned duration = Av(Ad/Ap) calculated with the AVERAGE(C3:C9) function

0.04833 Average of adjacent variations = Av(Delta) calculated with the AVERAGE(G4:G9) function

1.11283 Upper control limit for Ad/Pd = UCL(Ad/Pd) calculatged with the expression Av(Ad/Pd)+3*Av(Delta)/1.128

0.85574 Lower control limit for Ad/Pd = LCL(Ad/Pd) calculatged with the expression Av(Ad/Pd)-3*Av(Delta)/1.128

0.15795 Upper control limit for Delta = UCL(Delta) calculated with the expression 3.268*Av(Delta)

0 Lower control limit for Delta = LCL(Delta) set to 0 (cannot be less than 0)

Figure A-10 Step 3 of calculating control limits

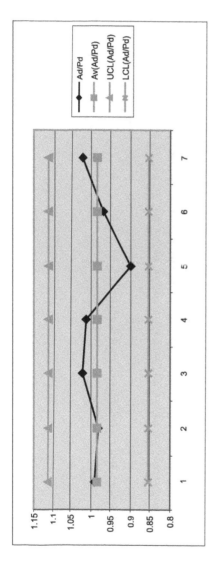

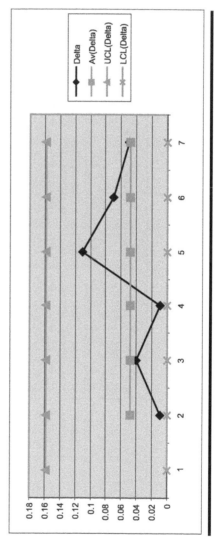

Figure A-11   Step 4 of calculating control limits

Annex B

Risk Assessment and Estimation of Losses

> Nothing that grieves us can be called little: by the eternal laws
> of proportion a child's loss of a doll and a king's loss of a
> crown are events of the same size.
>
> — Mark Twain

This annex tabulates Risk Exposure as a function of Likelihood, Vulnerability, and Impact. Values shown in the table presented below were derived with an application supporting the Probabilistic Risk Identification, Mapping, and Evaluation (PRIME) approach and can be useful to a Risk Analyst trying to quantify individual risks and their consequences, should these risks materialize.

The PRIME approach can be fairly complex. It is typically used to study the interaction of potentially large numbers of undesirable conditions and mitigation mechanisms in order to predict an outcome. In a sense, it is equivalent to predicting tomorrow's weather by studying winds, ocean currents, air pressure, and temperature gradients in the upper atmosphere. In many instances, most people only want to know if it will rain or if it will be sunny. In this case, it is therefore advisable to implement a simpler approach and to compute the exposure to losses for individual risks, without taking into account all interactions that come into play to produce detrimental outcomes. This may sometimes be over simplistic, especially when a large number of risks are consolidated. In fact, risks usually overlap and otherwise interact, and the occurrence of one may trigger the occurrence of others. Likewise, the avoidance of one may prevent other situations from deteriorating.

Nevertheless, for a relatively small number of risks (fewer than 10) or for risks that are unrelated, treating them individually facilitates their analysis and management, and is often all that is needed. The meaning associated with each parameter of the table is described below.

Likelihood characterizes, either intuitively or based on experience, the probability that an undesirable event will occur or the frequency at which it will happen. A value of 100 percent indicates a certainty that the event will occur; a value of 10 percent means that the event will occur infrequently, or on average, once in every 10 situations where this type of event could take place; a value of 50 percent means that the risk will occur, on average, once in every two situations.

Vulnerability characterizes, either intuitively or based on experience, the conditions that make it likely that a risk will deteriorate into the problem it suggests, as a result of deficiencies observed in a given initiative. A value of 100 percent means that the entity has no protection against the risk occurrence. A value of 10 percent means that few deficiencies were observed with respect to the risk in question. A value of 50 percent means that half of the measures that provide full protection are in place.

Impact characterizes, either intuitively or based on experience, the consequences of an undesirable event, should available protection fail to mitigate this event or prevent its occurrence. Impact is characterized as follows:

Impact	Description
1	Catastrophic
2	Critical
3	Severe
4	Serious
5	Moderate
6	Minor

Risk Exposure characterizes the normalized loss associated with the undesirable event, given its Likelihood, its Impact, and the Vulnerability of the initiative under consideration.

To use the table, first estimate the monetary loss resulting from a catastrophic event in a given initiative. For instance, a catastrophic event in an information technology (IT) initiative may be the inability to deliver an application and the loss of the market share that this application could have secured. It could also be the loss of a major customer for whom the application is intended, and all the benefits it could have generated for an organization. In safety critical systems, it could be a fatality and the compensation would then need to be paid out.

For a given risk, estimate the likelihood that the undesirable event to which it corresponds will occur. Estimate the vulnerability of the initiative to that event and its impact, as per the definitions given above. Finally, from the table, identify the risk exposure, and multiply the obtained percentage by the monetary loss resulting from a catastrophic event. This represents the expected loss for that risk.

For instance, assume a small business must weigh the pros and cons of undertaking the development of an application for a large customer. For this application, the catastrophic event consists of being unable to deliver within the acceptable period mandated by the customer, and of losing future short-term orders estimated at $1,000,000. This would put the business in a very difficult position because it needs these orders to expand. One of the risks identified relative to this development is that the company is dependent on one of its suppliers for a critical subsystem. The risk is therefore expressed as, "The supplier will not be able to deliver its subsystem as planned."

There are at least two other suppliers but the organization, being a small enterprise, has few resources. The time required to transfer knowledge associated with the system and to negotiate a contract would result in delays, which could jeopardize a successful delivery.

Given past experience acquired by the small business with the supplier, the likelihood that the subsystem will not be delivered on time with the required quality and functionality is estimated at 10 percent (very low). The impact of this risk is critical, given the difficulties of switching suppliers on the fly. The vulnerability of the small business is assessed at 60 percent (rather high), given its limited resources. As a result, the risk exposure is 30.02 percent, which corresponds to a monetary loss of $300,200.

Given this relatively large loss, it may be prudent for the small business to negotiate a loan (let's say for half the expected loss) in order to hire resources and to start negotiating and implementing a contract with one of the other two suppliers. This will not be money wasted because the resulting subsystems can be used in future orders.

It is estimated that the Vulnerability of the small business will have been reduced to 30 percent. The Impact, however, is left at Critical because there is nothing that assures the small business that the second supplier will be able to deliver its subsystem within the time constraints imposed by the customer. The result is a reduction of the Risk Exposure to 9.71 percent corresponding to a monetary loss of $97,100.

From the table below, it can be seen that a low vulnerability and a high likelihood of occurrence are preferable to a low likelihood of occurrence and a high vulnerability.

For instance, assume that the likelihood of the subsystem not being delivered on time with the required quality and functionality is estimated at 60 percent (rather high), and the vulnerability of the small business to this event is 10 percent (very low), because it has negotiated contracts with other suppliers for the subsystem. Impact remains Critical. The risk exposure would then be 8.68 percent. This corresponds to a monetary loss of $86,800, which compares favorably to the $300,200 obtained with a vulnerability of 60 percent and a likelihood of 10 percent.

This is simply Murphy's Law, which says that if something can go wrong, it will. Intuitively, it can be understood this way: if a risk has a high likelihood of occurring, but vulnerability is low, then there is a good chance that a given occurrence will not have any impact, or that it will somehow be mitigated. On the other hand, if a risk has a low likelihood of occurring, but vulnerability is high, then there is a good chance that every time a risk occurs, even if infrequently, it will translate into the worst forms of the problem it suggests. Among other things, this illustrates the importance of avoiding the dreaded single point of failure in any initiative.

Impact	Vulnerability	Likelihood	Risk Exposure	Impact	Vulnerability	Likelihood	Risk Exposure
1	10%	10%	2.80%	1	60%	10%	40.80%
1	10%	20%	4.60%	1	60%	20%	45.60%
1	10%	30%	6.40%	1	60%	30%	50.40%
1	10%	40%	8.20%	1	60%	40%	55.20%
1	10%	50%	10.00%	1	60%	50%	60.00%
1	10%	60%	11.80%	1	60%	60%	64.80%
1	10%	70%	13.60%	1	60%	70%	69.60%
1	10%	80%	15.40%	1	60%	80%	74.40%
1	10%	90%	17.20%	1	60%	90%	79.20%
1	10%	100%	19.00%	1	60%	100%	84.00%
1	20%	10%	7.20%	1	70%	10%	53.20%
1	20%	20%	10.40%	1	70%	20%	57.40%
1	20%	30%	13.60%	1	70%	30%	61.60%
1	20%	40%	16.80%	1	70%	40%	65.80%
1	20%	50%	20.00%	1	70%	50%	70.00%
1	20%	60%	23.20%	1	70%	60%	74.20%
1	20%	70%	26.40%	1	70%	70%	78.40%
1	20%	80%	29.60%	1	70%	80%	82.60%

Impact	Vulnerability	Likelihood	Risk Exposure	Impact	Vulnerability	Likelihood	Risk Exposure
1	20%	90%	32.80%	1	70%	90%	86.80%
1	20%	100%	36.00%	1	70%	100%	91.00%
1	30%	10%	13.20%	1	80%	10%	67.20%
1	30%	20%	17.40%	1	80%	20%	70.40%
1	30%	30%	21.60%	1	80%	30%	73.60%
1	30%	40%	25.80%	1	80%	40%	76.80%
1	30%	50%	30.00%	1	80%	50%	80.00%
1	30%	60%	34.20%	1	80%	60%	83.20%
1	30%	70%	38.40%	1	80%	70%	86.40%
1	30%	80%	42.60%	1	80%	80%	89.60%
1	30%	90%	46.80%	1	80%	90%	92.80%
1	30%	100%	51.00%	1	80%	100%	96.00%
1	40%	10%	20.80%	1	90%	10%	82.80%
1	40%	20%	25.60%	1	90%	20%	84.60%
1	40%	30%	30.40%	1	90%	30%	86.40%
1	40%	40%	35.20%	1	90%	40%	88.20%
1	40%	50%	40.00%	1	90%	50%	90.00%
1	40%	60%	44.80%	1	90%	60%	91.80%

Impact	Vulnerability	Likelihood	Risk Exposure	Impact	Vulnerability	Likelihood	Risk Exposure
1	40%	70%	49.60%	1	90%	70%	93.60%
1	40%	80%	54.40%	1	90%	80%	95.40%
1	40%	90%	59.20%	1	90%	90%	97.20%
1	40%	100%	64.00%	1	90%	100%	99.00%
1	50%	10%	30.00%	1	100%	10%	100.00%
1	50%	20%	35.00%	1	100%	20%	100.00%
1	50%	30%	40.00%	1	100%	30%	100.00%
1	50%	40%	45.00%	1	100%	40%	100.00%
1	50%	50%	50.00%	1	100%	50%	100.00%
1	50%	60%	55.00%	1	100%	60%	100.00%
1	50%	70%	60.00%	1	100%	70%	100.00%
1	50%	80%	65.00%	1	100%	80%	100.00%
1	50%	90%	70.00%	1	100%	90%	100.00%
1	50%	100%	75.00%	1	100%	100%	100.00%
2	10%	10%	2.06%	2	60%	10%	30.02%
2	10%	20%	3.38%	2	60%	20%	33.55%
2	10%	30%	4.71%	2	60%	30%	37.08%
2	10%	40%	6.03%	2	60%	40%	40.61%

Impact	Vulnerability	Likelihood	Risk Exposure	Impact	Vulnerability	Likelihood	Risk Exposure
2	10%	50%	7.36%	2	60%	50%	44.15%
2	10%	60%	8.68%	2	60%	60%	47.68%
2	10%	70%	10.01%	2	60%	70%	51.21%
2	10%	80%	11.33%	2	60%	80%	54.74%
2	10%	90%	12.66%	2	60%	90%	58.27%
2	10%	100%	13.98%	2	60%	100%	61.80%
2	20%	10%	5.30%	2	70%	10%	39.14%
2	20%	20%	7.65%	2	70%	20%	42.23%
2	20%	30%	10.01%	2	70%	30%	45.32%
2	20%	40%	12.36%	2	70%	40%	48.41%
2	20%	50%	14.72%	2	70%	50%	51.50%
2	20%	60%	17.07%	2	70%	60%	54.59%
2	20%	70%	19.42%	2	70%	70%	57.68%
2	20%	80%	21.78%	2	70%	80%	60.77%
2	20%	90%	24.13%	2	70%	90%	63.86%
2	20%	100%	26.49%	2	70%	100%	66.95%
2	30%	10%	9.71%	2	80%	10%	49.44%
2	30%	20%	12.80%	2	80%	20%	51.80%

Impact	Vulnerability	Likelihood	Risk Exposure	Impact	Vulnerability	Likelihood	Risk Exposure
2	30%	30%	15.89%	2	80%	30%	54.15%
2	30%	40%	18.98%	2	80%	40%	56.51%
2	30%	50%	22.07%	2	80%	50%	58.86%
2	30%	60%	25.16%	2	80%	60%	61.22%
2	30%	70%	28.25%	2	80%	70%	63.57%
2	30%	80%	31.34%	2	80%	80%	65.92%
2	30%	90%	34.43%	2	80%	90%	68.28%
2	30%	100%	37.52%	2	80%	100%	70.63%
2	40%	10%	15.30%	2	90%	10%	60.92%
2	40%	20%	18.84%	2	90%	20%	62.25%
2	40%	30%	22.37%	2	90%	30%	63.57%
2	40%	40%	25.90%	2	90%	40%	64.89%
2	40%	50%	29.43%	2	90%	50%	66.22%
2	40%	60%	32.96%	2	90%	60%	67.54%
2	40%	70%	36.49%	2	90%	70%	68.87%
2	40%	80%	40.03%	2	90%	80%	70.19%
2	40%	90%	43.56%	2	90%	90%	71.52%
2	40%	100%	47.09%	2	90%	100%	72.84%

Impact	Vulnerability	Likelihood	Risk Exposure	Impact	Vulnerability	Likelihood	Risk Exposure
2	50%	10%	22.07%	2	100%	10%	73.58%
2	50%	20%	25.75%	2	100%	20%	73.58%
2	50%	30%	29.43%	2	100%	30%	73.58%
2	50%	40%	33.11%	2	100%	40%	73.58%
2	50%	50%	36.79%	2	100%	50%	73.58%
2	50%	60%	40.47%	2	100%	60%	73.58%
2	50%	70%	44.15%	2	100%	70%	73.58%
2	50%	80%	47.82%	2	100%	80%	73.58%
2	50%	90%	51.50%	2	100%	90%	73.58%
2	50%	100%	55.18%	2	100%	100%	73.58%
3	10%	10%	0.57%	3	60%	10%	8.28%
3	10%	20%	0.93%	3	60%	20%	9.26%
3	10%	30%	1.30%	3	60%	30%	10.23%
3	10%	40%	1.66%	3	60%	40%	11.21%
3	10%	50%	2.03%	3	60%	50%	12.18%
3	10%	60%	2.40%	3	60%	60%	13.15%
3	10%	70%	2.76%	3	60%	70%	14.13%
3	10%	80%	3.13%	3	60%	80%	15.10%

Impact	Vulnerability	Likelihood	Risk Exposure	Impact	Vulnerability	Likelihood	Risk Exposure
3	10%	90%	3.49%	3	60%	90%	16.08%
3	10%	100%	3.86%	3	60%	100%	17.05%
3	20%	10%	1.46%	3	70%	10%	10.80%
3	20%	20%	2.11%	3	70%	20%	11.65%
3	20%	30%	2.76%	3	70%	30%	12.50%
3	20%	40%	3.41%	3	70%	40%	13.36%
3	20%	50%	4.06%	3	70%	50%	14.21%
3	20%	60%	4.71%	3	70%	60%	15.06%
3	20%	70%	5.36%	3	70%	70%	15.92%
3	20%	80%	6.01%	3	70%	80%	16.77%
3	20%	90%	6.66%	3	70%	90%	17.62%
3	20%	100%	7.31%	3	70%	100%	18.47%
3	30%	10%	2.68%	3	80%	10%	13.64%
3	30%	20%	3.53%	3	80%	20%	14.29%
3	30%	30%	4.38%	3	80%	30%	14.94%
3	30%	40%	5.24%	3	80%	40%	15.59%
3	30%	50%	6.09%	3	80%	50%	16.24%
3	30%	60%	6.94%	3	80%	60%	16.89%

Impact	Vulnerability	Likelihood	Risk Exposure	Impact	Vulnerability	Likelihood	Risk Exposure
3	30%	70%	7.80%	3	80%	70%	17.54%
3	30%	80%	8.65%	3	80%	80%	18.19%
3	30%	90%	9.50%	3	80%	90%	18.84%
3	30%	100%	10.35%	3	80%	100%	19.49%
3	40%	10%	4.22%	3	90%	10%	16.81%
3	40%	20%	5.20%	3	90%	20%	17.17%
3	40%	30%	6.17%	3	90%	30%	17.54%
3	40%	40%	7.15%	3	90%	40%	17.90%
3	40%	50%	8.12%	3	90%	50%	18.27%
3	40%	60%	9.09%	3	90%	60%	18.64%
3	40%	70%	10.07%	3	90%	70%	19.00%
3	40%	80%	11.04%	3	90%	80%	19.37%
3	40%	90%	12.02%	3	90%	90%	19.73%
3	40%	100%	12.99%	3	90%	100%	20.10%
3	50%	10%	6.09%	3	100%	10%	20.30%
3	50%	20%	7.11%	3	100%	20%	20.30%
3	50%	30%	8.12%	3	100%	30%	20.30%
3	50%	40%	9.14%	3	100%	40%	20.30%

Impact	Vulnerability	Likelihood	Risk Exposure	Impact	Vulnerability	Likelihood	Risk Exposure
3	50%	50%	10.15%	3	100%	50%	20.30%
3	50%	60%	11.17%	3	100%	60%	20.30%
3	50%	70%	12.18%	3	100%	70%	20.30%
3	50%	80%	13.20%	3	100%	80%	20.30%
3	50%	90%	14.21%	3	100%	90%	20.30%
3	50%	100%	15.23%	3	100%	100%	20.30%
4	10%	10%	0.093%	4	60%	10%	1.35%
4	10%	20%	0.153%	4	60%	20%	1.51%
4	10%	30%	0.212%	4	60%	30%	1.67%
4	10%	40%	0.272%	4	60%	40%	1.83%
4	10%	50%	0.332%	4	60%	50%	1.99%
4	10%	60%	0.392%	4	60%	60%	2.15%
4	10%	70%	0.451%	4	60%	70%	2.31%
4	10%	80%	0.511%	4	60%	80%	2.47%
4	10%	90%	0.571%	4	60%	90%	2.63%
4	10%	100%	0.631%	4	60%	100%	2.79%
4	20%	10%	0.239%	4	70%	10%	1.77%
4	20%	20%	0.345%	4	70%	20%	1.91%

Impact	Vulnerability	Likelihood	Risk Exposure	Impact	Vulnerability	Likelihood	Risk Exposure
4	20%	30%	0.451%	4	70%	30%	2.04%
4	20%	40%	0.558%	4	70%	40%	2.18%
4	20%	50%	0.664%	4	70%	50%	2.32%
4	20%	60%	0.770%	4	70%	60%	2.46%
4	20%	70%	0.876%	4	70%	70%	2.60%
4	20%	80%	0.982%	4	70%	80%	2.74%
4	20%	90%	1.089%	4	70%	90%	2.88%
4	20%	100%	1.195%	4	70%	100%	3.02%
4	30%	10%	0.438%	4	80%	10%	2.23%
4	30%	20%	0.578%	4	80%	20%	2.34%
4	30%	30%	0.717%	4	80%	30%	2.44%
4	30%	40%	0.856%	4	80%	40%	2.55%
4	30%	50%	0.996%	4	80%	50%	2.66%
4	30%	60%	1.135%	4	80%	60%	2.76%
4	30%	70%	1.275%	4	80%	70%	2.87%
4	30%	80%	1.414%	4	80%	80%	2.97%
4	30%	90%	1.553%	4	80%	90%	3.08%
4	30%	100%	1.693%	4	80%	100%	3.19%

Impact	Vulnerability	Likelihood	Risk Exposure	Impact	Vulnerability	Likelihood	Risk Exposure
4	40%	10%	0.690%	4	90%	10%	2.75%
4	40%	20%	0.850%	4	90%	20%	2.81%
4	40%	30%	1.009%	4	90%	30%	2.87%
4	40%	40%	1.168%	4	90%	40%	2.93%
4	40%	50%	1.328%	4	90%	50%	2.99%
4	40%	60%	1.487%	4	90%	60%	3.05%
4	40%	70%	1.646%	4	90%	70%	3.11%
4	40%	80%	1.806%	4	90%	80%	3.17%
4	40%	90%	1.965%	4	90%	90%	3.23%
4	40%	100%	2.124%	4	90%	100%	3.29%
4	50%	10%	0.996%	4	100%	10%	3.32%
4	50%	20%	1.162%	4	100%	20%	3.32%
4	50%	30%	1.328%	4	100%	30%	3.32%
4	50%	40%	1.494%	4	100%	40%	3.32%
4	50%	50%	1.660%	4	100%	50%	3.32%
4	50%	60%	1.826%	4	100%	60%	3.32%
4	50%	70%	1.991%	4	100%	70%	3.32%
4	50%	80%	2.157%	4	100%	80%	3.32%

Impact	Vulnerability	Likelihood	Risk Exposure	Impact	Vulnerability	Likelihood	Risk Exposure
4	50%	90%	2.323%	4	100%	90%	3.32%
4	50%	100%	2.489%	4	100%	100%	3.32%
5	10%	10%	0.011%	5	60%	10%	0.16%
5	10%	20%	0.018%	5	60%	20%	0.17%
5	10%	30%	0.024%	5	60%	30%	0.19%
5	10%	40%	0.031%	5	60%	40%	0.21%
5	10%	50%	0.038%	5	60%	50%	0.23%
5	10%	60%	0.045%	5	60%	60%	0.25%
5	10%	70%	0.052%	5	60%	70%	0.27%
5	10%	80%	0.059%	5	60%	80%	0.28%
5	10%	90%	0.066%	5	60%	90%	0.30%
5	10%	100%	0.072%	5	60%	100%	0.32%
5	20%	10%	0.027%	5	70%	10%	0.20%
5	20%	20%	0.040%	5	70%	20%	0.22%
5	20%	30%	0.052%	5	70%	30%	0.24%
5	20%	40%	0.064%	5	70%	40%	0.25%
5	20%	50%	0.076%	5	70%	50%	0.27%
5	20%	60%	0.089%	5	70%	60%	0.28%

Impact	Vulnerability	Likelihood	Risk Exposure	Impact	Vulnerability	Likelihood	Risk Exposure
5	20%	70%	0.101%	5	70%	70%	0.30%
5	20%	80%	0.113%	5	70%	80%	0.32%
5	20%	90%	0.125%	5	70%	90%	0.33%
5	20%	100%	0.137%	5	70%	100%	0.35%
5	30%	10%	0.050%	5	80%	10%	0.26%
5	30%	20%	0.066%	5	80%	20%	0.27%
5	30%	30%	0.082%	5	80%	30%	0.28%
5	30%	40%	0.098%	5	80%	40%	0.29%
5	30%	50%	0.114%	5	80%	50%	0.31%
5	30%	60%	0.130%	5	80%	60%	0.32%
5	30%	70%	0.147%	5	80%	70%	0.33%
5	30%	80%	0.163%	5	80%	80%	0.34%
5	30%	90%	0.179%	5	80%	90%	0.35%
5	30%	100%	0.195%	5	80%	100%	0.37%
5	40%	10%	0.079%	5	90%	10%	0.32%
5	40%	20%	0.098%	5	90%	20%	0.32%
5	40%	30%	0.116%	5	90%	30%	0.33%
5	40%	40%	0.134%	5	90%	40%	0.34%

Impact	Vulnerability	Likelihood	Risk Exposure	Impact	Vulnerability	Likelihood	Risk Exposure
5	40%	50%	0.153%	5	90%	50%	0.34%
5	40%	60%	0.171%	5	90%	60%	0.35%
5	40%	70%	0.189%	5	90%	70%	0.36%
5	40%	80%	0.208%	5	90%	80%	0.36%
5	40%	90%	0.226%	5	90%	90%	0.37%
5	40%	100%	0.244%	5	90%	100%	0.38%
5	50%	10%	0.114%	5	100%	10%	0.38%
5	50%	20%	0.134%	5	100%	20%	0.38%
5	50%	30%	0.153%	5	100%	30%	0.38%
5	50%	40%	0.172%	5	100%	40%	0.38%
5	50%	50%	0.191%	5	100%	50%	0.38%
5	50%	60%	0.210%	5	100%	60%	0.38%
5	50%	70%	0.229%	5	100%	70%	0.38%
5	50%	80%	0.248%	5	100%	80%	0.38%
5	50%	90%	0.267%	5	100%	90%	0.38%
5	50%	100%	0.286%	5	100%	100%	0.38%
6	10%	10%	0.00094%	6	60%	10%	0.014%
6	10%	20%	0.00155%	6	60%	20%	0.015%

Impact	Vulnerability	Likelihood	Risk Exposure	Impact	Vulnerability	Likelihood	Risk Exposure
6	10%	30%	0.00216%	6	60%	30%	0.017%
6	10%	40%	0.00276%	6	60%	40%	0.019%
6	10%	50%	0.00337%	6	60%	50%	0.020%
6	10%	60%	0.00398%	6	60%	60%	0.022%
6	10%	70%	0.00458%	6	60%	70%	0.023%
6	10%	80%	0.00519%	6	60%	80%	0.025%
6	10%	90%	0.00579%	6	60%	90%	0.027%
6	10%	100%	0.00640%	6	60%	100%	0.028%
6	20%	10%	0.00243%	6	70%	10%	0.018%
6	20%	20%	0.00350%	6	70%	20%	0.019%
6	20%	30%	0.00458%	6	70%	30%	0.021%
6	20%	40%	0.00566%	6	70%	40%	0.022%
6	20%	50%	0.00674%	6	70%	50%	0.024%
6	20%	60%	0.00782%	6	70%	60%	0.025%
6	20%	70%	0.00889%	6	70%	70%	0.026%
6	20%	80%	0.00997%	6	70%	80%	0.028%
6	20%	90%	0.01105%	6	70%	90%	0.029%
6	20%	100%	0.01213%	6	70%	100%	0.031%

Impact	Vulnerability	Likelihood	Risk Exposure	Impact	Vulnerability	Likelihood	Risk Exposure
6	30%	10%	0.00445%	6	80%	10%	0.023%
6	30%	20%	0.00586%	6	80%	20%	0.024%
6	30%	30%	0.00728%	6	80%	30%	0.025%
6	30%	40%	0.00869%	6	80%	40%	0.026%
6	30%	50%	0.01011%	6	80%	50%	0.027%
6	30%	60%	0.01152%	6	80%	60%	0.028%
6	30%	70%	0.01294%	6	80%	70%	0.029%
6	30%	80%	0.01435%	6	80%	80%	0.030%
6	30%	90%	0.01577%	6	80%	90%	0.031%
6	30%	100%	0.01718%	6	80%	100%	0.032%
6	40%	10%	0.00701%	6	90%	10%	0.028%
6	40%	20%	0.00862%	6	90%	20%	0.029%
6	40%	30%	0.01024%	6	90%	30%	0.029%
6	40%	40%	0.01186%	6	90%	40%	0.030%
6	40%	50%	0.01348%	6	90%	50%	0.030%
6	40%	60%	0.01509%	6	90%	60%	0.031%
6	40%	70%	0.01671%	6	90%	70%	0.032%
6	40%	80%	0.01833%	6	90%	80%	0.032%

Impact	Vulnerability	Likelihood	Risk Exposure	Impact	Vulnerability	Likelihood	Risk Exposure
6	40%	90%	0.01994%	6	90%	90%	0.033%
6	40%	100%	0.02156%	6	90%	100%	0.033%
6	50%	10%	0.01011%	6	100%	10%	0.034%
6	50%	20%	0.01179%	6	100%	20%	0.034%
6	50%	30%	0.01348%	6	100%	30%	0.034%
6	50%	40%	0.01516%	6	100%	40%	0.034%
6	50%	50%	0.01684%	6	100%	50%	0.034%
6	50%	60%	0.01853%	6	100%	60%	0.034%
6	50%	70%	0.02021%	6	100%	70%	0.034%
6	50%	80%	0.02190%	6	100%	80%	0.034%
6	50%	90%	0.02358%	6	100%	90%	0.034%
6	50%	100%	0.02527%	6	100%	100%	0.034%